THE SPIRIT IN SOCIETY

ESSAYS IN HONOUR OF WILLIAM K. KAY

THE SPIRIT IN SOCIETY

ESSAYS IN HONOUR OF
WILLIAM K. KAY

EDITED BY

ANDREW DAVIES
ANNE E. DYER

CPT

CPT Press
Cleveland, Tennessee

The Spirit in Society
Essays in Honour of William K. Kay

Published by CPT Press
900 Walker ST NE
Cleveland, TN 37311
USA
email: cptpress@pentecostaltheology.org
website: www.cptpress.com

Library of Congress Control Number: 2021942404 (paperback)

ISBN: 9781953358127 (paperback)
ISBN: 9781953358486 (hardback)

Dedication

To

William Kilbourne Kay

CONTENTS

Acknowledgments ix
Preface x
Abbreviations xi

Introduction 1

Chapter 1
William Kay – A Personal Sketch and Tribute
David Petts 3

Chapter 2
**Pentecostal Demographics, Definitions, and
the Changing Face of Global Christianity**
Allan Anderson 9

Chapter 3
The Orthodox Church and the Charismatic Movement
Andrew Walker 25

Chapter 4
**A Pentecostal Commentary on the Edinburgh 2010
Mission and Unity Conference**
Anne E Dyer 39

Chapter 5
The Paraclete – A Comforter for Pentecostals
Glenn Balfour 60

Chapter 6
Pneumatology and the Old Testament
Robin Routledge 85

Chapter 7
The Thousand Year Reign (Revelation 20.1-10)
John Christopher Thomas...107

Chapter 8
Ideology and 'Objective' Biblical Scholarship
Eryl W. Davies...131

Chapter 9
The Liberating Spirit: A Pentecostal Reading of Isaiah
Andrew Davies 147

Chapter 10
Personality and Charismatic Orientation: An Empirical Study
in Psychological Type Theory
Leslie Francis, Keith Littler, Mandy Robbins 159

Chapter 11
Psychological Temperament, Psychological Type, and
Attraction to the Charismatic Movement
Leslie Francis, Andrew Village, David Voas 179

Chapter 12
Ordinary Trinitarian Theology in the Assemblies of
God: A Qualitative Study
Mark J. Cartledge 199

Index of Biblical (and Other Ancient) References 221
Index of Authors 226

ACKNOWLEDGEMENTS

We thank all those who have contributed articles to this Festschrift in honour of Rev. Professor William K. Kay. They represent those who have worked alongside William in various stages of his life. One, David Petts, was an initial mentor as well as colleague. Another was once examined by William for his doctorate; another was supervised for a doctorate but all at some stage have been colleagues in colleges and universities in which William worked. We all wish to honour a pioneer in the field of Pentecostal studies for Britain in particular and globally in his latter contributions.

PREFACE

A long time in the making, finally this book has been produced as William Kay has become retired. So, we his colleagues, mentor and mentees wish to honour his work for the past several decades. Always an educationalist, William put those talents to work at Mattersey Hall Bible College, enabling that college to gain an academic footing. While there, his research rather inevitably went to the history of the college's own movement, that of the Assemblies of God, GB. However, by the mid-1990s he again broadened his research interests into education and then mixed the two interests – Pentecostalism and Education – before establishing at Bangor University, the Centre for Pentecostal and Charismatic Studies. He has been hailed around the world for his contributions and this book is here presented to him as an ongoing legacy from his contemporaries and the generation following his footsteps in establishing the credibility of Pentecostal studies worldwide.

The subject areas covered show his own wide-ranging interests from definitions and demography of Pentecostalism to theological comparisons, to missiological considerations and on to biblical studies Old and New Testaments, with ramifications for Eschatology and then on to ministerial psychological profiling! Ever interested in the empirical side the book ends with a study and outcomes of a 'typical' Assemblies of God church, from the area that triggered the Assemblies of God almost a century ago (98 years to be precise as the founding was 1924). After one century of development, it remains for future scholars to map the progress into the 21st century and that continues to open up future areas of study within Pentecostal and Charismatic studies. We thank William Kay for his many contributions on which we can build.

ABBREVIATIONS

BETS	Bulletin of the Evangelical Theological Society
CBQ	*Catholic Biblical Quarterly*
JBL	*Journal of Biblical Literature*
JEPTA	*The Journal of the European Pentecostal Theological Association*
JPT	*Journal of Pentecostal Theology*
JPTSup	Journal of Pentecostal Theology, Supplement Series
JSNT	*Journal for the Study of the New Testament*
JSNTSup	Journal for the Study of the New Testament, Supplement Series
NCB	New Century Bible Commentaries
TynBul	*Tyndale Bulletin*

INTRODUCTION

This book is a collection of essays, most of which are connected with Pentecostalism, all in honour of William K. Kay. He has had an influence on academic matters regarding Pentecostal and Charismatic studies for over three decades and on education before that. The first chapter provides an overview of his life as it is by his mentor, possibly counted among the first Pentecostals William had ever met, his lifelong friend David Petts.

The following chapter provides definitions of just what Pentecostal studies have been about over the past three decades, thanks to Allan Anderson's passion at trying to work out what Pentecostalism is both demographically and then theologically.

Meanwhile a comparison with the Orthodox Church's theology by Andrew Walker also contributes biographical details about William Kay that preceded his encounter with Christ directly. It is that encounter which directed the rest of William's life's work. Subsequent chapters indicate the range of interests held by William as he wrote himself and as he directed academic work in a following generation. At least three of the contributors are thankful for his work as their lecturer, some at BA others to PhD levels.

Prompted by the history of his own denomination for his own second doctorate (he has three!), William directed others to subsequent areas for study in their doctoral work. His global reach came when assisting various colleges from Finland to Philippines and it directed his more recent work in studying Asian Pentecostalism. Therefore, chapter four is geared to a Pentecostal response to the Edinburgh 2010 mission conference.

History alone never suffices in establishing the reason for the events recorded; the understanding of Pentecostals has to go into their epistemology found in theological and biblical studies. There-fore, chapters five to nine by various biblical studies scholars from Glenn Balfour, Robin Routledge, and Andrew Davies who worked with William at Mattersey Hall, to John Christopher Thomas our only American author, connected through his role at Bangor University north Wales; these show a range of studies from ancient Hebrew text to pneumatology to eschatology. While William may not have been a biblical studies expert, he did teach in all these areas, along with ethics at BA level triggering one of the editors into his special interest fields of OT, Ethics, and Hermeneutics. This brings us to ideology and Eryl Davies has provided an overview of how OT studies has been interpreted. I begin to wonder what William did not teach as he started with five-year-olds and then secondary school with his Eng-lish and RE backgrounds before his invitation to Mattersey Hall to develop Tertiary levels with a range of religious studies areas.

William has even delved into scientific epistemologies with re-search into Karl Popper's falsification theory as applied to history and the historiographical range of interpretation for Pentecostalism. That may bring us back to history perhaps, but we end the book with two chapters reflecting on his empirical (even statistical) work in cooper-ation with their authors, headed by Leslie Francis, on psychological theories of personality types and finally we come to an empirical and theological end with Mark Cartledge's discussion on a classically typ-ical Pentecostal (AoG) church in Birmingham.

We trust that this overview helps future students to get a wide breadth of possibilities for their future studies within this area of academic and ministerial issues.

1

WILLIAM KAY – A PERSONAL SKETCH AND TRIBUTE

DAVID PETTS[*]

William Kilbourne Kay was born in Margate, England, on the 15th of December 1945 to David and Alexandra Kay. Apart from his brother Peter, who was born on the 9th of August 1947, I know of no-one living who has known him longer than I have. It is, therefore, both a privilege and a joy for me to open this well-deserved *Festschrift* in honour of my good friend and colleague, by recounting something of my close association with him over many years and of his many and varied achievements. I am indebted to his wife, Anthea, for supplying many of the details of which I was previously unaware.

When William was 7 years old, he was sent to a boarding school in Oxford, Summerfield Preparatory School. His parents were divorced when William was just 9 and his mother moved to Kidlington, near Oxford. At the age of 13 he was sent to Eton College. At 18, after a year at the London School of Film Technique, he went up to Trinity College, Oxford, where he read English (1964-67). In 1966 as the Film Critic for *Isis* he went to hear Billy Graham in Earl's Court and it was there that he gave his life to Christ.

My first acquaintance with William was about a year later. I had graduated from Oxford in 1962 and was pastoring the Assemblies of God church in Colchester. I had also been appointed as Travelling

---

[*] David Petts (PhD, University of Nottingham) is the retired, former Principal of Mattersey Hall Bible College in Mattersey, England, UK.

Secretary to the Students Pentecostal Fellowship, the main purpose of which was preaching in universities and colleges on the Baptism in the Holy Spirit and praying for those who wished to receive. In 1967 one such meeting had been arranged in St John's College by Valentine Cunningham (then a postgraduate student at Keble College and later to become Professor of English Literature at Oxford). At the close of the meeting William was baptized in the Holy Spirit with the initial evidence of speaking in tongues.

Some time later, shortly after he had graduated, William wrote to me asking my advice as to what he might do to serve the Lord. I suggested that, as he had never had experience as a member of a local Pentecostal church, he might consider initially just joining a church and serving God as a member there. I also mentioned that I would be moving from Colchester to take over the pastorate of the Assemblies of God church in Basingstoke in January 1968. As a result, William decided to move to Basingstoke arriving there before me in late 1967.

William's purpose in coming to Basingstoke was to gain some experience in local church life and to be of what assistance he could to me in my new pastorate. He was not, therefore, unduly concerned about getting a well-paid job, wanting only enough to meet his everyday needs. So, he took a job as a pump attendant on the forecourt of a local petrol station. That was not to last for long, however. My father, Stanley Petts, who had just retired as the headmaster of a large comprehensive school in London, was visiting our church one Sunday morning and, after the service, in conversation with William was shocked to learn that an Oxford graduate was working at a petrol station. He encouraged William to set his sights higher and suggested that school-teaching might be a more fruitful avenue of service for the Lord. That conversation was to change the course of William's life and consequently of Pentecostal education not only in the United Kingdom but also much further afield.

William began his teaching career by teaching some 40 five-year-old children at a Church of England Primary School in Bramley, a village not far from Basingstoke. Later, at the invitation of Bill Champion, a local Christian headmaster, he moved to the Charles Chute Secondary School to teach Religious Education (1968-1973). From 1973 to 1974 he served as Head of Religious Education at the John Hunt of Everest School, and from 1974 to 1979 in the same capacity at Cranbourne School. During this time, he continued to improve his academic and professional qualifications. In 1974 he gained the *Certificate of Proficiency in Religious Knowledge* from the University of London. In 1977 he was awarded the degree of *Master of Education* from the University of Reading and four years later a *PhD* in Education from the same university. This led to the post of Research Officer and Lecturer for PGCE and MA at the University of Southampton (1981-1984).

Throughout this time William remained a loyal member of the local church. He served as a Sunday-School teacher, helped with the Friday night youth meeting, and drove the church minibus bringing people to the services. He later was appointed as a deacon and eventually as an elder serving as a valuable member of the Pastoral Oversight of the church. It was during this time that his ability and gift as a preacher became very apparent.

William's time at Basingstoke, however, was also noteworthy in that it was there that he met and married Anthea. Anthea Ruth Bell was a Christian school-teacher who joined our church in 1968. It was soon apparent to all that William and Anthea were ideally suited and, on the 30th October 1971, I had the joy of conducting their wedding, our daughters, Deborah and Sarah serving as bridesmaids. Their first son, Matthew, was born in 1973, their second, Samuel, in 1975. Matthew and Samuel are both now married and have children of their own, a great source of joy to both William and Anthea.

In 1977, I was asked to serve as acting-Principal of the Assemblies of God Bible College at Mattersey Hall and was confirmed as Principal by the vote of the Assemblies of God Conference in 1978. This, of course, meant relinquishing the pastorate at Basingstoke and it seemed that our relationship with the Kays would inevitably become less close. However, as the number of students at Mattersey began to grow it became apparent that an increase in the number of full-time staff was vitally important. William was an obvious possibility, but would the Board of Governors agree with my suggestion? At that time there was still a suspicion of academics among many Assemblies of God pastors and I wondered if William's PhD would count against him rather than for him! But as I was praying about this Isa. 48.15 came powerfully to my attention:

> I, even I, have spoken; yes, I have called him. I will bring him, and he will succeed in his mission.

This came as a word from God, not only to me, but also to William, and I brought his name before the Board of Governors who were happy to approve the appointment. So, William took up the post at Mattersey in 1984, buying a house in the nearby village of Everton, where he and Anthea lived until 2018. William's time as a full-time lecturer at Mattersey lasted for ten years. In addition to his work in the College he became actively involved in the local church as a member of the pastoral team and in 1985 was ordained as an Assemblies of God Minister. Other significant factors with regard to this period include William's second PhD (this time in Theology at Nottingham University) which he was awarded in 1989, his personal encouragement to me as I undertook my own PhD (1988-92), and his very practical help as we sought validation for our first BA degree course with the University of Sheffield (1994). It was also at this time that he became Secretary of the newly formed *Donald Gee Centre for Pentecostal and Charismatic Research* at Mattersey Hall, a role he continues to fulfil.

In 1994 William moved to Trinity College, Carmarthen, where he became Senior Research Fellow until 2001. From 2001 to 2004 his time was divided equally between King's College, London, as Senior Lecturer in Religious Education and Theology, and the University of Wales, Bangor, as Director of the Centre for Pentecostal and Charismatic Studies. In 2004 the post at Bangor became full time and was combined with that of Reader in Practical Theology in the School of Theology and Religious Studies. In 2009 William was awarded the degree of *Doctor of Divinity* by the University of Nottingham in recognition of his services to Pentecostal education. In the same year, he was offered and accepted the Chair which he occupied at Glyndwr University (Wrexham) with a further honorary professorial position with the University of Chester by 2011.

William's influence, however, has extended far beyond the confines of the universities where he has been employed. A prolific writer, he was Editor of the *Journal of the European Pentecostal Association* 2004-2018, and has authored or contributed to books and journals, far too numerous to mention, on topics including Pentecostal and Charismatic Studies, The Religious Development of Young People, Religious Education and Church Schools, and Comparative Education. He has presented papers and delivered lectures not only in England and Wales but as far afield as the Netherlands, Germany,

Poland, Norway and Finland, Virginia, Tennessee, Los Angeles, Jerusalem, and the Philippines with further research projects based around Pentecostal churches in Kuala Lumpur, Singapore, and Hong Kong. During the past decade or so, William was awarded the Society for Pentecostal Studies' Lifetime Achievement Award and, as mentioned earlier, was awarded his Doctor of Divinity from Nottingham University, for his contributions to scholarship in the numerous books he published.

From my perspective, perhaps the most valuable contribution that William has made, and where his influence will be appreciated for many years to come, is in the assistance he has been able to give to Pentecostal colleges in gaining validation for their degree courses. This is true not only of Mattersey Hall in the UK, but also to my certain knowledge of Iso Kirja College in Finland, Continental Theological Seminary in Brussels, and the European Theological Seminary in Germany, Philippines' AGTS and he even contributed to the development of one such college in Trinidad. As a result, through the influence of the now Reverend Professor William Kay, thousands of lives have been touched and educated by Pentecostal teachers with a passion to see men and women trained for Christian service in the power of the Holy Spirit. It is this, I believe, that will give him the greatest satisfaction. To refer once more to Isaiah 48.15, I say to William:

God did call you, God did bring you, and you did succeed in your mission.

2

PENTECOSTAL DEMOGRAPHICS, DEFINITIONS, AND THE CHANGING FACE OF GLOBAL CHRISTIANITY

ALLAN ANDERSON[*]

Changing Demographics

It is a widely established historical fact that during the twentieth century a remarkable shift in the global demographics of Christianity has taken place. At the beginning of the twentieth century Christianity was 80% European and North American. Its centre of gravity was in Europe. By the end of the century the centre had moved southwards and eastwards into Africa and less than 40% of its adherents were Europeans and North Americans.[1] Hundreds of millions of Africans, Asians, and Latin Americans had become Christians and a significant proportion of them were Pentecostal, Charismatic, or of a 'Pentecostal' type (with an emphasis on the practice of spiritual gifts), or at least of a sort that did not follow traditional European and North American ecclesiastical patterns. As *The Atlas of Global Christianity* observed, 'The churches growing in the South, whether Anglican, Roman Catholic or Pentecostal, have a strong supernatural orientation

[*] Allan H. Anderson (DTh, UNISA) is the retired Chair of Mission and Pentecostal Studies at the University of Birmingham, UK.
[1] Todd M. Johnson and Kenneth R. Ross (eds.), *Atlas of Global Christianity 1910-2010* (Edinburgh: Edinburgh University Press, 2009), pp. 8-9.

emphasising healing, prophecy and, in some cases, prosperity'.[2] Pentecostalism has not only contributed enormously to this southward shift of Christianity's centre of gravity but its spectacular growth also casts considerable doubt on the meta-narratives of the inevitable process of secularization that have become popular in the sociology of religion in the western world. During the second half of the twentieth century the most significant changes in the global demography of Christianity have occurred through the growth of Pentecostalism, which began in a series of revival movements at the beginning of the century occurring within a few years of each other in different parts of the world.

In Europe, William Kay has been in the forefront of the study of Pentecostalism, not only through his many and varied publications, but also in his encouraging and mentoring others to study the subject at a postgraduate level, for which the scholars of Pentecostalism at the University of Birmingham are particularly grateful. His books and articles on Pentecostalism have been pioneering and based on extensive field research and comprehensive surveys. This is particularly true of those books on Pentecostalism in Britain, where he tackles subjects never before covered in academic research and reveals some surprising results.[3] Although these studies hold interests far beyond the British Isles, his latest books on Pentecostalism branch out into the study of global Pentecostalism beyond anything he has attempted before.[4] I will discuss this further below. Pentecostalism has almost certainly been the fastest growing religious movement in the contemporary world and a phenomenon that has to be reckoned with, especially in countering the sometimes prevalent view that secularization is the inevitable outcome of an historical process. Ironically, most of the growth of Pentecostal and Charismatic Christianity in all its diversity, both inside and outside the older churches, has occurred during the very period when secularization in Europe was at its height and there was a dramatic change in the religious affiliation

---

[2] Johnson and Ross, *Atlas of Global Christianity*, p. 51.
[3] William K. Kay, *Pentecostals in Britain* (Carlisle: Paternoster, 2000); William K. Kay, *Apostolic Networks in Britain* (Carlisle: Paternoster, 2007).
[4] William K. Kay, *Pentecostalism* (London: SCM, 2009); William K. Kay, *Pentecostalism: A Very Short Introduction* (Oxford: OUP, 2011).

of ordinary people, who simply stopped going to church.[5] The un-anticipated global expansion of Pentecostalism in recent times poses significant questions regarding the role of religion in the contemporary world, including its societies, ideologies, and politics.

Probably the main reason for the growth of Pentecostalism is that it is above all else a missionary movement. This is how to understand the primary motivation for its global expansion throughout the twentieth century. Pentecostalism sees itself primarily as a movement of mission and evangelism that must communicate its message to as many people in as many countries and cities as possible in the shortest possible time.[6] Sometimes its outreach has been aggressive and insensitive to the religions and cultures around it, but it has probably turned more people from other or no faiths to Christianity than most other Christian missionary movements have done. Its message is a simple one of repentance and conversion to faith in Christ as Saviour (as social scientists put it, a radical break with the past), but this is also accompanied by the power of the Spirit bringing healing, deliverance from evil forces, and supernatural signs to confirm its message. Despite their sometimes confrontational attitude, Pentecostals see all this as positive aspects of their growth and confidently proclaim a message they are convinced has answers for both global and local problems.

At the beginning of the twentieth century, global Pentecostalism started as a restoration or revitalization movement among radical evangelicals who were expecting a world-wide, Holy Spirit revival before the imminent coming of Christ. They believed that their movement was a revival of New Testament, miracle-affirming Christianity that had awakened a church that had largely lost its power. The fundamental conviction of Pentecostals is that the power they receive through the Spirit is to evangelize all nations and so glorify Jesus Christ. It was estimated that Pentecostalism had reached fifty different nations within the first decade of its existence. Although growth was at first modest, as the world of the twentieth century lurched

---

[5] Hugh McLeod, 'The Crisis of Christianity in the West: entering a post-Christian era?' in Hugh McLeod (ed.), *The Cambridge History of Christianity: World Christianity c.1914-c.2000* (Cambridge: Cambridge University Press, 2006), pp. 323-47; *idem, The Religious Crisis of the 1960s* (Oxford: OUP, 2010); Callum G. Brown, *The Death of Christian Britain* (New York: Routledge, 2001).

[6] Allan Anderson, *Spreading Fires: The Missionary Nature of Early Pentecostalism* (London: SCM, 2007).

through two devastating world wars and colonial empires crumbled, Pentecostalism expanded and adapted to the changing world. Perhaps more than any other form of Christianity, it was able to utilise popular religious cultures in different parts of the world, to respond to the felt needs of the poor, and to address the desire for a more indigenous form of Christianity independent of foreign forms – all of which helped its transition into the Majority World and its rapid growth. As one observer put it,

> Pentecostalism has thrived in the Global South amongst peoples marginalised from power precisely because it both incorporates their cultural values (emphasis on the emotional and the spiritual world) and responds to their deeply felt needs for healing and a voice in the midst of great poverty and socioeconomic and political marginalisation.[7]

Key to this transformation was the role of local leaders who took the Pentecostal message into the interiors of the southern continents, East Asia, and to the islands, often using innovations that addressed more directly local needs than the western missionaries had done. By the twenty-first century Pentecostalism had become predominantly a non-western phenomenon, with thousands of mutations from large urban mega-churches with high-tech equipment and sophisticated organizations to remote village house churches meeting sometimes in secret with handfuls of believers. The largest Pentecostal churches in the world are now found in sub-Saharan Africa, Latin America, and the Asian Pacific rim. One needs to visit Lagos, Seoul, and Rio de Janeiro to see the largest churches – not London, Berlin, or Los Angeles.

Pentecostal and Charismatic Christianity in all its diversity, both inside and outside the older churches, was probably the fastest expanding religious movement worldwide in the twentieth century. According to one debatable estimate, it had some 614 million adherents by 2010, a quarter of the world's Christian population; at least that is what this most generous statistic tells us.[8] Even if these figures are inaccurate or inflated, no observer of Christianity can deny the

---

[7] Johnson and Ross, *Atlas of Global Christianity*, p. 67.
[8] Todd M. Johnson, David B. Barrett, and Peter F. Crossing, 'Christianity 2010: A View from the New *Atlas of Global Christianity*', *International Bulletin of Missionary Research* 34.1 (2010), pp. 29-36 (36).

significance of Pentecostalism in today's religious world. In countries like Nigeria, Kenya, the Philippines, South Korea, Brazil, and Argentina, its presence is everywhere, often dominating the media and sometimes even the political arena. It is a growing force in China and India, the most populous and rapidly developing nations on earth. Considering that this movement had only a tiny number of adherents at the beginning of the twentieth century, its growth has been phenomenal. The many varieties of Pentecostalism have contributed to the reshaping of the nature of global religion itself and this has enormous implications. Its adherents are often on the cutting edge of the encounter with people of other faiths, although sometimes confrontationally so. The future of Christianity is affected by this seismic change in the character of the global Christian faith. It is no accident that the southward shift in Christianity's centre of gravity over the twentieth century has coincided with the emergence and expansion of Pentecostalism. It will be important to trace both the contours of the changing nature and the demographics of global Christianity and the contribution of Pentecostalism to these features.[9]

Making sense out of the bewildering varieties of Pentecostalism found throughout the contemporary world is not an easy task. In fact, it is becoming increasingly difficult to refer to all these different movements as 'Pentecostalism' at all, as the following will reveal. There is much disagreement about the correct use of terms, if indeed there is a 'correct' term. But despite its diversity, there are certain universal features and beliefs held in common throughout its many manifestations, most of which emerged in the early twentieth century, but were also found in various movements throughout the history of Christianity. This is not a homogeneous movement, for there are literally thousands of different Pentecostal denominations and many movements independent of those forms founded in North America and Europe at the start of the twentieth century. Notwithstanding these very significant differences, however, these varieties may all be described as 'Pentecostal' in character, theology, and ethos. Whether we need to describe them thus is a huge issue that needs further discussion. What is even more problematic is when people use statistics for their own ideological or expansionist purposes.

---

[9] Allan H. Anderson, *To the Ends of the Earth: Pentecostalism and the Transformation of World Christianity* (Oxford: OUP, 2013).

None of this, however, should detract from the remarkable and irreversible changes that have occurred in global Christianity.

Defining Pentecostalism

Kay acknowledges the difficulties in defining Pentecostalism and writes that however we do it, 'our definitions will be more or less inclusive'.[10] Inclusiveness is fraught with difficulties when it comes to global Pentecostalism, and this is why Kay, like so many scholars, does not offer any working definition.[11] Although the term 'Pentecostalism' is now widely used by scholars of religion (especially by social scientists) and that most of these scholars seem to know what it means, 'Pentecostalism' has been used to embrace large movements as widely diverse as the ascetic and celibacy-practising Pentecostal Mission in India, the Seventh-Day and 'Oneness' True Jesus Church in China, the uniform-wearing, highly ritualistic Zion Christian Church in Southern Africa (together with other African Zionist and Apostolic churches), and Brazil's equally enormous prosperity and deliverance-oriented Universal Church of the Kingdom of God, now expanding internationally. These diverse denominations are gathered together by some scholars under one label with classical Pentecostal denominations like the Assemblies of God and the various Churches of God, the Catholic Charismatic movement, 'neo-Charismatic' independent churches with prosperity and 'Word of Faith' theologies. It includes the so-called 'Third Wave' evangelical movement with their use of spiritual gifts framed within a theology differing considerably from the 'initial evidence' theology of classical Pentecostalism, and many other forms of Charismatic Christianity as diverse as Christianity itself. Clearly, such a widely inclusive definition is difficult to sustain. Classical Pentecostal scholars have sometimes implied that Johnson and Barrett's statistics establish the numerical strength of their particular form of Pentecostalism.[12] These scholars begin at Los Angeles (or Topeka, Kansas) and state rather triumphalistically, that

---

[10] Kay, *Pentecostalism*, p. 8.

[11] Part of what follows is adapted from Allan Anderson, 'Varieties, Definitions and Taxonomies', in A. Anderson, M. Bergunder, A. Droogers, and C. van der Laan (eds.), *Studying Global Pentecostalism: Theories and Methods* (Los Angeles: University of California, 2010), pp. 13-29.

[12] Vinson Synan, *The Holiness-Pentecostal Tradition: Charismatic Movements in the Twentieth Century* (Grand Rapids, MI: Eerdmans, 1997).

Pentecostalism has grown to half a billion members without analysing either what are included in these figures or what are the very different historical trajectories that brought about such simultaneous diversity and growth. Although Kay has managed to avoid this trap, his analysis of the numbers involved in Johnson and Barrett's figures does suggest that more consideration should be given to analysing the largest group within these statistics, the non-western 'neo-Charismatic' and independent churches.[13]

Looking at Johnson et al.'s latest (2016) annual offering, where these statisticians of global Christianity from Barrett's stable state that there are 657 million 'Pentecostals/Charismatics' in the world in 2016 (a figure projected to rise to over a billion by 2050).[14] The statisticians have departed from their three distinct forms, where the term 'Neocharismatic', numerically by far the largest of the three, was included. Although not expressly defined in this article, presumably 'Pentecostal' here means 'classical Pentecostal' as defined below; 'Charismatic' means those who practice spiritual gifts in the older Catholic, Anglican, and Protestant denominations (with Catholics forming the great majority); and it also includes all others, especially the vast number of independent churches – perhaps two-thirds of the total, previously termed 'Neocharismatic'. The change in terminology shows how much confusion there is in terminology. Kay follows the broad three-fold analysis, but I do think that this last group needs much more careful analysis by scholars, not an easy task. In many cases, movements and churches here might not consider themselves 'Pentecostal' at all, nor would they be considered as such by local Christians. So, we have to ask ourselves to what extent does the study of Pentecostalism in the western world make constructs that might be useful for academic discourse but bear little relevance to the grassroots movements it is trying to represent? Social scientists and other scholars place all these movements under the generic title 'Pentecostalism', based on phenomenological evidence but with little regard to the significant theological and historical differences. I hope that future scholarly analyses will help unravel these complexities, even though any attempt at definition will fall short of precision.

---

[13] Kay, *Pentecostalism*, pp. 11-15.

[14] Todd M. Johnson, Gina A. Zurlo, Albert W. Hickman, and Peter F. Crossing, 'Christianity 2016: Latin America and Projecting Religions to 2020', *International Bulletin of Mission Research* 40.1 (2016), pp. 22-29 (26).

We should no longer assume that there are over 650 million 'Pentecostals' in the world without further qualification, as only a fifth of these are classical Pentecostals with direct or indirect connections to the North American revival at the beginning of the twentieth century. A hundred and fifty million or so classical Pentecostals after only a century, however, is still an impressive statistic. But if we are to do justice to this global movement of the Spirit, we must include an analysis of its more recent expressions in the Charismatic and Neo-charismatic movements, perhaps making allowances for our categorising to remain diffuse. Johnson himself once placed all these movements into an all-embracing term 'Renewalists',[15] but this term has since been abandoned. This term did not give sufficient recognition to the thousands of churches started by the entrepreneurial initiatives of Africans, Asians, Pacific and Caribbean islanders, and Latin Americans, who did not seek to renew older forms of Christianity but to form new ones from scratch.

So, what exactly do we mean when we talk of 'Pentecostalism'? There is no 'exact' way to answer this question – and debates will rage on. Defining anything is a hazardous exercise, as Kay has observed.[16] Jacobsen has pointed out that from its earliest times Pentecostalism has defied precise definition. It is 'clear to everyone with regard to its general meaning but impossible to define in detail in a way that will satisfy everyone'. The nearest Jacobsen gets to a definition is, 'In a general sense, being Pentecostal means that one is committed to a Spirit-centred, miracle-affirming, praise-oriented version of the Christian faith', but concludes that 'there is no meta-model of Pentecostalism – no essence of Pentecostalism or normative archetype'.[17] Any attempt to define the term is bound to have detractors. The scientific accuracy of the various statistics is a massive issue, but the western reader familiar with classical Pentecostalism must also beware of confusing this specific section of Pentecostalism with other forms that form the greater portion in the statistics. Global Pentecostalism is more diverse than any other Christian tradition precisely because its different forms of expression are rooted in local

---

[15] Johnson and Ross, *Atlas of Global Christianity*, p. 102.
[16] Kay, *Pentecostalism*, 5; Allan Anderson, 'Varieties, Definitions and Taxonomies', pp. 13-29.
[17] Douglas Jacobsen, *Thinking in the Spirit: Theologies of the Early Pentecostal Movement* (Bloomington: Indiana University, 2003), pp. 11-12.

contexts. Pentecostalism's localness makes any attempt to understand the dynamics of Pentecostal globalisation a difficult exercise. Kay begins his textbook on Pentecostalism with descriptions of different Pentecostal services, as I did in the first edition on *An Introduction to Pentecostalism*.[18] He then suggests that these different expressions have certain common features:

> What they have in common is a willingness to be open to the Holy Spirit. There is a confidence that God is an interventionist God and that the Holy Spirit can be felt and manifested through human agency in Christian gatherings. There is a belief in charismatic gifts, whether these are gifts of healing or utterances in unknown tongues ...[19]

Once again, this suggests that the family resemblance consists of an emphasis on the practice of spiritual gifts. My own desire to do justice to the forms of Pentecostalism found outside the western world and to be inclusive in my definition of 'Pentecostalism' is a perspective that sometimes solicits controversy among western-founded classical Pentecostals. There are sometimes unwitting double standards here: classical Pentecostals cannot at the same time claim that there are 650 million in 'their' movement while at the same time exclude those groups within this inclusive definition that they do not consider 'Pentecostal' at all. The alternative is to abandon the statistics game altogether.

Classifications

Pentecostalism has considerably mutated from its diverse beginnings a century ago into several different forms today, each with its own family resemblances. I have attempted to classify these forms with broad strokes to include the following, each with its own sub-types:

Classical Pentecostals

These are those who can be shown to originate in the evangelical revival and missionary movements of the early twentieth century, particularly in the western world. Considering theological differences,

---

[18] Allan Anderson, *An Introduction to Pentecostalism: Global Charismatic Christianity* (Cambridge: CUP, 2004), pp. 1-9.

[19] Kay, *Pentecostalism*, p. 5.

these can be further divided into: (a) Holiness Pentecostals, whose roots are in the nineteenth century holiness movement with a belief in a second work of grace called 'sanctification' and a third stage experience called 'baptism in the Spirit', usually accompanied by speaking in tongues; (b) 'Finished Work' Pentecostals, who differ in their approach to sanctification, seeing it as a consequence of conversion to be followed by Spirit baptism with speaking in tongues (often seen as 'initial physical evidence') as a second work of grace; and from the latter stem: (c) Oneness Pentecostals, who reject the doctrine of the Trinity and posit a Unitarianism that includes the absolute deity of Christ; and (d) Apostolic Pentecostals, both Oneness and Trinitarian, who emphasize the authority of present-day 'apostles' and 'prophets' and are especially strong in West Africa. These four categories apply mostly to those denominations emanating from western Pentecostalism, such as the significant number of Apostolic Pentecostals in West Africa influenced by the Apostolic Church in Britain, including such large African denominations as the Church of Pentecost (Ghana) and the Christ Apostolic Church (Nigeria and Ghana). All of these groups have a theology of a subsequent experience of Spirit baptism usually accompanied by speaking in tongues.

Older Church Charismatics
These include Catholic, Anglican, and various Protestant Charismatics, the majority being Catholics. These movements are widespread and worldwide and sometimes approach the subject of Spirit baptism and spiritual gifts from a sacramental perspective. These Charismatics differ from each other in the same ways that their denominations differ in theology, but they also constitute a powerful force for ecumenical contact. In some countries like Nigeria and the Philippines, they constitute a large percentage of the Christian population. One of the best known of these movements is the Catholic El Shaddai movement in the Philippines, with over seven million members much larger than any Pentecostal denomination there.

Older Independent Churches,
Examples of these include especially the 'Old Three-Self Churches' and newer house churches in China of a 'Pentecostal' nature, the Indian Pentecostal churches emanating from the (Ceylon) Pentecostal Mission and the Indian Pentecostal Church of God, and the multitudes of 'Spirit churches' in sub-Saharan Africa. China has a long

tradition of independent Pentecostal churches like the True Jesus Church and the Jesus Family, but new unregistered churches in this vast country are proliferating by the thousands and are mostly of a fundamentalist and Pentecostal type. Similarly, in India, the older independent churches have given rise to many new ones who selectively borrow older ideas and practices. The older independent churches differ considerably from each other; they sometimes (but often do not) have links with classical Pentecostalism, they do not always have a clearly defined theology nor (in the case of China and Africa) necessarily see themselves as 'Pentecostal', but their practices of healing, prayer, and spiritual gifts are decidedly so.

Neo-charismatic Churches
These churches are also termed 'Charismatic' independent churches, including megachurches, and consisting of many, often overlapping kinds: (a) 'Word of Faith' churches and similar churches where the emphasis is on physical health and material prosperity by faith, predominating in North America and Africa; (b) 'Third Wave' churches (a misnomer, but that is another issue), who usually conflate Spirit baptism with conversion and see spiritual gifts as available to every Christian believer without there being a necessary 'crisis' experience subsequent to conversion – these are mostly based in the North; (c) new Apostolic churches, who have reintroduced an apostolic leadership to their governance not unlike that of the earlier Apostolic Pentecostals; and (d) probably the largest group, consisting of all other different independent churches that overlap and vary considerably in their theology between 'Third Wave', 'Word of Faith', and various kinds of classical Pentecostal, and are therefore even more difficult to categorize. Some of the churches in the 'new church' category are among the largest Pentecostal churches in the world, among them the Universal Church of the Kingdom of God (with origins in Brazil) and the Redeemed Christian Church of God (originating in Nigeria). These various churches are constantly mutating and proliferating, creating new forms of independent churches, literally every week.

There are indeed fundamental and substantial differences between classical Pentecostals and Charismatics on the one hand, and between Pentecostalism in the global South and that in the North on the other. Even within classical Pentecostalism (sometimes within the same Pentecostal denomination) there are similar fundamental differences to those between classical Pentecostals and Charismatics. But there are far more commonalities between these different groups than there are differences, essential emphases common to all that distinguish them from the rest of Christianity, and these theological and historical commonalities justify such an inclusive definition. There are admittedly inherent dangers in such an approach. I prefer to adapt the definition of the social historian Robert Mapes Anderson,[20] whose American-focussed study admittedly cannot be applied to the rest of global Pentecostalism without qualification. So, 'Pentecostalism' includes all those movements and churches where the emphasis is on the experience of the Spirit and the practice of spiritual gifts. The experience of the Spirit may or may not include speaking in tongues as 'initial evidence' of baptism in the Spirit, what for many classical Pentecostals is an essential characteristic. But it will always include an emphasis on a spiritual experience and the practice of spiritual gifts as found in Paul's first Corinthian letter, or what Kay calls a belief in 'an interventionist God and that the Holy Spirit can be felt and manifested through human agency'.[21] In particular, distinctive spiritual gifts include those that are most unusual in the Christian church: prophecy, healing, and speaking in tongues. This, for me, is what Pentecostalism is all about. Using a narrower theological definition (as some classical Pentecostals do) like 'initial evidence', 'speaking in tongues', or even 'baptism in the Spirit' is fraught with difficulties when there are numerous exceptions all over the world. This is even the case with those who can indirectly trace their origins to the USA, such as in most forms of European classical Pentecostalism. Establishing what the criteria for our definitions are is essential, for it is often easier to criticise the 'inclusive' definitions of others without providing a clear alternative. I do not pretend or assume that 'Pentecostal', 'Charismatic', and 'Neopentecostal' (or 'Neocharismatic') are identical or interchangeable terms, but they often do overlap.

Nobody can adequately treat the subject of classical Pentecostalism in contemporary Christianity without noting its constant interplay with and influence on the Charismatic and Neocharismatic movements. Many of the best-known leaders of the Charismatic movement were either classical Pentecostals themselves or were

---

[20] Robert Mapes Anderson, *Vision of the Disinherited: The Making of American Pentecostalism* (Peabody MA: Hendrickson, 1979).
[21] Kay, *Pentecostalism*, p. 5.

influenced by classical Pentecostalism, and they played catalytic roles in the emergence of the Charismatic and Neocharismatic movements. Similarly, the liturgies of classical Pentecostalism, particularly styles of worship and song, have been fundamentally affected and changed by the Charismatic movement. The independent churches in Africa, China and elsewhere have been indelibly influenced by their own encounters with classical Pentecostalism. It would be simplistic to deny these associations, for we live in a globalized world where religious acculturation is a fact of life. The present needs to be understood in the light of the past, and this is essential in any attempt to make sense of the contemporary proliferation of global Pentecostalism.

Emerging Scholarship

William Kay has played a significant role in the emerging scholarship, both in Britain and in the Majority World. Studies on global Pentecostalism outside the western world have only recently begun to emerge. One of the most notable is that of Amos Yong, a Chinese American theologian born in Malaysia, who attempts to use his data on global Pentecostalism for suggesting that a global, pneumatological theology is possible. His selective treatment of a mass of reading is purposeful: to justify his theological position that Pentecostalism is diverse, practical, holistic, and with strong connections to the marginalized of this world, and to introduce his contention that a 'reconstruction' of a global Pentecostal theology is possible.[22] The study has a pneumatological focus: it is the experience of the Spirit in all its diversity in global Pentecostalism that informs a global theology. For Yong, Pentecostal theology is grounded in soteriology, a soteriology that is 'thoroughly pneumatological', but also multidimensional. His method is also dynamic and progressive, and therefore open-ended. The experiences of global Pentecostalisms mean that the 'multidimensionality' of salvation is expanded comprehensively and holistically to include personal, family, ecclesial, material, social (race, class, and gender), cosmic, and eschatological salvation. Donald Miller and Tetsunao Yamamori's fascinating book also treats global

---

[22] Amos Yong, *The Spirit Poured Out on All Flesh: Pentecostalism and the Possibility of Global Theology* (Grand Rapids, MI: Baker Academic, 2005), pp. 79-80.

Pentecostalism, but in a less theoretical way than Yong's. Using extensive fieldwork in several countries across the globe, they portray
Pentecostalism as a complex new social movement of many different
varieties, focussing on those forms of Pentecostalism with active social ministries, which they term 'Progressive Pentecostalism'.[23] The
massive Templeton-funded project directed by Miller and Yamamori
has revealed a wealth of new information on Pentecostalism in the
Majority World and in former communist bloc countries.

Scholars of Pentecostalism in Europe tend to be more cognisant
of the influence of the Majority World on global Pentecostalism than
their North American counterparts are. William Kay's 'core text' Pentecostalism is an example. In his descriptions of Pentecostal services,
he includes examples from Kenya and South India.[24] He describes
Pentecostalism as 'revivalistic' following revival traditions of the past,
adding that 'Patterns of revival behaviour became part of Pentecostal
worship. There was lay leadership and emotion and unpredictability.'[25]
He links the revivals in Korea, Wales, and India at the start of the
century, together with that in Azusa Street, Los Angeles, with the beginnings of Pentecostalism.[26] Kay's four familiar examples of denominational consolidation all originate in the western world (the
USA, Norway, Americans in South Africa, and Britain). There were,
of course, many examples of denominations consolidating without
western influence in Africa, Asia, and Latin America. These histories
have begun to be written and need further integration into histori-
ographies of global Pentecostalism.[27] However, the chapters on Asia,
Latin America, and Africa compensate for this, show Kay's increasingly interest in and knowledge of Pentecostalism in the Majority
World, and demonstrate the global character and considerable variety
within Pentecostalism. More attention, however, could be given to
the vibrant new Pentecostal and Charismatic churches in these continents. The history of the healing and Latter Rain revivals, the Charismatic and post-Charismatic movements, and in fact, the rest of the
book dealing with Pentecostal theology and sociology, is

[23] Miller and Yamamori, *Global Pentecostalism*, p. 2.
[24] Kay, *Pentecostalism*, p. 4.
[25] Kay, *Pentecostalism*, p. 59.
[26] Kay, *Pentecostalism*, pp. 60-70.
[27] A major theme of Anderson, *To the Ends of the Earth*.

overwhelmingly western-oriented. This is more of a reflection of Kay's own background and experience than a weakness in his research.

What Kay has achieved in these and other studies is to challenge the stereotypical views of Pentecostalism, particularly those that have characterized the theological and historical studies emerging over the past half century. The synchronic and diachronic links between the various movements we call 'global Pentecostalism' today can be demonstrated historically. Links and influences between classical Pentecostalism and independent churches throughout the world (both contemporary and early twentieth century), those in the middle of the century between classical Pentecostals and the Charismatic movement, and those towards the end of the century between the earlier movements and the new independent 'Neocharismatic' churches are illustrated in these publications.

When I wrote the first edition of *Introduction to Pentecostalism* in 2003, I had only a little evidence to substantiate my conviction that the Azusa Street revival was but one significant event in a whole series of global revivals in early twentieth century evangelical Christianity, and that this event by itself did not constitute the beginning of global Pentecostalism.[28] I think Kay would agree wholeheartedly in this analysis, one that resisted popular stereotyping and was global in orientation. But this book created some controversy among more conservative American Pentecostal scholars. The research undertaken for *Spreading Fires*, completed in 2006, and my two subsequent books, confirmed my earlier hunch that Pentecostalism, or rather, the global Pentecostalisms as we know them today, have been formed by long processes of interweaving events and have taken decades to emerge.[29] Nevertheless, all these studies have traced the early histories of some of the non-western founders in a conscious attempt to debunk the 'made-in-the-USA, exported-to-the-rest-of-the-world' syndrome that has plagued some American histories of Pentecostalism. In these books I was passionate about drawing attention to some of the things I saw as shortcomings in the Pentecostal movement needing correction, such as the rather appalling record on ecumenism, social activism, gender equality, and racism. If the considerable work left to be

---

[28] Anderson, *Introduction to Pentecostalism.*
[29] Anderson, *Spreading Fires.*

done by scholars of Pentecostalism provokes people enough to cause them to be more culturally and theologically sensitive, more politically and socially aware, and more globally oriented, then we will have succeeded.

This essay has tried to show that Pentecostalism today has had an enormous role in changing the nature of global Christianity in its southwards shift during the twentieth century. Perhaps more than any other Christian sector has done, it has been a catalyst in transforming Christianity from being predominantly a religion of the northern continents (with Catholics in Latin America and small pockets of Christians in Asia and Africa) to one where two thirds of its members are in the Majority World or the global South. This remarkable change has happened not only with the help of the rapidly increasing numbers of adherents of Pentecostal and Charismatic churches, but also in the 'Pentecostalisation' of older, mainstream Christianity, Catholic, Anglican, and Protestant. This is a factor that will remain with us for this generation and perhaps, for many generations yet to come. That Christianity will never be the same again is without doubt; whether Pentecostalism will continue to be robust in the face of the pressures of urbanisation, economic growth, and secular materialism will remain to be seen. Clearly there is need for the kind of pioneering research done by William Kay to continue well into the twenty-first century, so that the impact of Pentecostalism upon global religion and the challenges of our time might be more clearly defined, while its weaknesses, corruptions, and sometimes scandalous exploitations might also be analysed. Rigorous, honest, and reflective scholarship by Pentecostal scholars like William Kay can be a prophetic voice in this regard.

3

THE ORTHODOX CHURCH AND THE CHARISMATIC MOVEMENT

ANDREW WALKER[*]

I am privileged and proud to contribute to this *Festschrift* for Professor Kay. I have included here a new personal preamble, an earlier Orthodox critique (and the only one) that I previously published of classical and neo-Pentecostalism.[1]

Preamble to the Original Publication

A favourite metaphor for the religious life in Christianity is 'the journey'. We can find it in the poetry of the psalms ('Though I walk through the shadow of the valley of death I will fear no evil', [Psalm 23]); in the parables of Jesus ('A man was going down from Jerusalem to Jericho', [Luke 10:30]); and in the descriptions of life-changing encounters with the Risen Christ of the apostles ('And as he journeyed he [Saul] came near Damascus and suddenly a light shone round him from heaven', [Acts 9:3]).

In the 4th century, Helena, the mother of the Emperor Constantine, hijacked the metaphor by turning it into what was to become a standard motif in the literary genre of the late middle Ages. The genre can best be described as Medieval Romance and the motif was

---

[*] The late Andrew Walker (PhD, Goldsmiths, University of London) was Emeritus Professor of Theology, Religion, and Culture at King's College, London.
[1] D. Martin and P. Mullen (eds.), *Strange Gifts: A Guide to Charismatic Renewal* (Oxford: Basil Blackwell, 1984), pp. 163-72. Reprinted here with permission from the publisher.

'the quest'. In Helena's case the quest was to find the one true cross of Christ which according to some traditions she did. So impressed was the Byzantine Church by this discovery that Helena is one of the few woman in Christendom to receive the accolade 'equal to the apostles'. Splinters of the cross (true or not) were to fuel the relish for relics in Europe and were to become a roaring trade until the Protestant Reformation.

The most enduring quest story of Medieval Romance is the Arthurian legend and the search for the Holy Grail. Quests by virtue of the long and drawn-out journey usually appear in saga or epic form both in oral and literary cultures. *The Lord of the Rings* is probably the most well-known 20th century inheritor of the medieval quest motif. But a second and far more potent tradition also emerged in the Middle Ages, which kept alive the journey as spiritual metaphor: and this, of course, was the pilgrimage. Chaucer's *Canterbury Tales*, though not religious in nature, are grounded in the significance of pilgrimage for cleansing of soul and renewal of faith. To be a Pilgrim (a traveller) transcended Catholic Culture and became both a proper noun for the Puritan *émigrés* from Old England to New England – The Pilgrim Fathers – and also emerged as a mainstay of Christian literature and piety, with allegories such as John Bunyan's *Pilgrim's Progress* and C.S. Lewis's *The Pilgrim's Regress* being obvious examples. The Orthodox East have also ferried this tradition across the centuries. In Russia, Orthodox spirituality is at its most inspirational in the anonymous authored books of the nineteen-century, *The Way of the Pilgrim*, and *The Pilgrim Continues his Way*.[2]

Journeys like following Chesterton's drunken English Road may lead to nowhere in particular or slowly meander to some kind of destination in the end. Main roads, however, since the 'Royal Road' of the Bible (Num. 21.17-19, NAB) have a special place in the annals of spiritual journeys. Roads swollen with searchers looking for objects (questers) or places (pilgrims) jostle with fellow travellers who are 'just looking' (tourists) and stragglers and loners (seekers) trying to find a way of being Christian they can square with their conscience – a 'form of life worth living' as Wittgenstein might have put it.

Given this heavy traffic heaving in both directions it is not surprising that William Kay and myself nearly missed each other despite

---

[2] See my foreword to *The Way of the Pilgrim* (London: SPCK, 1995).

both being seekers travelling on the same road. But then he was mov-ing west while I was going east, and it is easy to get lost in a crowd. William, on his maternal side, comes from an aristocratic family of White Russians who were part of the first great wave of the Russian Diaspora of 1917-1920. One of William's uncles was Prince Dimitri Obolensky, who was also a knight of the realm and Professor of Russian and Balkan History at Oxford. William Kay was baptised into the Russian Orthodox tradition but was not really nurtured or tutored in it to any great extent. His father was an English intellectual and not, like his mother, overtly religious. Consequently, William lived most of his early years in a religious no-man's-land increasingly out of touch with his mother's 'Holy Russia' but not fully embedded into the secular intellectual English world of his father. Perhaps the one Orthodox religious spark that fired him up and helped put him on the main road was a visit to his home from the Russian priest Fr. Anthony Bloom, later to become the senior Russian bishop in West-ern Europe, Metropolitan Anthony of Sourozh. A scientist and med-ical doctor not a theologian by training, the bishop was asked by the still-at-school William Kay how it was intellectually credible in the light of the enormity of the cosmos and the vast unknowableness of an unfathomable universe to believe in God. To the surprise of the young agnostic the bishop's reply said nothing about intellectual sat-isfaction or metaphysical speculation. He simply said, 'what matters is that you are loved'.

By contrast I was born a working-class son of a Pentecostal pastor and after a brief flirtation with bible college in London became an agnostic; after a decade or more had passed an unsettling dream opened up the possibility of faith again and I set off on the road looking for someone I might recognise as Lord and somewhere I could feel I belonged. In the event I was to find my spiritual home in the Russian Church William had left behind, while he pitched his tent with the Pentecostals I had abandoned. I would describe William and myself as nomads or dwellers rather than hunters or settlers. We re-main loyal members of our freely-chosen Confessions but have not become denominational proselytes or retrenched isolationists. Wil-liam has not cut himself off from the historic churches and the wider reaches of Christendom, as his highly respected work on religious education demonstrates.

As for me since 1973, despite my Orthodox conversion, my major sociological field work has been on the new church (or house church) movements and I have participated at Spring Harvest, Anglican Renewal Conferences, and been the keynote speaker at various Pentecostal venues from Oral Roberts University in Tulsa to Elim Bible College when it was in Nantwich, Cheshire. In 1980, shortly before this chapter was first mooted in its original form, I visited the World Council of Churches Consultation on the Charismatic Movement as a lay Orthodox theologian and as a member of the British Council of Churches contingent that included New Testament scholar Professor James Dunn and Michael Harper, the founder of the 'Fountain Trust' – arguably the major influence on the Charismatic Renewal Movement in England and Wales in the late 1960s and 1970s. I have continued to contribute sociological and theological bits and pieces on the Pentecostal world for the academy, the ecclesia and the media but it is William who has done more than any one in Britain to provide empathetic but objective data on the Charismatic movements. Some of my reservations concerning aspects of Pentecostal and Charismatic practices and beliefs are shared by William (as he was a cradle Orthodox, I like to think he may carry within him a subliminal residue of Patristic cautiousness into the contemporary Pentecostal world).

Ironically, I was commissioned to be a missioner of the Orthodox Church by the same Metropolitan Anthony who helped William Kay on the road to Pentecost all those years ago. His commission to me was simple: build bridges to those you have left behind. It seems to me taking William's work as a whole that he too has built bridges; he certainly has not burnt them. If he had then we would never have spotted each other on the road but would have passed each other by like land-locked ships in the night.

I have attached this preamble as a prefix to the main text because I do not see things in quite the same way I did when this chapter appeared in its original form: in those days (early 1980s) my major concern was to demonstrate the differences between charismatic and institutional religion, Bible and tradition, experience, and reason. I find at the present time that I can no longer keep these apparent dualities apart. This year, as I pass from in-house academic to wandering emeritus, Orthodox and Pentecostal Christianity look increasingly alike to me. The liturgical form is of course different, the cultural styles still hostile to each other, the weight and balance of ancient and modern uneven between them, but the 'feel' and 'taste' of the spirituality is much the same.

I am not the first person to feel this way. Pentecostal pioneer. Alexander Boddy, the Anglican clergyman who played such a strategic role in the early Pentecostal revivals and edited *Confidence*, the most influential Charismatic publication in Britain for many years, had himself travelled to Russia and was deeply impressed with the spirituality of the pilgrims and the devotion of the peasants to their faith. It was the Russian Cross he chose to put round his daughter's neck when he baptised her and we know from her own account when she became an adult that he was open to the use of icons which were prominently displayed in his vicarage in Monkwearmouth.[3]

And so to the original article.

The Marginality of the Charismatic Movement to Eastern Orthodoxy

Perhaps the most interesting and significant feature of the modern Charismatic Movement is the extent to which it has taken root in the historic churches. While 'enthusiasms' of many kinds have existed in these churches, the advent of a Pentecostalist revivalism under the less threatening title of 'Charismatic Renewal' was not altogether to be expected. The effect of this renewal, growing and flourishing in the traditional soils of Roman Catholicism, Lutheranism, and Anglicanism appears to be grafting the sectarian offshoots back upon the original stemmata.

The seeds of renewal, however, have not been so successful when sown into the ground of Eastern Orthodoxy. As far as the peoples of Eastern Europe, Greece, and the Middle East are concerned, the seeds of charismatic revival are a Protestant and Western phenomena that do not directly concern them. Orthodox communities in the traditional heartlands are barely aware of the western crop of neo-Pentecostalism. There are rumours of charismatic plantings in Romania and the student population of Lebanon but gossip hardly constitutes evidence. It would seem, for the moment, that Orthodox soil is either

---

[3] G. Wakefield, *Alexander Boddy: Pentecostal Anglican Pioneer* (Carlisle: Paternoster, 2007).

too sterile (or, perhaps, too rich) for charismatic spores to fructify, or else the renewal has simply not yet reached the east with any germinating power. The new Pentecostalism has sprung up in the Third World in Protestant and Catholic countries; in no sense, therefore, should the renewal be seen as a purely western phenomena (as some Orthodox erroneously think).

In the west, where the Orthodox diaspora exists in a pluralistic Christendom, charismata have made a showing. Individual members of Orthodox churches have participated in charismatic meetings, and some have laid claim to the experience which is still usually called 'the baptism of the Holy Spirit'. Official reaction is mixed. Archbishop Paul of Finland, in *The Faith We Hold*,[4] has warned of the superficialities and sentimentality of charismatic experiences, whilst Metropolitan Anthony of Sourozh in England prefers to judge each case on its merits rather than openly endorse the whole Charismatic Movement or condemn it out of hand. A Serbian priest (who has recently become a bishop in the Orthodox Church of America) was involved in the Renewal Movement for some years. He supported it, on the whole, whilst worrying about the lack of discipline. Cryptically, he used to say 'When you open the window to let in the fresh air, you also invite bad smells'.

The Greek Orthodox Church in America is the only major Orthodox community in the west that has seen the Charismatic Movement flourish on its home ground. Influenced by Protestant and Catholic renewalists, an Orthodox journal, *Logos*, was the focal point for the movement. There followed considerable controversy, personality clashes, and the eventual official curtailment of one of the leading charismatics, Fr Stephanou. In the last few years, the movement has become somewhat muted, and the new charismatic journal, *Theosis*, and its whole editorial staff, are notably less 'Protestant' than the earlier leaders. Indeed, the movement has dropped the word 'charismatic' for the more Orthodox phrase, 'Spiritual Renewal'.

The Charismatic Movement in America has challenged the nominal commitment of many Orthodox Christians, and a number of priests and lay people have welcomed the emphasis (seen as Orthodox) on repentance and a strong personal commitment to Christ. However, even among those Orthodox who see much of positive

---

[4] Archbishop Paul of Finland, *The Faith We Hold* (Oxford: Mowbray, 1978).

worth in the Renewal Movement (the late Fr Lev Gillet, for example) there are aspects which genuinely concern them. Other Orthodox writers such as Hiermonk Seraphim Rose[5] have seen the rise of the new Pentecostalism as demonic whilst some Orthodox priests at the World Council of Churches, consultation on the Charismatic Movement in 1980, tended to see the whole thing as the final twitchings and convulsions of a dying western Christianity.

Western Christians often have a view of Orthodoxy that has very little grounding in reality: they sometimes see it as a monolithic, unchanging religion dominated by men with long beards and funny hats; in short, an antiquated and antiquarian corner of eastern Christendom where the people are convinced that they are right on all matters doctrinal and spiritual, and the west is simply wrong. Such a caricature (not without some merit) fails to see the quarrelsomeness of Orthodoxy within its own ranks, and the extraordinary freedom of beliefs and practices that surround the commonly held dogmatic position (which is primarily the insistence on the original Nicene creed as being the most consonant with the biblical good news). For most Orthodox, many of the questions and issues of what has become known as the Charismatic Movement are issues of private opinion, pious opinion (views of a non-dogmatic nature by fathers of the church), and theological opinion (*theologoumena*). This being so, it is not the case that the Orthodox Church – in whatever ethnic guise – is likely to pronounce on the phenomenon with any great authority. Pronouncements, pontifications, and the 'correct line' are not popular nor traditional ways of defending the faith. The rest of this study will attempt to outline Orthodox opinions concerning neo-Pentecostalism and raise one crucial dogmatic issue concerning charismatics' understanding of the Holy Trinity.

Orthodox Responses to the Charismatic Movement

Whilst it is true that the Charismatic Movement remains marginal to world Orthodoxy, Orthodox Christians living in the west have nevertheless had to face the issues of neo-Pentecostalism as a matter of ecumenical imperative. As already remarked, some Orthodox have

---

[5] Hiermonk Seraphim Rose, *Orthodoxy and the Religion of the Future* (Platina, CA: St Herman Press, 1979).

made their views known in print or by word, but on the whole the approach has been investigative. An abiding memory of many of the delegates to the World Council of Churches consultation on the renewal in 1980, was of the Greek Metropolitan, who attended nearly every charismatic prayer meeting because he simply wanted to know what it was all about.

This sense of curiosity and the investigative stance that follows from it has led a number of Orthodox Christians to be convinced that the Charismatic Renewal is primarily a mutation from classical Pentecostalism. To ask an Orthodox Christian what he thinks of the Charismatic Movement is really to ask him what he thinks of Pentecostalism. There are really no new questions thrown up by the Renewal that are not already raised by its sectarian parent: questions concerning the so-called 'baptism'; questions concerning the nature of tongues and the gifts of the Holy Spirit as outlined by St Paul in 1 Corinthians 12; and questions concerning the nature of Pentecostalist spirituality and liturgy.

The phrase, 'baptism in the Holy Spirit' is in fact known to the Orthodox east. It was used by St Symeon the New Theologian, who clearly believed not so much in a second (or third) blessing, but in a continual infusion of the holiness of God the Holy Spirit. This insistence on the holiness of God, the necessity of repentance and the subjective reality of knowing God's presence was for him objectified by a sign – or seal – from God. Unlike Pentecostals, however, he did not see glossolalia as the outward sign of an inner presence, but tears. Tears remain in Orthodoxy as a spiritual gift, but it distinguishes the tears of ascesis and prayer from the normal outflow of human emotion. St Symeon is one of the great mystics and poets of the Orthodox east, but his experiences and explanations of the 'baptism of fire' would not be the only, or primary, rebuttal of the Pentecostal experience as a distinctive phenomenon. The Orthodox, like Roman Catholics and some Anglicans would want to know what the sacramental status of a Pentecostal baptism would be, and whether it was truly biblical.

Concerning the issue of glossolalia per se, many Orthodox would be prepared to argue the matter. Certainly, it is the case that the phenomenon is not unknown in the private prayer of individuals. As to whether this phenomenon is indeed the biblical speaking in tongues is disputed, in, the same way as it is within the evangelical constituency (it is interesting to compare Packer's reflections on tongues in the 1970s with Orthodox opinion).[6] For many Orthodox Pentecostals confuse glossolalia with xenoglossy (though this is less prevalent than it was not least because of the influence in the ecclesia and the academy of New Testament Pentecostal scholar Gordon Fee). The distinction between 'tongues of ecstasy' (as the short-lived New English Bible put it) and the ability to speak a foreign language is important for Orthodox believers because it seems to them that the primary phenomena witnessed and experienced by the disciples on the day of Pentecost was not one of glossolalia, but of a mighty rushing wind, descending tongues of fire, and the charism of speaking recognisable foreign languages as the Holy Spirit 'gave them utterance'. The evidentialist approach to the 'baptism of the Holy Spirit' tends to insist on the hallmark of glossolalia as the defining characteristic of Pentecostal experience. Even if this were true, to conflate 1 Corinthians 12, 13, 14 with the theophany of Acts 2 is not really helpful and in fact strictly speaking the chosen title of this movement of enthusiasm as 'Pentecostal' is a misnomer. Several classical Pentecostal movements do not insist on tongues as the initial evidence confirming the Spirit baptism; the Elim Movement does not, for example.)

Concerning the issue of divine healing, Orthodox Christians would never deny God's ability to heal the sick. Charismatic leaders are often unaware that praying for the sick to recover physically is not only a regular practice within the Orthodox church, but that it has been recognised that some men and women have the gift of healing. Such a gift, however, is not a licence to set up practice either outside the Church or against its teachings and sacramental practices. The question of healings, miracles, visions, prophecies, etc., within the Charismatic Movements throughout the world is a question for most Orthodox of discerning the hand of God, or the machinations of psychological and psychosomatic processes from the work of the Devil. It follows, therefore, that a watchful Gamalielism in a spirit of sobriety is the hallmark of a truly Orthodox approach. A simple rule of thumb is to measure rigorously the spiritual gifts outlined by Paul in Corinthians by the spiritual fruits spelled out by the same Apostle

---

[6] J.I. Packer, 'Theological Reflections on the Charismatic Movement', 2 parts, *The Churchman*, 94.1 (1980).

in the letter to the Romans. A more elaborate approach would be to see how charismatic experiences are consonant with the Word of God and the teachings of the Church. As we shall soon note, there are issues here which are not only issues of opinion (*in dubiis libertas*), but of the fundamentals of the faith (*in necessitatibus unitas*).

The nature of spirituality in charismatic circles is a puzzle for the Orthodox Christian. It is not that enthusiasm is a peculiar feature of Pentecostals. Neither is it unknown in Orthodoxy. In Russia, for example, Fr John of Kronsdat was not only a famous healer, but in some respects spirituality under his direction had a strong emotional appeal to the peasants and the new working classes of the late nineteenth century. His famous book, *My Life in Christ* would not seem out of place in the latter stages of the 2nd 'Great Awakening' of American evangelicalism. However, in no way did he radically tamper with the Divine Liturgy (with the possible exception of mass public confessions). Charismatic worship, conversely, remains a mystery to most Orthodox.

Hence Orthodox observers of the Renewal note that at the very moment that charismatics claim to have rediscovered forgotten biblical truths, and the supernatural power of God's kingdom, they also adopt practices which seem to militate against those truths. Why, the Orthodox ask, does the charismatic experience seem to lead to freewheeling liturgies and the adoption of secular music (often of a wildly enthusiastic nature with rock, march, waltz or ragged timing)? Dancing and drums and shrieks and shouting seem to an Orthodox eye and ear to be outward signs of emotionalism, subjective individualism, and a lack of self-control amounting almost to exhibitionism. At Bossey in Switzerland, the site of the World Council of Churches 1980 consultation on the Renewal, both the Orthodox delegation and some of the Africans saw the white Protestant (and Catholic) usage of shaking, mumbling, and ritualistic raising of hands as a manifestation of Renewal that they would rather do without. They saw in it as an unconscious cultural imperialism. Paradoxically, many Orthodox do not object to the exuberance of many black Pentecostal churches. This is not simply because it looks more natural than the rather stilted copying of secular practices within the western white churches, but also because the black emphasis appears more liturgical to Orthodox eyes: clapping to God in worship as a congregational body without the emphasis on solo singer, or individualist expression seems to capture the spirit, although not the resonance, of Orthodox worship. Admittedly, it is the case that contemporary black Pentecostal worship does not have the liturgical shape of say slave music in the antebellum period of American history. It is true, also, that many charismatic services are more restrained than some of the classical Pentecostal counterparts. What they all seem to share in common, however, is a deep-rooted sentimentality that the church fathers always saw as the enemy of a mature spirituality. Not that Orthodox can afford to be triumphalistic in this matter: many Greek, Coptic, and Russian icons bear the very marks of sentimentalism that Orthodox see as the hallmark of western spirituality and in particular Protestant pietism. (Many Orthodox see the Renewal – even in its Catholic setting – as essentially pietistic.)

Orthodox believers can see the personal response to God, and the concomitant repentance, as a positive feature of the Charismatic Movement. Rejoicing at this, however, is tempered by a concern that the sheer noise and chatter of Pentecostalism, which seems to be so often accompanied by a marked self-consciousness, will stifle the quiet still voice of the Holy Spirit. Charismata are always gifts from God, who in his sovereignty responds to the faith of his children. Such faith, which is itself God's gift, is not an invitation to laziness or a denial of ascesis: charismatic power without self-control is the 'cheap-thrill' response to God's action; and power without responsibility is dangerous in any situation. When Michael Harper, in *Charismatic Crisis* pointed out that fun and wholeness need to give way to holiness and discipleship in order that the renewal should move onto a new maturity, he was at least speaking a language which Orthodox understand.[7]

Not that central features of charismatic spirituality are that clear to interested Orthodox. Why are so many 'prophecies' and the interpretation of tongues, which are presumably understood as coming directly from God, taken so lightly and casually? Why is it that so many charismatic believers forget so easily God's messages?[8] The messages themselves seem to be so often banal, or the sort of homilies that a good priest or preacher comes up with every Sunday. Does

---

[7] M. Harper, *Charismatic Crisis* (Hownslow: self- Published, 1980).

[8] A. Walker and J. Atherton, 'Time of Blessing', *Sociological Review* 19.3 (August 1971), 367-87. Cf. Colin Urquhart. *Faith for the Future* (London: Hodder and Stoughton, 1982).

the omnipotent Holy Trinity speak in this way? Individual practices (not shared by many sections of the Pentecostal world) seem particularly strange. 'Slaying in the Spirit' whereby the charismatic leader touches a 'prayer line' seeker (usually on the forehead), who subsequently swoons to the ground in an apparent faint or trance, seems an odd New Testament methodology. Or again, the 'word of knowledge', whereby the person with this 'gift' claims to diagnose some sickness or sin appears more like a method of mediumship rather than a Christian response to the prompting of God the Holy Spirit. Clearly St Paul in 1 Corinthians 12 distinguishes word of wisdom (*sophia*) from word of knowledge (*gnosis*), but how does this relate to modern day charismatic practices? If these are issues on which Orthodox are seeking elucidation in order to ground a Christian critical response (*in omnibus caritas*), there is an issue of a dogmatic nature that is of far greater importance.

Is the Charismatic Movement Trinitarian?

Since the beginning of classical Pentecostalism there has been a dispute concerning the formula to use for water baptism. The 'Jesus only' faction claimed that the New Testament Church does not record a single Trinitarian baptism. Even to this day, some American and African Pentecostals, some branches of the House Church Movement continue to baptise in the name of Jesus only. But whilst it is the case that most classical Pentecostals and renewalists have rejected this formula, it is by no means clear that, in practice, charismatics adhere to a biblical doctrine of the Holy Trinity.

Although Orthodoxy is often seen as a mystical religion, it is firmly committed to the God of revelation, and in that commitment, it sees the essential mystery of the Godhead as trinitarian. The belief that western Christianity has been essentially binitarian (with the person of the Holy Spirit being relegated to a function of Christ) or even unitarian is not a peculiarly Orthodox notion. Theologians in the Presbyterian Reformed tradition have said as much for years (Professors Tom and James Torrance, for example). In some senses the Charismatic Movement sees itself as rediscovering the lost person of the Trinity. Professor Nissiotis has claimed, in Orthodox Ethos, that enthusiasm and charismatic revival are nostalgia for the God who is lost.[9] To rediscover God the Holy Spirit, the Lord and Giver of Life, can only be truly Christian if that discovery is rooted in the Trinitarian Godhead. To see this as a fundamental issue of faith, grounded in the scriptures and the Nicene creed, seems often to be of no interest to the charismatics aflame with the immediate religious experience: who needs creeds, one might argue when the Holy Spirit, *Deus Absconditus* has been persuaded to tarry for a while?

Without a balanced Trinitarian doctrine, in which all the Persons of the God are worshipped and honoured, and without a recognition of the unique function of each Person (*Hypostasis*) within the one nature of God, an unhealthy and lopsided Christianity develops. And yet we find in so many charismatic circles, not an 'up-raising' of the *Paraclete* to a position of glory, but an understanding of the Holy Spirit as 'power for living', or a kind of spiritual energy emanating from Christ. In short, a Christocentric theology emerges where the lordship of the Spirit somehow loses his holiness, and the creative role of the Spirit in creation and incarnation is lost.

At least a Christocentric theology preserves the Lordship of Christ (but for many Orthodox, western theology has over concentrated on the centrality of the atonement at the expense of incarnation). Whilst this is not as preferable as a consistent Trinitarian faith, it is less dangerous than that other imbalance within Pentecostalism, *pneumatomonism*. When God the Spirit usurps the unique position of the Father (*monarchia*) in charismatic theology, then the risk is run of despotic charismatic leadership that is more dangerous and oppressive than any clericalism. At its worst, this can become the hell of the Jones cult, or give rise to the false prophet of David Moses of the Children of God sect. At its best, it bears the hallmarks of discerption, schism, anti-institutionalism, and 'triumphalism'. The triumphalism of some charismatic movements is characterised by the barely controlled smugness that God is only really alive and working in their own fellowships and churches.

Triumphalism is not a feature of Pentecostalism *per se*. What westerner could doubt that Eastern Orthodoxy is not without its fair share? In order to avoid any misunderstanding, I would like to stress that Orthodox responses to the Charismatic Movement and perhaps

---

[9] Nikos Nissiotis, 'The Importance of the Doctrine of the Trinity for Church Life and Theology', in A.J. Philippon (ed.), *The Orthodox Ethos* (Leighton Buzzard: Faith Press, 1964), pp. 32-69.

even more so to the classical Pentecostals, are responses of friendship. The above remarks may seem like a strange form of friendship, but politeness and western good manners are not really a feature of Eastern Orthodoxy: rudeness is a sign that friendship has a cutting edge as well as the ability to agree to differ. For the Orthodox living in the west, the charismatics are in many ways natural allies standing as they do for the fundamentals of the gospel, and against modernism in theology. 'Speaking the truth in love' (Eph. 4.15) is a much-overworked phrase: love has to be demonstrated, and the truth defined and defended, but it is the speaking that comes first as a sign that interaction has begun. In that sense, this study is an attempt to begin dialogue, not to dismiss Pentecostals as unworthy of attention, devoid of any truth or insignificant.

4

A Pentecostal Commentary on the Edinburgh 2010 Mission and Unity Conference

Anne E. Dyer[*]

Rev. Professor William K Kay has been my supervisor and senior colleague for many years. Without his help and wise counsel, I would not be doing what I have been doing – teaching, equipping, and enabling students to go into ministry, serving God in mission wherever they are. It was mission that created my PhD focus. Mission to me is the mark of a true 'Pentecost'. For that reason, I have chosen to write on mission and Pentecostals in the light of the Edinburgh Mission and Unity Conference in 2010 to mark the Centennial of the first 'Ecumenical Missions conference' at Edinburgh in 1910. I managed to become a delegate at the last minute and found 25 Pentecostals from around the globe, many who were also scholars.

How do Pentecostals relate to the wider church universal? Do they march on 'doing the job' oblivious to other Christians around them, maverick, independent evangelists? Or do they learn from others, how not to reinvent wheels but encourage others into an experience of the power of God's Holy Spirit?

It was a privilege to be a delegate at this historic conference, the centenary of the 1910 conference. Edinburgh 2010 had 300 delegates

[*] Anne E. Dyer (PhD, University of Wales, Bangor) was on the staff of the Assemblies of God Bible College, Mattersey Hall (2000-2020) and is now a freelance tutor with several colleges and independent students.

and other guests representing at least 60 nationalities with so many denominational groups: that made it so special.[1] There was such diversity yet with a hope of caring interaction between groups. Mission from a basis of unity was the original aim of 1910 and was continued in 2010. However, there were some great differences between each of the conferences. Not least of these was the presence in 2010 of at least 25 Pentecostals of 15 nationalities.[2] In 1910 none were present even from those with the 'Pentecostal experience' from the mainline denominations as far as can be told.[3] So for this chapter I wish to consider the results of the common call from a personal and Pentecostal perspective.[4]

Introduction to the Edinburgh 2010 Conference

In 1910 John Mott[5] called for the evangelisation of the world in 'this generation'. He was the coordinator for this conference, since he led both the YMCA and World Christian students' movement, based in the USA. Participants in the original Edinburgh conference felt they were at the cusp of a wave or the apex of missionary work; the Archbishop of Canterbury prophesied of potential to see the Kingdom of God come in power.[6]

Edinburgh 2010 is the 13th conference[7] since Edinburgh 1910 if one includes the 1961 New Delhi incorporation of the International Missionary Council.[8] This figure does not include the series of

---

[1] Initially written just after this conference, this article is now updated slightly.

[2] Countries represented by Pentecostals included Canada, Burkina Faso, Cook Islands, Finland, Ecuador, Honduras, Ghana, Korea, Malaysia, Nepal, Philippines, Russia, Samoa, Switzerland, UK, and the USA.

[3] See note 16.

[4] I personally have experienced both the charismatic scene and the classical Pentecostals as well as having been a practicing cross-cultural missionary, with experience of at least three cultures other than Britain's English population.

[5] John R. Mott, Nobel Laureate, http://www.nobelprize.org/nobel_prizes/peace/laureates/1946/mott-bio.html [accessed May 2017]

[6] Stanley, *The World Missionary Conference*, p. 1.

[7] See Conference report http://www.towards2010.org.uk/downloads_int/1910-PlaceHistory.pdf [accessed 7 June 2010]

[8] This 1961 conference was *not* mentioned by Dana Roberts in her introductory and indeed far more passionate summary of the Edinburgh then and now than other plenary sessions. She only referred to the conference at Mexico City 1963 since it was a missions conference more than a WCC one but 1961 saw the IMC

diverging mission conferences now associated with the Lausanne Movement. Since the 1961 New Delhi WCC Conference where the International Missionary Council was merged into the WCC, the evangelical agencies for mission branched off to form their own, starting with Berlin 1966.[9] 'Berlin's conference under Stanley Mooneyham's leadership led on to the 1974 Conference in Lausanne.[10] Their statement has been 'The whole Church taking the whole Gospel to the whole world'. Even in this group, Pentecostals were not represented until the 1989 Manila conference. There was a far wider range of churchmanship represented at 2010's Cape Town Lausanne gathering but like Edinburgh 1910 it was focussed more on mission agencies than church denominations whose agencies were represented. Edinburgh 2010 did not have so many representatives of mission agencies present, save in the fact that denominations have their own departments for mission, since its stance is that *Missio Dei* is more important: the Church's mission is derived from God's mission.

Instead of duplicating missions, John Mott wanted to work from a place of cooperation even unity at least in purpose. Did the subsequent conferences achieve this unity? The World Council of Churches certainly points back to 1910 as the beginning of the ecumenical movement. Yet Evangelicals, and Pentecostals with them, have eschewed the older denominational stance on ecumenism until more recently. Mel Robeck was one almost lone Pentecostal ecumenist after David Du Plessis' legacy; he has attempted to bridge the gap for Pentecostals for over 25 years.[11] In more recent years others have

---

merge with WCC. The American AoG warned the British Pentecostal leader Donald Gee not to attend the New Delhi conference even as an observer, but his friend David du Plessis did attend to the subsequent loss of his ministerial credentials with AG America. The more 'liberal stance' of the WCC regarding matters like inspiration and infallibility of scripture [and hermeneutics] caused a schism to eventuate. This was why the evangelicals established their own international conferences as of Berlin 1966 and the Lausanne 1974, 1989 and on to the Cape Town Lausanne 2010 meeting.

[9] There is no need to cite every gathering or the sponsors, but the initial sponsors were Carl Henry and Stanley Mooneyham and the Billy Graham association. C.F. Henry and W. S. Mooneyham, *One Race, One gospel, One Task* VOL 1 (Minnesota: World Wide Publications, 1966).

[10] http://www.lausanne.org/global-congresses.html [accessed 12/06/2010]

[11] E.g., see – V-M Kärkkäinen 'Anonymous Ecumenists"? Pentecostals and the Struggle for Christian Identity', *JES* 37.1 (2000), pp. 13-27; H.D. Hunter, 'Two

joined him. All too often relationships with other churches have, as Keith Warrington says, 'resulted in hurt and suspicion on the part of all'.[12]

The book written for the conference, *Edinburgh 2010: Mission Then and Now*,[13] shows how differently the world works now and how therefore mission has had to change. After a 100 years of schisms and new churches developing, the Global Church it has scarcely developed unity but rather further diversity! Even among the Anglicans there have been divisions (1922 group) and yet four of the British Methodist groups merged in 1932 – but has ongoing tensions.

The Edinburgh 1910 conference has been taken as an early stage of what became the Ecumenical movement, leading to the creation of the World Council of Churches in 1948. Such ecumenism was rightly demonstrated at Edinburgh 2010. The need for careful diplomatic wording of the 2010 plenary sessions showed how sensitive interdenominational relationships still are. However, the evangelicals were in attendance, whereas many backed out of the New Delhi WCC/IMC conference of 1961. By 2010 more groups were also incorporated: the mainline Protestant stream was joined by Roman Catholic, Orthodox, Pentecostal, and African Independent and Independent representatives. Notably the Pentecostals were treated as a 'free-standing' group and not counted as a subgroup of evangelicals, nor for that matter were the African Independents treated as a subgroup of Pentecostals despite their similar 'flavour' at times.

There had been previous invitations to wider groups. Even as far back as 1961's WCC conference in New Delhi, Pentecostals were invited as observers and yet only one attended – David Du Plessis, known elsewhere among Denominational Renewalists as 'Mr Pentecost'. Donald Gee, friend of Du Plessis, was advised strongly not to attend by the American Assemblies of God; he therefore did not

---

Movements of the Holy Spirit in the 20th Century? A Closer Look at Global Pentecostalism and Ecumenism,' *One in Christ* 38.1 (2003), pp. 31-39. Cecil M. Robeck Jr., 'Roman Catholic-Pentecostal Dialogue: Some Pentecostal Assumptions', in *JEPTA* 21 (2001), 3-25; C.M. Robeck Jr., 'Mission and the Issue of Proselytism', *IBMR* 20.1 (1996), pp. 2-8; idem, 'Do We Agree as to When Evangelism Becomes Proselytism?' *Ecumenical Trends* 29.10 (November 2000), pp. 7/151-14/158.

[12] K. Warrington quotes these in 'Cracked or broken? Pentecostal Unity' a paper from the EPCRA Conference, OCMS Oxford, August 12-15, 2009.

[13] David A. Kerr and Kenneth R. Ross (eds.), *Edinburgh 2010 Mission then and now*, (Oxford: Regnum Books International, 2009).

attend despite his proactive stance on bridging gaps as editor of *Pentecost,* the magazine of the Pentecostal World Conference (PWC). That Conference had first emerged in 1947 under Leonard Steiner's organisation in Zurich, aided spontaneously by David Du Plessis; they have had a conference in different places around the world every three years since then;[14] in 2010 (August) the PWC returned to the Philadelphia Church in Stockholm; the European Pentecostals had joined together there in 1938. At least 60 different Pentecostal denominations are recognised by this gathering.[15] One of the PWC's statements is that they gather to encourage mutual cooperation in world mission.

The conference of Edinburgh 2010 then served as a commemoration of all three movements – of the World Council of Churches, Lausanne, and the Pentecostal World Conference and church gatherings on a global scale. Together they wrote 'The Common Call' as a call to action and means all should apply it to each context. Pentecostals can take on the challenge.

Introduction to the Pentecostals

One could say that it is due to Pentecostals coming on to the scene that there have been so many more new denominations and groups emerging. Pentecostals have been marked not only for supernatural phenomena claimed but also for their urgency in relation to mission. L. Grant McClung cites F. Bruner as noting that Pentecostalism and mission are almost synonymous; Pentecostal missionaries set out from their home bases almost as soon as they were filled with the Holy Spirit.[16] Planting churches results in new networks or indeed denominations.

---

[14] In Zurich (1947), Paris (1949), London (1952), Stockholm (1955), Toronto (1958), Jerusalem (1961), Helsinki (1964), Rio de Janeiro (1967), Dallas, Texas (1970), Seoul (1973), London (1976), Vancouver, British Columbia, Canada (1979), Nairobi (1982), Zurich (1985), Singapore (1989), Oslo (1992), Jerusalem (1995), Seoul (1998), Los Angeles, California (2001), South Africa (2004), and Indonesia (2007). http://www.pentecostalworldfellowship.org/ [accessed 12/06/2010]
[15] http://www.pentecostalworldfellowship.org/ [accessed 12/06/2010] lists 60 organisations with links to many of their websites.
[16] G.L. McClung, 'Try to get people saved', in M.W. Dempster et al (eds.), *The Globalization of Pentecostalism, a religion on the move* (Carlisle: Regnum Books International, / Paternoster 1999), p. 32.

The independent spirit of Western individualism and entrepreneurship[17] simply contributed to the cultural willingness of Pentecostals to go and witness, making disciples of all nations. This 'Go' was once regarded as the essential imperative; now much exegesis focuses on the imperative to 'make disciples'. A community of disciples of the Lord Jesus Christ should be what the church is. The 'Going' is a result and a consequence of bringing others into relationship with God through Christ.

The reasons for Pentecostal mission arose from the individual response to the infilling of the Spirit. The scriptural foundation of Acts 1.8 was vitally relevant since it declared to the early Pentecostal believers seeking revival of the church that the promise of the Father to empower his church to witness was indeed being revived. This was the result of people seeking God. Triggered as it seems to have been by William Seymour at the Azusa Street Apostolic Faith Mission in Los Angeles there were many other areas of the world affected by revival fires in the early years of the 20th century.[18] Since Charles Parham's defining moment in January 1901 at his school in Topeka, Kansas, the baptism of the Spirit was to be associated with the speaking in unknown tongues 'as at the beginning'.[19] The languages were regarded as signs for mission, even as xenolalia; that soon subsided as it 'did not work'. 'Baptism in the Holy Ghost' with its attendant glossolalia was the media focus at Azusa Street but beyond all the hype and debate, came many missionaries who then went out across the world to witness *to*[20] and *for* and *about* Christ to the millions who had never heard about the Saviour of the World. Pentecostals simply sensed a call to go and make disciples and went; they were known

---

[17] Cf. J.-D. Plüss, 'Globalisation of Pentecostalism or Globalisation of Individualism', in M.W. Dempster et al (eds.), *The Globalization of Pentecostalism, a religion on the move* (Carlisle: Regnum Books International, Paternoster 1999), pp. 170-82.

[18] Allen Anderson in his book *Spreading Fires* (London: SCM 2007) had to concede to C.M. Robeck, Jr. with his emphasis on Azusa Street in *Azusa Street: Mission and revival*, (Nashville, TN: Thomas Nelson, 2006), that while there were other centres of revival the biggest catalyst for global Pentecostalism was Azusa Street. The revivals of Mukti in India (1906), Pyongyang in Korea (1906), and Azusa (1906) could all be said to have had links to the Welsh Revival of 1904; what happened in Wales was the trigger catalyst!

[19] Cf. Michael Harper's book title as he described the rise of Pentecostalism for those being renewed in the Spirit across mainline churches in Britain in 1964 onwards. M. Harper, *As it was in the beginning* (London: Hodder and Stoughton 1965).

[20] 'Witnessing to Christ' was the title of Edinburgh 2010's conference.

often as the people of the 'one way ticket'. Many never returned home; many died but they went boldly in the first place.

The *organisation* of Pentecostal mission began however, at least for Britain, with the two Anglicans who organised the first Pentecostal conferences in Sunderland, Rev. Alexander A. Boddy and Cecil Polhill. Polhill, a wealthy landowner, had been one of the original Cambridge Seven who had gone out with Hudson Taylor's mission to China (CIM) in 1885. Together these men formed the Pentecostal Missionary Union (PMU) in 1909,[21] a year before the Edinburgh Conference. Polhill was apparently in Scotland in 1910[22] but may not have qualified as a delegate to the conference as the rules stated the conference was 'composed of delegates from foreign missions societies actively supporting missionaries in the field and spending no less than £2000 on their foreign work annually.[23] Perhaps the PMU did not qualify and yet the China Inland Mission, his original sending organisation with the Cambridge Seven in 1885, could have provided him with a way into the Edinburgh conference. The PMU was virtually financed by Polhill himself with the assistance of funding from people associated with the Sunderland conference; this had only commenced its annual meeting in 1909 so hardly had time to register for Edinburgh with just the PMU's first missionaries – two women, Miss Kathleen Miller and Miss Lucy James; they were only sent in 1909.[24]

---

21 AA. Boddy and Cecil Polhill, *Confidence*, 1.2 (January 1909), pp. 13-15, ed. A.A. Boddy, full announcement cited in W.K. Kay ancd A E Dyer, *Pentecostal and Charismatic Studies: a reader* (London: SCM, 2004).

22 According to the PMU Minutes of the week preceding the Conference (June 13th, 1910) Cecil Polhill was in Scotland that week visiting his Pentecostal Missionary Union colleague H. Small who had a church not far from Edinburgh at East Wemyss or with the Beruldsens at Leith. So, while he was not a delegate, restricted by the financial outlay requirement for attendance of any agency, he may well have attended the associate meetings. Of his Cambridge Seven friends, D.E. Hoste attended Edinburgh 1910 representing CIM as its General Director and C.T. Studd had a copy of all the documentation. Polhill's own papers were destroyed at the time of WW2 when Howbury Hall was used by the military.

23 Missionary Research Library Archives: Section 12 Finding Aid, World Missionary Conference Records, Edinburgh, 1910, p.2. http://www.columbia.edu/cu/lweb/img/asets/6398/MRL12_WMC_FA.pdf

24 Polhill and Boddy (eds.) in *Confidence* 2.3 (1909), p. 75. They were probably not new missionaries but ones who like Miss Elkington later were established with other missions like the Zenana and Bible mission but had since received a Pentecostal experience and were not comfortable in their old mission agency. Cf. J. Andrews, 'Regions Beyond' (PhD thesis, Bangor University 2004), p. 97.

Comity was the intent and hoped for outcome of the Edinburgh 1910 conference; comity was intended to work so that there was no duplication and crossing of other agencies' areas by new missions but it has a broader meaning; it implies a 'courteous consideration towards others that allows for collaborative methods of working together and shared standards leading to mutual benefits'.[25] The Pentecostal Missionary Union, as a faith mission with an Anglican home leadership, intended to work collaboratively on the mission fields with other missionary organisations while not allowing itself to compromise its Pentecostal identity. The overall purpose was to enable the whole world to be reached with the good news of Jesus Christ. As yet it seems this collaboration has not truly eventuated; nor has the full purpose been achieved, neither for Pentecostal nor any other missionary movement of the Christian church. There is still a large number of people and generations who do not know what the Good News is about and, over a century later, that number now includes the western world from which the Edinburgh 1910 agencies largely came. Did the Christian presence and therefore witness become compromised? World wars and strife disillusioned a large proportion amidst a perception of church that had no strong call morally or missionally. It could be asked in the light of the chaos of the 20th century if the Edinburgh 1910 conference ultimately failed to motivate the churches to rally in unity for God's Mission and create 'peace on earth'? And if it has, are the chances of Edinburgh 2010 ultimately succeeding any better? To answer this question, as we go through the Common Call made in 2010's conference I will comment on the various themes consequent on this title 'Witnessing to Christ' in the light of a Pentecostal perspective.

The Edinburgh 2010 Common Call: Witnessing to Christ

The content of the Common Call is prefaced:

As we gather for the centenary of the World Missionary Conference of Edinburgh 1910, we believe the church, as a sign and symbol of the reign of God, is called to witness to Christ today by

---

[25] L. Goodwin, 'The Pentecostal Missionary Union (PMU): A case study exploring the missiological roots of early British Pentecostalism' (PhD thesis, Chester University, 2013).

sharing in God's mission of love through the transforming power of the Holy Spirit.[26]

'Witnessing to Christ' was the title of the whole 2010 conference. The first concept I found intriguing concerning the whole conference was the very concept of Witnessing *to* Christ. Normally speaking for Evangelicals and Pentecostals the word 'witnessing' is the word used to declare who Christ is *to* those who do not know him! It is done for Christ, not to[wards] him. Witnessing is done *to* those who have never heard or heard incorrectly about Christ. It is possible to speak *to* a proposal in terms of a debate, but Pentecostals do not speak *to* Christ of himself. The uniqueness of Christ in a pluralist world is a concept worthy of witnessing about to those who have no knowledge of him. John the Baptist *testified* or *bore witness* that Jesus is the Son of God from what he had seen. Christ said as he left Earth that his disciples would be '*his* witnesses' or 'witnesses of him to others'. As disciples of Christ today this is what Pentecostals also do – testify that Jesus is the Son of God and as John's gospel states, that he is the Way to the Father, the Truth and Life. 'He is the Christ, the Son of God and by believing this we have life in his name' (John 1.34, 14.6, 20.31).

This concept of witnessing *to* Christ may lie in the objectifying of a concept, in trying to make it sound less like propagating the Gospel of Christ for persuasion and conversion purposes, i.e. proselytizing, which at the 2010 conference still had (almost unspoken) connotations of 'poaching' from other faiths, including other Christian denominations and hence is not 'politically correct' for the company kept among the delegates of Edinburgh 2010. The uniqueness of Christ and the exclusive claim that this entails does not sit well in a pluralist world. Presence evangelism was a preferred option to the proclamation type of evangelism known among evangelicals and Pentecostals. I wonder if the faith missions of the Edinburgh 1910 conference and its subsequent Continuation committee which became the International Missionary Council, would recognise the phrase 'witnessing *to* Christ'?

The 1910 Conference did not have representation from Latin America as a condition for the Anglo-Catholic delegation to attend

---

[26] http://www.edinburgh2010.org/fileadmin/Edinburgh_2010_Common_Call_with_explanation.pdf.

since it was considered a 'Christian nation' not in need of mission *per se*; they did not wish to encourage any idea of 'poaching' by 'evangelical proselytism' from the Catholic nations.[27] The same principle also applied to the Orthodox church areas from Russia to Ethiopia. Europe was not considered a continent to be 'missioned' either since it was very much Christendom of ancient times and had the job of sending out Christianity from the west to the rest in terms of bringing 'civilisation'. They were probably unaware of their own patronising attitude in this. 'Carrying the gospel to all the non-Christian world' was the 1910 motto. Indeed, the non-Christian world did seem to be the non-western world then; who could have foreseen the maps now presented in Todd Johnson's *Atlas of World Christianity*, presented at Edinburgh 2010? It shows the centre of Christianity to be firmly in the Global South, in Africa 'the dark continent' of 1910.

So, it may be semantics to quibble over 'to' or 'for' Christ as in 'normal' Evangelical and Pentecostal terminology. It does reflect the 21st Century's more pluralist attitude. However, Luke's words in Acts 1.8 are still very much to the fore in Pentecostal thinking and includes the term witness as a noun – Christ's witnesses *in* Jerusalem, Judaea, Samaria, and to the ends of the earth. That may be interpreted as presence evangelism but was certainly demonstrated by Peter equipped and empowered by the Holy Spirit by proclamation. This has continued ever since as basic to evangelism, particularly in the Pentecostal world. The debate of the 1960s over social and proclamation gospels showed the wide chasm between the evangelicals and the WCC mainline denominations and yet it could be said that Charismatic movements showed the way forward to being inclusive of both styles and 'holistic mission' is the favoured approach today. This is not to say that Pentecostals – or Evangelicals – never had social action in their missionary activity. There is strong evidence for physical care and elementary educational aspects in their outreach and one means was to establish training centres for nationals to reach their own people – and beyond.[28]

[27] B. Stanley, *The World Missionary Conference Edinburgh 1910*, (Grand Rapids, MI: Eerdmans, 2009), p. 13

[28] See M.W. Dempster, 'Evangelism, Social Concern and the Kingdom of God' in M.A. Dempster, B.D. Klaus, and D. Petersen (eds.), *Called and Empowered* (Peabody, MA: Hendrikson, 1991), pp. 22-43 and scattered throughout the Minutes of

From here onwards I will comment on the nine statements made in the Edinburgh 2010 Common Call.

1. Trusting in the Triune God and with a renewed sense of urgency, we are called to incarnate and proclaim the good news of salvation, of forgiveness of sin, of life in abundance, and of liberation for all poor and oppressed. We are challenged to witness and evangelism in such a way that we are a living demonstration of the love, righteousness, and justice that God intends for the whole world.[29]

The key of the first introductory phrase for Pentecostals is the phrase 'sharing in God's mission of love through the transforming power of the Holy Spirit'. That is something Pentecostals delight in seeing. As a result of all forms of ministry, in the light of the triangular formula of Pentecostal Mission – Eschatology, Experience, and Evangelism – the result is seen in transformed lives which eventually transform society. Extraordinary examples have been found and recorded on video by George Otis from Cali, Columbia, a South American city of well over a million people. The result of work there over decades was a commitment to church unity across the city. Other examples can be quoted, though they are also contested.[30]

The 2010 Conference made no mention of this sort of transformation. Leading on from the introductory sentence, this Call was based on Track 1.1 Foundations for Mission. While evidently including the basic gospel of salvation and forgiveness with consequent abundant life, it led on to more emphasis on ethical issues like justice

---

the British AOG mission department – which succeeded the PMU as the Home Missionary Reference Council till 1942, then Overseas Missions Council and World Action, there are reports of many social action projects (Donald Gee Archives, Mattersey Hall).

[29] http://www.edinburgh2010.org/fileadmin/Edinburgh_2010_Common_Call_with_explanation.pdf.

[30] See http://www.christian-witness.org/archives/van2001/video13.html for a protagonist view and http://herescope.blogspot.com/2006/02/george-otis-transformation-spiritual.html for one of the opposition sites. The term 'transformation' now has connotations detrimental to the obvious meaning of change which arises in mission terms from people becoming followers of Christ – conversion! See also D.E. Miller and T. Yamamori, *Global Pentecostalism: The new face of Christian social engagement* (Los Angeles: University of Southern California, 2007).

than Pentecostals have normally done.[31] From time to time the conference seemed to prefer an ecological answer that transforms the world from the political, social, and economic devastation to a Kingdom of God, without the political connotation of Christendom's concept of 'Kingdom'. Pentecostals would agree with the need for this, but also keep in mind the eschatological transformation of a future hope of final fulfilment of the Kingdom of God dependent on individual's lives being transformed from the domination of sin to life in Christ. Interestingly Charismatics have proved more interested in the social, economic, and indeed ecological side of holistic mission.[32]

> 2. Remembering Christ's sacrifice on the Cross and his resurrection for the world's salvation, and empowered by the Holy Spirit, we are called to authentic dialogue, respectful engagement, and humble witness among people of other faiths – and no faith – to the uniqueness of Christ. Our approach is marked with bold confidence in the gospel message; it builds friendship, seeks reconciliation, and practises hospitality.[33]

A first reaction to this leads to a belief that the basic soteriological gospel is in place alongside the pneumatological means of asserting it. This sits happily with Pentecostals until they meet the awkward word 'dialogue'. However, the subsequent phrase mollifies the previous connotation on 'dialogue' as since the 1970s that phrase has been a source of contention against the WCC from evangelicals. Finding out about other faiths by talking to their leaders is one thing, but making disciples of Jesus Christ is another. The uniqueness of Christ is well hailed, but definitions could lead to a version of monolatry instead of monotheism for the pluralist world we live in. There are many recent books on the theology of religions and the debates on God's revelation in general to the whole world apart from Christ.

---

[31] This was rectified at least at the European Pentecostal Theological Association's 2010 Conference, Mattersey Hall, 6-9 July 2010. The theme is Pentecostals and Justice with a keynote speaker Joel Edwards from the Micah Project. Around the Majority World Pentecostals are becoming involved in government to seek to establish justice in society too; cf. Brazil, Colombia, Ghana.

[32] Consider the last issue of Bryn Jones' *Restoration Magazine* published by Harvest Time which illustrates these aspects.

[33] http://www.edinburgh2010.org/fileadmin/Edinburgh_2010_Common_Call_with_explanation.pdf.

Suffice it to say here that for the Pentecostal in the streets of our nations, the revelation is full and complete only in Christ. Friendship, reconciliation, and hospitality are normal means of evangelism across denominational groups, not least among Pentecostals. Our busy lives have to make room for the people who need to hear the message of reconciliation and take in the demonstration of the love of Christ which can only be seen through Christians of any ilk being the body of Christ.

> 3. Knowing the Holy Spirit who blows over the world at will, re-connecting creation and bringing authentic life, we are called to become communities of compassion and healing, where young people are actively participating in mission, and women and men share power and responsibilities fairly, where there is a new zeal for justice, peace and the protection of the environment, and re-newed liturgy reflecting the beauties of the Creator and creation.[34]

Julie Ma, the Pentecostal representative on the Edinburgh 2010 council, read this statement attempting to be all inclusive as indeed the Spirit enables. Again, the concept of pneumatology whirling around creation is well accepted among Pentecostals[35] and they surely have a few things to learn there. However, it may seem that Pentecostal's preference for eschatology is declining in favour of ecology as the idea of the 'last things' [*eschaton* ...] shrinks to the home [*oiko – eco*]; they seem to consider *this* world more important than when Christ comes to reign; eschatology for the future designation of believers had motivated the first missionaries. Few Pentecostals would ever be willing to concur that *kosmos* as in Jn 3.16 refers *only* to the ecological natural world.[36] Charismatic emphasis on Kingdom Now, or realised

---

[34] http://www.edinburgh2010.org/fileadmin/Edinburgh_2010_Common_Call_with_explanation.pdf.

[35] There are now broader understandings among certain Pentecostals like Amos Yong of how the Spirit moves in and even through other religions' adherents, than would have been given by a Pentecostal world statesman like Donald Gee: e.g., A. Yong, *Discerning the Spirit* (JPTSup 20; Sheffield: Sheffield Academic Press, 2000), *Beyond the Impasse; Towards a Pneumatological Theology of Religions* (Grand Rapids, MI: Baker Academic, 2003), *The Spirit poured out on all Flesh* (Grand Rapids, Mich.: Baker Academic, 2005); 'The Spirit of Hospitality: Pentecostal Perspectives towards a Performative Theology of Interreligious Encounter, *Missiology* 35.1 (Jan 2007), pp. 55-74.

[36] I did hear the concept voiced at Edinburgh 2010 by a younger delegate. Track 3, Theme 2.

eschatology, may have influenced Pentecostals more than is realised, at least in western theological training situations. A right balance is called for.

What is a more normal default for Pentecostals in this third call is the reference to 'healing'? Miracles were recorded in Azusa Street's publication *Apostolic Faith* and throughout the British periodical *Confidence* (1909-1925) published by the Anglican minister of the Sunderland church All Saints, Alexander Boddy. Testimonies of healing are exciting and attractive in terms of evangelism. They show that God is active in the here and now. He is attributed with the power, but it usually is for individuals. Communities of compassion and healing tend more to be in the other denominations' groups like the Base Communities of Latin America. However, there are many demonstrations of God's compassion at work in and through local churches. Where the Pentecostal contribution comes in is in the ministry of healing physical and even emotional needs, with laying of hands, and anointing of oil, usually by evangelist, healers, and ministers.[37] When John Wimber arrived on the global scene in the 1980s, he encouraged ordinary people in the congregation to pray for others, cutting out the lay-ordained division.

This Common Call notes how all can contribute to the compassionate communities, young and old, women and men. This is a healthy promotion of the body of Christ working together which will result in witness. This is more than a healing of bodies as per a Smith Wigglesworth or Reinhard Bonnke campaign; it is a holistic healing for communities. No doubt Pentecostals can learn more of community life from other groups, but they can offer to teach as did David

---

[37] There is no need to go into the variety, the extremes, the Faith Prosperity groups here. Taken as potentially general contribution from 'Pentecostalism', the world is far more conscious of supernatural healing than we might expect, especially if the British newspaper *The Daily Mirror*, could place a photo of Beckham's foot requesting people pray over it for the 2006 world cup game! The concept of Divine Healing has been a part of supernatural church life for centuries but highlighted this past century in particular, since A.B. Simpson in 1880s, John Dowie in Zion City 1890s through the Healing Evangelists noted in the *Voice of Healing* published by J. Gordon Lindsay starting in 1948. see David Edwin Harrell, *All Things Are Possible: The Healing and Charismatic Revivals in modern America* (Indiana: Indiana University Press, 1978) and on to Benny Hinn and others seen as tele-evangelists often regarded as controversial even among Pentecostals.

Du Plessis[38] the power of the Holy Spirit to enable such groups demonstrate the healing compassionate power of God.

> 4. Disturbed by the asymmetries and imbalances of power that divide and trouble us in church and world, we are called to repentance, to critical reflection on systems of power, and to accountable use of power structures. We are called to find practical ways to live as members of One Body in full awareness that God resists the proud, Christ welcomes and empowers the poor and afflicted, and the power of the Holy Spirit is manifested in our vulnerability.[39]

Power is always an issue. Misuse of power is more probable than right use when left in the hands of weak human beings. The church has never been immune. The life of the Body of Christ has to be demonstrated among us to bring into fulfilment the prayer of Jesus in John 17 – that we may be one, so that we may be sent as Christ was sent by the Father. Repentance is never an easy thing, never something imposable on any. The Holy Spirit has to be recognised as leading. Indeed, historic revivals were times of repentance as seen in Wales 1859, 1904, Korea 1904-1906 and Pensacola 1995, even if not so obvious in Azusa Street. Each denomination no doubt had its just cause in being founded, and yet if that corrected something missing in a prior group it may have led to pride in their new recovery of that missing element. All sides therefore need repentance as a footstool before the presence of God before they can go out into the world effectively. Yet is that why we often do not go out in the right power? Pentecostals are known for their emphasis on 'power' as evangelists yet even their growth has become limited in the West – if not the rest of the world. Can Pentecostals start again with repentance and mutual seeking of forgiveness? Most British Pentecostals do work with other churches in their towns; acceptance has been shown by most. Let there now together be a welcome and empowering of the poor and afflicted in physical and indeed emotional or spiritual terms, in the power of the Holy Spirit. Are Pentecostals willing to be vulnerable? Once hurt by rejection in the early 20th century, the Pentecostals

---

[38] The one Pentecostal involved initially in WCC circles from the 1950s onwards.

[39] http://www.edinburgh2010.org/fileadmin/Edinburgh_2010_Common_Call_with_explanation.pdf.

formed their exo-skeletons, frameworks that became new denominations, to protect themselves. Can Pentecostals ensure that these do
not need to be worn again? There is power in vulnerability.

> 5. Affirming the importance of the biblical foundations of our
> missional engagement and valuing the witness of the Apostles and
> martyrs, we are called to rejoice in the expressions of the gospel
> in many nations all over the world. We celebrate the renewal ex-
> perienced through movements of migration and mission in all di-
> rections, the way all are equipped for mission by the gifts of the
> Holy Spirit, and God's continual calling of children and young
> people to further the gospel.[40]

Amazingly that is what Pentecostals did from the beginning. Being
multi-national, the colour line being washed away in the tide, Azusa
Street's original church of 1906 was led by William Seymour, a Black
American, a son of freed slaves; Blacks, Chinese, Hispanics, and
Whites all attended, seeking God's power. People left there to go all
over the world bearing witness as the Holy Spirit empowered them
to do in a repeat of Acts 1.8 – from L.A. to California, to the rest of
the USA, and the whole world; in that we rejoice. Pentecostals were
on fire with the Good News of Jesus Christ and with eschatological
impetus, they travelled. All too soon however, that colour culture
came back, and denominations formed according to colour.[41] Pentecostals may have betrayed what the Spirit wanted to establish. Now,
a century later, are they willing to accept the ministry of any and all
colours? Ideally 'Yes' but with a caution not to generalise. Does that
include the African churches now dominating the church growth
rates *in* western nations? Can they also integrate the westerners
among whom they live? Many intend to but do not perhaps contex-
tualise sufficiently to have many western nationals stay! It could at
least be argued that the same mistakes westerners made are happening all over again – in reverse.[42]

---

[40] http://www.edinburgh2010.org/fileadmin/Edinburgh_2010_Common_
Call_with_explanation.pdf.

[41] Frank Bartleman's famous phrase 'the color line was washed away in the
blood' (of Christ) was soon forgotten – Whites dominated USAG, Church of God,
vs Black Church of God in Christ, as early examples in the USA.

[42] For more on reverse mission in Europe see Claudia Waehrisch-Oblau, *Bringing Back the Gospel: The Missionary Self-perception of Pentecostal/Charismatic Church Leaders from the Global South in Europe* (Leiden: Brill 2009).

Valuing the witness of all who have gone before includes the many witnesses, apostles and martyrs of the past century not just centuries. Many an early Pentecostal missionary became known as those of the one-way ticket, not just because they spent their all on a single outward going ticket but because they died of malaria or black water fever all too soon after arriving on a mission field. Violence against its workers is not unknown in the history of Pentecostals. Amazing growth across the nations is what has earned Pentecostals notice in the world church. In Latin America, Korea, even India, as well as Africa Pentecostal church growth is 'normal', expected and seen. Faith, the miraculous, preaching the Word of God and seeing God at work is what Pentecostals are famous for. At last, this is recognised. It does not mean that Pentecostals are 'right' all the time any more than Anglicans or any other group. The renewal of the awareness of the Gifts of the Spirit may be the contribution of Pentecostals; we can all learn how to use these tools – in love.

During the Edinburgh 2010 Conference, Young Hoon Lee, the successor to Yonggi Cho in the Yoido Church of Seoul addressed the whole conference. The last paragraphs of his address alert us to the fact that Pentecostals can learn as they do mission. The Korean churches at the time of the 2010 conference were able to support 23,000 missionaries from national wages which average just one third that of salaries in the USA.[43] Why do they go? There are many reasons yet surely, 'Without the Holy Spirit touching our hearts we cannot even practice love; this is the true expression of the spirit's empowering presence'.[44]

6. Recognising the need to shape a new generation of leaders with authenticity for mission in a world of diversities in the twenty-first century, we are called to work together in new forms of theological education. Because we are all made in the image of God, these will draw on one another's unique charisms, challenge each other to grow in faith and understanding, share resources equitably worldwide, involve the entire human being and the whole family

---

[43] David Taylor, 'Today's Imperative and Tokyo 2010', *Mission Frontiers*, Sept-October 2009 http://missionfrontiers.org/pdf/2009/04/06-12%20Discipling%20All%20Peoples.pdf

[44] Young-Hoon Lee, 'Christian Spirituality and the Diakonic Mission of the Yoido Full Gospel Church', Plenary 2 Mission worldwide: Friday 4 June 2010.

of God, and respect the wisdom of our elders while also fostering the participation of children.[45]

Leadership has to be missional. No longer is mission divorced from church, missionary from pastor. The *missio dei* is also that of the *missio ecclesiae* when the church regains its perspective. It is noted in at least British theological educational institutes that Pentecostal flavours have permeated worship styles;[46] also, non-Pentecostal students attend Pentecostal colleges, and probably vice versa. We all 'draw on one another's unique charisms' as the quoted part 6 of the Conference Statement above declares. So, ecumenism need not be a divisive word any longer when leaders understand the ethos from which each other come and learn to share in different ways of speaking about and doing things. When it comes to sharing resources, Pentecostals may yet have a lot to learn but Classical Pentecostals whom I know, do want to be all inclusive from old to young, from different ethnic backgrounds, from different theological perceptions. Leadership has changed from the 'one-man-band' and if it has not, it needs to do so. New generations of leaders need not only to like the idea of team and congregational participation but act on it.

> 7. Hearing the call of Jesus to make disciples of all people – poor, wealthy, marginalised, ignored, powerful, living with disability, young, and old – we are called as communities of faith to mission from everywhere to everywhere. In joy we hear the call to receive from one another in our witness by word and action, in streets, fields, offices, homes, and schools, offering reconciliation, showing love, demonstrating grace, and speaking out truth.[47]

Only with that all-inclusive participation will this call be achieved. Where are Christians in society? Do 'we all' 'look saved' as Archbishop of York, John Sentamu asked in the closing meeting of the Edinburgh 2010 conference? His call was for this sort of mission as we come from the altar of commitment and sacrifice and see the river of life run into the desert of the world bringing life. It was a joy to

---

[45] http://www.edinburgh2010.org/fileadmin/Edinburgh_2010_Common_Call_with_explanation.pdf.

[46] Kay and Dyer – survey among tertiary colleges' theological and ministry training institutions re styles and curricula. *Quadrant* 2006.

[47] http://www.edinburgh2010.org/fileadmin/Edinburgh_2010_Common_Call_with_explanation.pdf.

see the Scotland African mass choir celebrating 'with lots of joy'; a Pentecostal expression of spiritual life? An African one indeed. Let that spread into our British offices, homes schools ... as we make disciples of all groups of people!

> 8. Recalling Christ, the host at the banquet, and committed to that unity for which he lived and prayed, we are called to ongoing co-operation, to deal with controversial issues and to work towards a common vision. We are challenged to welcome one another in our diversity, affirm our membership through baptism in the One Body of Christ, and recognise our need for mutuality, partnership, collaboration, and networking in mission, so that the world might believe.[48]

From meeting the other delegates, this call to ongoing co-operation and a spirit of unity should be contagious and needs to permeate the various churches we all come from. No doubt there are controversies even over baptism that have lasted millennia, but can Pentecostals work with those with differing doctrines – e.g. paedo-Baptists? Of course, it is possible! There are some Pentecostals with Bishops and some with congregational government. It is probable that among the many variations of Pentecostal churches they demonstrate every form of church government and baptism styles, women in ministry and not, Trinitarian-oneness issues ... every controversy might well be duplicated. Can we learn from history, build bridges, and cooperate for the sake of the one body of Christ? This is a challenge to the many variations of Pentecostal groups.

> 9. Remembering Jesus' way of witness and service, we believe we are called by God to follow this way joyfully, inspired, anointed, sent and empowered by the Holy Spirit, and nurtured by Christian disciplines in community. As we look to Christ's coming in glory and judgment, we experience his presence with us in the Holy Spirit, and we invite all to join with us as we participate in God's transforming and reconciling mission of love to the whole creation.

A fine general conclusion. Holistic, all inclusive, idealistic? The global context has now changed dramatically since 1910 and indeed since

---

[48] http://www.edinburgh2010.org/fileadmin/Edinburgh_2010_Common_Call_with_explanation.pdf.

1982. The new CWME statement made from the meeting at Ghana 2011 reflected this.[49] Just as the CWME statement on what defines mission for the 21st Century was reworked from its 1982 statement in 2012, can Pentecostals be renewed in their sense of urgency to fit the 21st Century?

There was an emphasis on integration of church and mission at Edinburgh 2010; integration seems the obvious course of action for ecumenical and indeed even among evangelical interdenominational missions there is no single preferred ecclesial system to be imported.[50] The early 20th century saw many interdenominational agencies commence to enhance unity for mission across the world, yet they often missed the ecclesiological aspect of mission. The parachurch organisations took on mission and the churches left off their responsibilities except in donations to these organisations. Maybe this is an overstatement but is it what the Pentecostals did? Not quite: Pentecostals formed their own agencies, attached to the multiple denomination/networks that Pentecostals established through both renewals and schism. Ecclesiology was not the strongest part of their pneumatological spontaneity!

Can Pentecostals get over their individualism, their desire to do it 'our way' and replace it with his way, in community with others in his Body? Spontaneity can lead to maverick independent attitudes. Experiential Pentecostalism of all brands can be dangerous without good scriptural foundations. Can Pentecostals learn from the past hundred years? Can the sense of 'being sent by the Holy Spirit' be conveyed again to Pentecostals as much as Orthodox or Charismatic groups? Can Pentecostals just 'get on with mission' as the earliest Pentecostals did back in 1906 ... but this time do it in cooperation

---

[49] CWME = the World Council of Churches' Commission for World Mission and Evangelism https://www.oikoumene.org/en/what-we-do/cwme; compare the updated statements and all previous conferences' statements are available through that site. [accessed 22/05/2017]. 2012 saw Jooseop Keum's edited paper published: https://www.oikoumene.org/sites/default/files/File/Together%20towards%20Life_Mission%20and%20Evangelism.pdf.

[50] E.g. OMF (the Overseas Missionary Fellowship International) had to designate certain fields 'baptistic' or Anglican but in Thailand there is a blend under the ACT churches that are the plants from OMF missionaries, even if more baptistic perhaps in taking on adult baptism. However, the missionaries may not even know their missionary colleagues' original denominations; they do not matter. The extension of the Kingdom of God is what matters and is attempted contextually depending on the surrounding cultures.

with every other church we meet? Otherwise, we defeat the whole purpose not only of Edinburgh 1910 and 2010, but also of the Great Commission that Christ gave us. Let us move on in Christ, together to extend his kingdom.

Jesus completed his redemptive ministry by giving orders to his disciples by the Holy Spirit about their imminent Spirit-baptism and empowering (Acts 1.2, 5, 8).

5

THE PARACLETE – A COMFORTER FOR PENTECOSTALS

GLENN M. BALFOUR[*]

Classical Pentecostalism generally treats Johannine Pneumatology badly. It tends either to ignore it altogether or to interpret it from a heavily Lukan perspective.[1] This essay uses a narrative-critical methodology to make a 'non-Pentecostal' proposal for Jn 20.19-23.[2] The proposal offers support, nonetheless, for a Classical Pentecostal model.

1. The Proposal

1.1 The lead-up to John 20.19-23

At the start of 'Resurrection Sunday', Mary Magdalene comes to the tomb where Jesus had been hastily buried (19.42) and sees that the stone has been rolled away from the entrance (20.1). While the point

---

[*] Glen M. Balfour (PhD, University of Nottingham) served at the Assemblies of God GB Bible College (Mattersey Hall) for many years, including in the role of Principal. He is currently Theologian in Residence for AoG GB, and continues to serve at the college (now Missio Dei).

[1] See U. Luz, 'Empowerment and Commission in the New Testament', *JEPTA* 26 (2006), pp. 1-15.

[2] A new 'narrative-critical' approach to *John's Gospel* was introduced at the start of the 1990's, as part of the post-modern range of critical methodologies. Eg M. Stibbe, *John as Storyteller* (Cambridge: CUP, 1992). Rather than asking 'modernist' questions such as, 'Do I think this happened?', narrative criticism engages with the text in the way it would have been engaged with initially – as a piece of drama.

is not made explicit, the inference is clear – Jesus is risen from the dead. For how long has Jesus been raised? The answer is between 'three days' and 'very recently'. The most appropriate narrative-critical answer must surely be, 'very recently'. All four canonical Gospels suggest that the body of Jesus remains in the tomb 'for three days and three nights' before he is raised from the dead (e.g. Mt, 12.39-40 [compare 16.4]; Mk 8.31; 9.31; Jn 2.19-21.), or that Jesus is raised 'on the third day' (e.g. Lk. 9.22; compare 1 Cor. 15.4). By any reckoning, this brings us to the end of Saturday night. In other words, Jesus has very recently risen from the dead.

Mary runs off to tell two other disciples what she has seen (Jn 20.2). While they run ahead to carry out their own investigation (20.3-8), she presumably makes her own way back to the tomb, because that is where we find her in 20.11. After a brief conversation with two angels, Jesus himself appears to Mary (v. 14). It is easy to overlook the significance of this moment – this is the first appearance of the risen Christ (at least in John's Gospel).

Let us look again at the time scale. We have established that when Mary first gets to the tomb, the resurrection has only recently occurred. So how much time has elapsed between then and now? We cannot be sure, but by any account it cannot be a lot. Within the drama, we need to allow enough time for Mary to run back to the disciples, to walk back to the tomb, for the two disciples to leave, and for Mary to be left alone and have had the brief conversation with the two angels. To allow a couple of hours for this should be sufficient. The point is that this first appearance of Jesus, to Mary Magdalene, is relatively soon after the resurrection itself.

At risk of indulging ourselves, let us ask two more questions. Where has the risen Christ been? What has he been doing? Such questions are often idle and pointless. On this occasion, however, there is a point to them. Where, then, has the (recently) risen Jesus been? Perhaps a more acceptably Johannine form of this question is in the negative: where has the (recently) risen Jesus *not* been? Jesus himself shortly tells Mary (v. 17) – 'I have not yet ascended to the Father'. [3] This may seem a little surprising, since in John's Gospel the completion of Jesus' mission is marked by his return to the Father (e.g. 13.1, 3; 14.28; 16.28; 17.5). The risen Christ, then, seems to be

---

[3] All NT translations are made by the author.

'holding off' this final act. Let us make a conjecture. The (recently) risen Jesus has been nowhere – he has been waiting in the garden!

What has the (recently) risen Christ been doing? We have offered an answer to this question: he has been waiting in the garden. Nevertheless, it deserves further examination. Why has he been waiting in the garden? Why has he not yet returned to the Father? The answer seems clear. He has not yet returned to the Father because he has been waiting to talk to Mary Magdalene. Undoubtedly, he wishes to comfort her (notice his concern over her weeping). There is, however, a more obvious and crucial reason for him waiting. He has a vitally important message for Mary to take to his disciples.

Mary Magdalene recognises Jesus in what comes down to a two-word exchange between them (v. 16). The next two verses (vv. 17-18) are hugely significant for Johannine Pneumatology. With Mary having realised that this is Jesus, he gives her two instructions. He begins by instructing her, 'Do not touch me' (v. 17a: μή μου ἅπτου). It would be a mistake to think that Jesus is telling Mary not to make any 'physical contact' with him, for two reasons. First, what would be the purpose of such a command? A popular Christian notion seems to be that somehow if Mary physically touches Jesus (or he puts a comforting arm around her, etc.), the 'divine agenda' would be ruined – that somehow Jesus would be sullied, unclean, or rendered imperfect. This is hardly tenable – especially for the Johannine Christ.

Second, the Greek shows that Jesus' command is a command *to stop an action already started*. That is because the construction uses the negative (μή) plus the present imperative.[4] This puts paid to any notion that the risen Christ cannot tolerate physical contact yet. Far from it, the implication in the Greek is that Mary – thoroughly understandably – has *already* grasped hold of Jesus. He is back, or so she thinks!

In fact, then, Jesus begins by instructing Mary to let go of him. Why would Jesus say this? Surely, it is because he needs to go – he is on his way somewhere. The question is: to where? We do not have to wait any longer for the answer. Jesus tells Mary why she must let go of him (v. 17b) – 'for I have not yet ascended to the Father'. The

---

[4] See G.M. Balfour, *A Step-by-Step Introduction to New Testament Greek* (Mattersey: MUP, 2005), p. 329. This tends to be reflected in most translations, e.g. NRSV and NIV, 'Do not hold on to me'.

answer to our question is intimated here. Jesus *is* going somewhere. He is 'ascending' (ἀναβέβηκα) to the Father.

Jesus now gives Mary a second instruction. This involves passing a message back to his disciples (v. 17c): '… but go to my brothers and tell them, 'I am ascending to my Father and your Father, to my God and your God'. This is precisely why the Johannine risen Christ has put the 'divine agenda' on hold. This is the message he has stayed behind to give. He has not yet ascended to the Father in order to pass on the message to his 'brothers' (ἀδελφούς) – *via* Mary Magdalene – that that is where he is (now) going.

1.2 Excursus: The Lukan schema

Let us divert our attention to the Lukan schema and look at the period from Jesus' resurrection to the descent of the Holy Spirit. The traditional way the Lukan schema is understood – especially within the Pentecostal context – may be represented by the following diagram:

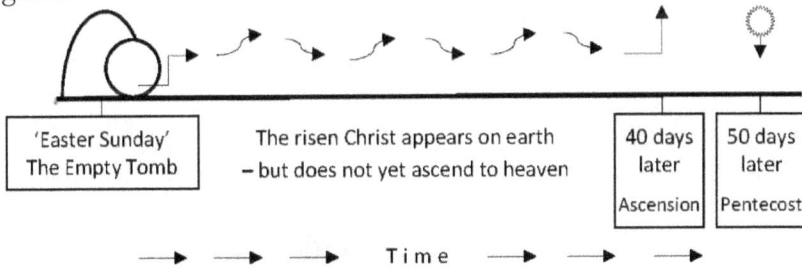

'Easter Sunday' The Empty Tomb	The risen Christ appears on earth – but does not yet ascend to heaven	40 days later Ascension	50 days later Pentecost

→ → → T i m e → → →

This diagram portrays a number of salient features. Jesus rises before daybreak on the Sunday morning. He then appears to various disciples over the next 40 days. However, he does not (read, 'cannot'?) ascend to heaven during this time. He ascends to heaven 40 days later, to make no more earthly appearances (notwithstanding 1 Cor. 15.8). There is a 10-day gap, after which the Holy Spirit descends on the Day of Pentecost.

Two features of this schema are questionable, on two counts. First, they do not reflect the Lukan text that well. Second, they do not make much sense. The first questionable feature involves the 40 day period between the resurrection and the ascension recorded in Acts 1.9. The 40 day period is perfectly in order. The implicit notion tagged on to it – that Jesus does not (read, 'cannot'?) ascend to heaven during these 40 days – is the questionable part.

Since this feature relies heavily on a reading of the Lukan corpus, we will use the Lukan corpus to take issue with it. In Lk. 24.15, Jesus appears to two disciples on the road to Emmaus. The question for us is: from where does Jesus appear? Without wishing to be simplistic, we either have a 'materialising and de-materialising' risen Christ who is 'stuck' here on earth; or we have a risen Christ who has free exchange between the Father and his disciples. The second alternative makes eminently more sense.

In Lk. 24.31, we read that these two disciples recognised Jesus as he broke bread and gave it to them, 'and he disappeared from their sight'. Again, we have a similar question: to where does Jesus disappear? There are the same two options: either he disappears to 'another earthly location'; or he disappears to 'heaven' (i.e. the Father). In *Lk.* 24.36, we read that Jesus 'stood among his disciples'. Our question again is: from where does Jesus appear? Again, we have the same two options – 'heaven' or 'earth'. On this occasion, we also need to ask another question: *when* does Jesus go?

To answer this question, we need to turn to Lk. 24.50-51. The traditional reading of these verses (supported by most modern English editions of the Bible) is to see a gap between v. 49 and v. 50. At the end of v. 49 Jesus leaves the disciples – although this is not mentioned. We then jump forward 40 days – although this is not mentioned. Before the start of v. 50 Jesus returns to his disciples – although this is not mentioned. Luke 24.50-51 can now be read as a précised version of the ascension into heaven recorded in Acts 1.4-9.

It might be that this interpretation is correct. However, we may offer another – at least equally plausible – interpretation. There is no gap between v. 49 and v. 50. Jesus finishes the conversation with the disciples by telling them to wait in Jerusalem until they have been clothed with power from on high (v. 49). He then leads them out to Bethany and blesses them (v. 50). While he is still doing this, 'he left them and was taken up into heaven' (v. 51).

This interpretation may be continued into Acts 1.1-2. Here the writer reminds Theophilus that in his former book (Luke's Gospel) he wrote about everything Jesus began to do and to teach, 'until the day he was taken up'. Now in his second volume, the writer picks up where he left off. By this reading, the ascension 40 days later (Acts 1.9) is a *subsequent* ascension.

One does not need to be persuaded by this interpretation of Lk. 24.50-51. The essential point is that when Jesus appears to various disciples over the 40 days following his resurrection, he is not 'earth bound'. Rather, he appears to them from the vantage point of heaven itself. Of course, the question arises: so, when does Jesus *first* ascend to the Father? We will address this on our return to Jn 20.17-18.

The ascension 40 days later now takes on a different significance. This event is special not because it is the *first* time Jesus ascends to the Father (which is suggested nowhere in the text). Rather, it is special because it is the *last* time he ascends to the Father. Indeed, both Jesus and two other figures insist that the disciples should now stop waiting for any more appearances – the next time Jesus returns will be in his own good time (see Acts 1.6-11).

The second questionable feature involves the 10 day gap in the traditional Lukan schema between this (final) ascension and the descent of the Holy Spirit on the Day of Pentecost. The latter part of it is fine – the Holy Spirit does descend 10 days later at Pentecost (Acts 2.1-2). It is the former part of it with which we take issue.

If there is a 10 day gap between Jesus being with his disciples and them receiving the Holy Spirit, who is with the disciples for these 10 days? This may appear to be a mere technicality – it is only 10 days after all. Nonetheless, it is important. Of course, if we do not care for a hiatus between the ascended Christ and the descended Spirit, the question arises: so, when might the post-resurrection believers receive the Holy Spirit at an earlier time than the Day of Pentecost? We come back to this question as we return to John's Gospel.

1.3 John 20.17-18

We return to Jesus' words to Mary Magdalene in Jn 20.17. One question raised near the end of our excursus may be dealt with now: when does Jesus *first* ascend to the Father? The message the risen Christ has for Mary to take to the disciples is: 'I am ascending to my Father and your Father, to my God and your God'. Let me make two suggestions regarding it.

First, we should take it at 'face value'. What Jesus tells Mary he is (now) going to do, he does. In other words, at the end of this brief conversation between Jesus and Mary, the two part company: Mary returns to the other disciples (v. 18); and Jesus ascends to the Father. This is *exactly* how we would read this passage if we had just John's Gospel to read. (Indeed, it is only because of our reading of the

Lukan schema – an erroneous reading, to boot – that we do not read it this way.) Moreover, this is how John's Gospel was intended to be read. In other words, whatever level of interplay there may have been with the Synoptic Gospels, this is how John's Gospel would have been engaged with by its target audience.

Incidentally, we may also recall how the writer describes the completion of Jesus' mission at the start of the Private Discourse material. Jesus is to leave this world and go *to the Father* (13.1); he has come from God and is to return *to God* (13.3). We should surely expect to see the completion of this mission in John's Gospel itself. This moment in Jn 20.17-18 marks the completion of that mission. Indeed, the very words of Jesus' message here appear to be a deliberate allusion to the words used back in Jn 13.1, 3 – 'I am ascending *to my Father* and your Father, *to my God* and your God'.

The second suggestion is one we have already proposed. Jesus' message offers an explanation for why he does not ascend to the Father straight from the empty tomb (i.e. before daybreak on that Sunday morning). It is not because he *cannot*; rather, it is because he *will not*. That is to say, he wants to talk to Mary Magdalene before he 'goes'; and he needs her to pass on a vital message to his disciples. Let us paraphrase: 'Mary, this is not me "back" yet. In fact, I have not yet "gone". I am now "going" – and please tell my brothers.' The point behind the message is clear. With Jesus' glorification (his return to the Father) complete, there is one more thing to happen – the Comforter must come! (See Jn 7.39; 16.7, etc.) [5]

There is little to add regarding Jn 20.18 itself. Mary goes away to do what she needs to do – pass the message on to the disciples. By implication, Jesus does what he needs to do – ascend to the Father. One objection to this reading might be that Jesus' ascension is not explicitly referred to. We do not see him go, so to speak. Surely the writer would narrate the event of Jesus ascending to the Father if that is what happens, especially since it is so crucial.

There are two counters to this objection. The first is that Jesus has already given his word to Mary Magdalene. What else do we need

---

[5] Some early Pentecostals did note the reference to an ascension here and spoke in terms of a 'Double Ascension' (one here and one in Acts 1.9). This language can be misleading, however, since it refers specifically to *two* ascensions. Our proposal is that the risen and ascended Christ now has 'open access' between the Father and his disciples.

from the (Johannine) Christ? Indeed, we have already noted that if we were basing our understanding of the post-resurrection events purely on John's Gospel, the notion that Jesus ascends here would be all too obvious.

Second, this would not be the only crucial event in the Passion Narrative that is not narrated. The writer does not narrate the resurrection of Jesus either. (No NT writer narrates it.) Rather, we just have the account of the empty tomb *ex eventu*. People turn up after the event and are told what has happened, or they arrive at their own conclusions. Indeed, in John's Gospel Jesus is quite at pains not to point out to people things they should be capable of realising for themselves (e.g. see 2.19-21; 7.37-39; 11.12-13.) Let us also pose one final question here. If Jesus does not ascend to the Father now, where *does* he go? The only alternative is the far less credible one we have already mentioned. He goes nowhere – he is an 'earth bound' risen Christ (for the next 40 days).

1.4 John 20.19-23

We come to what we regard as the climactic action of Jesus in John's Gospel – Jn 20.19-23. This unique piece of Johannine tradition marks the culmination and fulfilment of the promise of the Holy Spirit, the 'other Paraclete' (14.16). In short, the disciples receive the Holy Spirit.

Before we deal with the passage, we should remind ourselves of the importance in John's Gospel of Jesus completing his work by returning to the Father. The night before Jesus is crucified, he begins to orchestrate things, 'so that he can return to the Father' (13.1). Indeed, the events that mark the beginning and the completion of Jesus' mission are that he came from God and will depart back to God (13.3). In Jn 13.31-32 the death of Jesus is typically described in terms of him being 'glorified'. [6] This language is so appropriate to John's Gospel, because the death of Jesus is an integral part of his returning to the *glory* he shares with the Father (compare 13.33; 16.28; 17.5).

By the time we get to Jn 20.19, Jesus has completed his mission and returned to the Father – to his Father and the disciples' Father, to his God and their God. It remains for him to give the disciples

---

[6] The Verb 'I glorify' ($\delta o \xi \acute{a} \zeta \omega$) is used five times in this passage. (Compare 3.14; Isa. 52.13.)

what he has promised he would give when he left – the Spirit, his Spirit (7.39; 16.7). We see how this unfolds in the following verses.

1.4.1 John 20.19-21

It is the evening of that same day – 'Resurrection Sunday'. The disciples are together, except for Thomas, with the door locked because they are afraid of 'the Jews' (οἱ Ἰουδαῖοι). There is already a leading question worth asking here: why have the disciples met together? We do not have a definite answer for this. The only distinct possibility offered by the text (in particular the previous two verses), however, is that it is in response to the message Mary has just brought them. In other words, this is not just a regular meeting. Rather, the message the disciples have just heard – that Jesus is (now) going to the Father, to God – has made them aware that something extraordinary is happening. Perhaps the Private Discourse material Jesus spoke to them only a few nights before – the last time he was with them – means that they are half-expecting something else extraordinary to happen now. The 'Paraclete passages' (Jn 14.15-18, 25-26; 15.26-27; 16.5-15) would be especially resonant.

Jesus comes and stands among them. Without wishing to labour the point, we could ask the question one more time: from where does Jesus come? The answer is implicit in the text. Jesus comes from where he has just told Mary Magdalene is going – the Father. Jesus says to the disciples, 'Peace be with you' (εἰρήνη ὑμῖν) At one level this is a typical Semitic greeting – 'Shalom!'[7] It is apparent, however, that it has a loaded meaning here – indeed, Jesus repeats the words a second time (v. 21). What, then, *is* its loaded meaning? Elsewhere in John's Gospel, 'peace' (εἰρήνη) is associated with the receiving of the Holy Spirit (see especially 14.27; 16.33).[8] We suggest, then, that with these opening words of Jesus, the disciples (and the audience) are being 'cued' for what comes next.

Jesus shows the disciples his hands and side, and they are overjoyed to see him. He repeats his greeting to the disciples – 'Peace be with you' (εἰρήνη ὑμῖν) As already noted, the repetition of these words points to their heightened significance. Jesus and the writer are

---

[7] Compare Lk. 24.36; Mt. 28.9.
[8] Outside of its three appearances in John 20 (vv. 20, 21, 26), this noun appears only in these two places in John's Gospel.

drawing attention to the corollary of peace – the imminent introduction of the Holy Spirit (compare 14.27). [9]

Jesus continues, 'Just as the Father has sent me, I also am sending
you'. These words are deeply significant here in John's Gospel. The
writer often uses *dualistic* imagery to emphasise the conviction that
Jesus comes 'from above', while every other person is 'from below'
(3.31-32). One expression of this is in his 'sending' language. He
stresses that Jesus is sent (from the Father);[10] and he equally stresses
that no-one else is sent. So, for example, there is no reference in
John's Gospel to Jesus sending out any of the Twelve during Jesus'
earthly ministry. There is also an almost total absence of the term
'apostle' (ἀπόστολος). [11]

This, then, is the first time the disciples are 'sent' in John's Gospel.
It is something special and unique. It signals that something highly
distinctive is about to happen. The disciples are about to enter a new
sphere of ministry. They are being *commissioned*.

1.4.2 John 20.22

Jesus now 'breathes on' (ἐνεφύσησεν) the disciples.[12] There are two
things to draw out from this action. First, Jesus' action here is pneumatologically *significant*. He is imparting his own breath – his own
pneuma (πνεῦμα) – into the disciples. There is a strong emphasis in
John's Gospel that the Holy Spirit is the on-going presence of Jesus
in the life of the believer – that the Holy Spirit being in the disciples
is Jesus (and the Father) being in the disciples.[13] This act of 'infusing'
is a perfect demonstration of that emphasis.

Second, Jesus' action here is pneumatologically *reminiscent*. It echoes – surely deliberately – his pun to Nicodemus near the start of his

---

[9] J.L. Martyn, *History and Theology in the Fourth Gospel* (Nashville: Abingdon,
1968), pp. 24-36, coined the phrase 'two-level drama' to describe this double perspective in John's Gospel.

[10] E.g. See Jn 5.23, 36-38; 6.29, 38-39; 7.16, 28-29; 8.18, 26, 29, 42, etc. This is
referred to by German Johannine scholars as *Sendungschristologie*.

[11] Its one Johannine usage is in Jn 13.16. Its sense here is distinctly anti-hierar-
chical (so much so that most modern English translations choose not to translate
the term as 'apostle').

[12] This is the Verb ἐμφυσάω – 'I breathe on' or 'I breathe into'. It appears only
here in the NT. It appears in the Septuagint in the highly significant Gen. 2.7
(ἐνεφύσησεν) and Ezek. 37.9 (ἐμφύσησον).

[13] Brown, *John*, II, pp. 1139-43, rightly describes the Holy Spirit in John's Gospel
as 'the alter-ego of Jesus'.

public ministry (Jn 3.8) [14] It also echoes – again surely deliberately – a host of passages from the Jewish scriptures, which refer to God's breath, or Spirit, entering people and creating life (including Gen. 1.2; 2.7; Ezek. 37.9-10).

Why does all this matter? It matters because it means that everything Jesus has said and done so far in this immediate context alludes to the Holy Spirit: his reference to 'peace'; his words of 'sending'; and his act of 'breathing on / into' the disciples. It would be difficult to write this better if one tried! So, what Jesus says next takes on even greater significance. He commands his disciples, 'Receive [the] Holy Spirit' (λάβετε πνεῦμα ἅγιον).[15] This command is radically new, different and surprising; and yet it is thoroughly understandable, explicable, and perhaps even inevitable once we appreciate the Johannine drama for what it is (e.g. 7.39; 16.12-16).

We should take careful note of what is happening here – Jesus is speaking a word of command. Given the high presentation of Jesus in John's Gospel – particularly its implicit Logos Christology – it is hardly tenable that Jesus' command here is not obeyed or fulfilled.[16] It is also worth mentioning some Greek grammar at this point. The tense of the command 'Receive!' here is *Aorist*,[17] and the Aorist tense in Greek is fundamentally a simple (or 'punctiliar') tense.[18] So, the sense is not, 'Keep receiving', 'Receive some time later', 'Start receiving' or 'Receive one by one'. Rather, the sense is, 'Each of you receive, and receive now'.

---

[14] 'The wind (πνεῦμα) blows wherever it wants to … So it is with everyone who is born of the Spirit (πνεῦμα).' The writer does not *have* to use the word πνεῦμα here to refer to the wind – he could use the word ἄνεμος. (He uses this word the only other time he refers to the 'wind', in Jn 6.18.) In other words, the play on the word πνεῦμα here is intentional.

[15] In John's Gospel, both the Father and the Son send the Holy Spirit (*e.g.*, compare 14.16; 15.26; 16.7). Albeit somewhat controversial at the time, the *Filioque Clause* (*filioque* is Latin for 'and the son') was added to the Nicene Creed in 589 CE in order to reflect this 'Double Procession'. This uniquely Johannine involvement of the Son in the sending of the Spirit should make us all the more sensitive towards this command spoken by Jesus for the disciples to receive the Spirit.

[16] E.g. Jesus' words are 'all-powerful' in John's Gospel (e.g. 2.7-9; 4.50-53; 5.8-9; 9.7; 11.43-44 [compare 5.25]; 18.5-6). Jesus never lays hands on anyone to impart healing or life in John's Gospel; rather, he just 'speaks the word' (e.g. 4.50-53).

[17] It is second person plural second aorist imperative active of λαμβάνω ('I take', 'I receive').

[18] See Balfour, *Step-by-Step*, pp. 184, 190.

Some theologians raise objections to the notion that the disciples receive the Holy Spirit here. The point usually made is not that 'nothing happens here'. Rather, it is that what happens is 'prophetic symbolism' or 'proleptic anticipation'. This point was first put forward by Theodore of Mopsuestia (about 350 – 428 CE).[19] More usually it is put forward by Classical Pentecostals.[20] This is unfortunate, since a genuine reception of the Holy Spirit here in Jn 20.22 can be used to support a Classical Pentecostal pneumatology.

Our objection to the 'prophetic symbolism' understanding of Jn 20.22 is simple. Arguments have to be seen for what they are; and this argument means precisely what its protagonists do not want it to mean – 'Nothing happens here'. However, one cuts it, this argument posits that when Jesus says, 'Receive the Holy Spirit' (having just breathed into the disciples), the disciples do *not* in fact receive the Holy Spirit.

Some theologians note that the definite article ('the') does not appear here – what Jesus actually commands is: 'Receive Holy Spirit'. [21] The point made is that the disciples receive an 'influence' of the Holy Spirit, but do not actually receive the Holy Spirit. There are two flaws in this argument. The first relates to the data. The distinction in meaning in between those times in the NT the definite article appears and those times it does not appear is by no means clear. The data is ambiguous (e.g. compare Acts 1.8; 2.4). The second relates to the argument itself. The distinction is too vague to be especially meaningful – as if someone can receive 'the *influence* of the Spirit' without receiving 'the Spirit'.

We propose, then, that, at least within the Johannine drama, this is when the disciples receive the Holy Spirit. This is the plain reading of the passage – especially for the target audience, who are 'hearing' and engaging with John's Gospel on its own terms. This interpretation alone, moreover, allows for John's Gospel to offer its own conclusion, its own finale, to Jesus' mission.

---

[19] He was excommunicated by the Council of Constantinople in 553 CE – partly for this 'heresy' (!).
[20] For example, see D. Petts, *The Holy Spirit: An Introduction* (Mattersey: MHP, 1998), pp. 47-48.
[21] See D. Pawson, *The Normal Christian Birth* (London: Hodder and Stoughton, 1989), pp. 320-24.

This event marks the fulfilment of Jesus' words to Nicodemus (Jn 3.3-7). His disciples are now 'born of the Spirit' – they are now 'born from above'. It is the fulfilment of Jesus' words to the woman of Samaria (Jn 4.13-14). He now gives the water that becomes in his disciples 'a spring of water that wells up to eternal life'. Indeed, the time has now come when 'the true worshippers will worship the Father in spirit and truth.' (Jn 4.21-24)

This is the fulfilment of Jesus' words at the Feast of Tabernacles (Jn 7.37-39). He has now been 'glorified' – he has now returned to the Father, and to the glory he shared with him. So those who believe in him can now 'receive ($\lambda\alpha\mu\beta\acute{\alpha}\nu\omega$) the Holy Spirit'. From now on, streams of living water will flow out of the believer – just as the scripture said would happen of the Temple, the place in which God dwells by his Spirit (e.g. Zech 14.8).[22]

This is the fulfilment of Jesus' promise of the Paraclete (Jn 14.15-17, etc.). The (other) Paraclete has come to the disciples, with all that this implies. Until now he has lived *with* them, but from now on he lives *in* them (Jn 14.17; 16.7). Jesus has not left the disciples as orphans; he has returned to them (Jn 14.18). From now on Jesus – who is in the Father – is in the disciples, and they are in him (Jn 14.20). Jesus and the Father have now made their 'home' ($\mu o\nu\acute{\eta}$) in the disciples (Jn 14.23). Jesus has now given the disciple peace – peace that will not be taken away (Jn 14.27).

In short, the event recorded in Jn 20.22 marks the final, climactic, 'baton passing' moment between Jesus Christ and the Holy Spirit. The Comforter has come!

1.4.3 John 20.23

Jesus continues, 'If you forgive anyone their sins, their sins are forgiven; if you do not forgive them, their sins are not forgiven.' We should not get embroiled in a 'Systematic' treatment of these words here. Instead, we will limit ourselves to a discussion of the text.

Within the Johannine narrative, Jesus nowhere proclaims forgiveness of sins for anyone. That is to say, in John's Gospel Jesus does not forgive anyone's sins during his earthly ministry. (This is in contrast to the Synoptic Gospels, e.g., Mk 2.5; Mt. 9.2; Lk. 5.20.) In

---

[22] The notion of 'realised eschatology' in John's Gospel, which is implicit here, was first championed in C.H. Dodd, *The Interpretation of the Fourth Gospel* (Cambridge: CUP, 1953).

light of this, some earlier words of Jesus become especially pertinent. A little before introducing the Holy Spirit as the Paraclete for the first time, Jesus says, 'I am telling you the absolute truth: the one who believes in me will do the works I do and they will do greater works than these (μείζονα τούτων ποιήσει), because I am going to the Father' (Jn 14.12).

What are the 'greater works' the believer will do? The traditional answer is to suggest that the works are greater in *quantity* – after all, it would be unthinkable that the believer should 'improve' on the works of Jesus. So, where there was only 'one' Jesus doing the works of the Father during his earthly ministry, by virtue of his indwelling Spirit in the believer there will now be 'many' of him. This is something of a 'fudge'. It is not really doing *greater* (μείζων) works; it is doing *more* (πλείων) works.

A more authentic answer must be that the works are greater in *quality*. Initially, of course, this is the answer we all seek to avoid. After all, how can Jesus' believers do *greater* works (*qualitatively* greater works) than he did?[23] Let us explore this a little more. In stark contrast to the Synoptic Gospels, in John's Gospel the disciples perform no 'works' while Jesus is with them on earth – whether healings or miracles. The effect of this is that, right up to the time Jesus is crucified, his disciples have done no 'works'. This makes Jesus' promise in 14.12 all the more stark and surprising.

We can now put these three bits of the jigsaw together – Jesus not yet having forgiven anyone's sins, the disciples being told they will do 'greater works' than Jesus did, and the disciples now being commissioned to forgive sins – to make a convincing picture. Within the Johannine schema, it is this 'releasing' of people from their sins that forms the 'greater works' Jesus' disciples will do. Indeed, some scholars have referred to this moment as the 'Johannine Commission' (akin to the 'Matthean Commission' of Mt. 28.18-20) – in the same way that some scholars have referred to the previous moment (Jn 20.22) as the 'Johannine Pentecost' (akin to Acts 2.1-4). We must be careful not to load the schema of the distinct Gospels on to each other without care; but this at least illustrates the significance of this Johannine moment. And what better time to 'send out' the disciples,

[23] This may seem all the more perplexing when we bear in mind the Johannine presentation of Jesus.

to do the greatest work of all – to release people from their sins? They have just received the Comforter, the Holy Spirit!

Let us promote this reading a little more. In Jn 14.12 Jesus gives a vital clue as to why the disciples will do 'greater works' than he did – 'because I am going to the Father'. The significance of Jesus going to the Father is surely that it allows for the disciples to receive the Holy Spirit. That is to say, it allows for the 'baton passing' moment from Jesus Christ to the Holy Spirit. Jesus' explanatory words, then, may be understood as, 'because you have received the Holy Spirit'. (It is equally because the disciples do not have the Holy Spirit 'abiding' in them hitherto that they have done no 'works' up to now.)

Jesus has returned to the Father (Jn 20.17-18); he has infused his disciples with the Paraclete (Jn 20.22); it makes eminent sense that now (20.23) he *commissions* them with the 'greater works' they are to do, arguably the greatest work a human can ever do – the supreme, necessarily post-resurrection, work of separating people from their sins.

As we finish dealing with this passage, let us return to the diagram we saw a little earlier. We have adjusted it to suit our examination of John's Gospel. It portrays the Johannine schema. It also incorporates the Lukan schema and makes the implicit point that the two can be superimposed on each other while doing full justice to both.

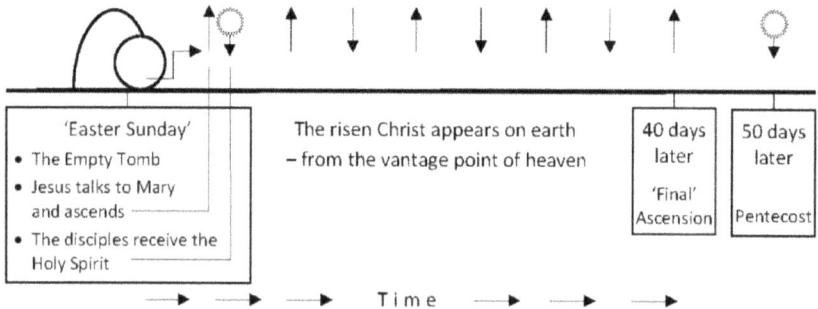

'Easter Sunday'	The risen Christ appears on earth	40 days	50 days
• The Empty Tomb	– from the vantage point of heaven	later	later
• Jesus talks to Mary and ascends		'Final'	
• The disciples receive the Holy Spirit		Ascension	Pentecost

Time

2. A Defence

After all this, the Classical Pentecostal reader of John's Gospel can remain the most resistant to this proposal. It is not so much the proposal *per se* that proves the sticking point. Rather, it is the sense that the proposal somehow undermines the integrity of the reception of the Holy Spirit recorded in Acts 2.1-4. In the light of this, let us offer a defence of our proposal. Much of this involves the countering of any remaining objections to the notion that the disciples actually receive the Holy Spirit in Jn 20.22.

2.1 The 'Overlap' between Jesus Christ and the Holy Spirit

Our own final objection to the traditional understanding of the Lukan schema was that it requires a ten-day hiatus between Jesus Christ 'leaving' and the Holy Spirit 'arriving'. Someone could raise a similar objection to our Johannine proposal. That is to say, there is *still* a hiatus between Jesus Christ 'leaving' and the Holy Spirit 'arriving'. Of course, it is much smaller than the ten days between the final ascension and the Day of Pentecost – it is only the time between Jesus and Mary parting on 'Resurrection Sunday' (morning?) and Jesus coming back to the disciples that same evening. Nonetheless, it remains a hiatus all the same.

Our response to this objection is simple. The idea that there is a hiatus (however small) between Jesus Christ 'leaving' and the Holy Spirit 'coming' in John 20 is in fact purely illusory. Our contention is that it is much more biblical (not to mention, sensible) to regard the 40 days following 'Resurrection Sunday' as accommodating not a risen Christ who is 'earth bound', but rather a risen Christ who has free and full access to both heaven and earth (i.e. to both the Father and the disciples). Indeed, what happens 40 days later is not that Christ ascends to the Father *for the first time*. It is that Christ *stops appearing on earth 'physically'*. His need to prove to his disciples that he is raised from the dead is now over (compare Acts 1.3; 1 Cor. 15.3-7). This means that Jesus' return to the Father after his conversation with Mary does *not* mark the time he finally 'leaves' the disciples. Rather, it is his ascension 40 days later in Acts 1.9 that marks this moment.

Given that the disciples receive the Holy Spirit on 'Resurrection Sunday' evening, far from there being a 10 day hiatus between the risen Christ and the descended Spirit, there is in fact a 40 day 'overlap'! Of course, this could raise the opposite objection – we end up with 'two Paracletes' at once! At one level this analysis is perfectly true. Nevertheless, the objection is essentially specious. First, we still have those 'two Paracletes' with us! That is the whole point of the disciples receiving the Spirit – it is not to take the place of Jesus, but to ensure that he (like the Father) remains with the disciples forever. Second, Jesus appears to his disciples 'physically' over the next 40 days; but this is not in the same sense that he was with them before the crucifixion. It is not an ordinary and continuous presence; rather, it is an extraordinary and occasional presence. He is not so much bringing his followers to true discipleship as he is reassuring them of the reality of his resurrection and preparing them for the future. Ultimately, of course, one has either the conundrum of 'two Paracletes' for 40 days; or 'no Paraclete' for 10 days! Which would you prefer?

2.2 Consistency of argument

The following issue is in some ways a more serious one. It is generally accepted among Johannine scholars that John's Gospel is a 'spiritual gospel'.[24] Different scholars may mean different things by this; but all are agreed it means that the Gospel's narrative framework primarily serves the Gospel's *theological* agenda, rather than any post-enlightenment Western connotation of history. Of course, any NT scholar worth their salt will tell you this is true of all four canonical Gospels – Luke's Gospel included. A dabble into *Redaction Criticism* makes so much abundantly clear. But the point for John's Gospel is that this is 'doubly true' – the writer has no qualms whatsoever about the fact that he uses his narrative-drama to serve his theological agenda. Quite the opposite, he positively celebrates it.[25]

So far, fair enough. But how far does one wish to take this?[26] Some scholars go so far as to apply this to the events here in Jn 20.19-23 – we should not take these events as 'historical' but as 'spiritual'. This in part is where the terms 'Johannine Pentecost', 'Johannine Ascension', and 'Johannine Great Commission' come from. That is to say, these events narrated in the Synoptic Gospels are given a new context and rendering in John's Gospel, fundamentally for the sake of theological purpose. Indeed, it is noted how the events that 'round off' the other early Christian Gospels are concertinaed here in John's Gospel into a single event.

One might not be altogether comfortable with this; but at least there is a logic to it. Moreover – and this is the fundamental issue

---

[24] This description of John's Gospel was first used by Clement of Alexandria (about 150 – 215 CE).

[25] E.g. R.A. Culpepper, *Anatomy of the Fourth Gospel* (Minneapolis: Fortress, 1983), especially chapter six ('Implicit Commentary').

[26] This marks one of the divides between critical scholarship of a more 'conservative' and a more 'liberal' nature. For an example of the latter, see P.M. Casey, *Is John's Gospel True?* (London: Routledge, 1996). For an example of the former, see J.W. Wenham, *The Easter Enigma* (Grand Rapids, MI: Revell, 1993²).

here – either way it does not impinge on how we should read Jn 20.19-23 at a *narrative level*. At a narrative level, it is clear what is going on. Jesus breathes on his disciples, commands them to receive (now) the Holy Spirit and sends them out. Whether or not one wishes to view this dramatic narrative as 'history' – an actual historical event – is a separate matter of biblical interpretation.

What some scholars do, however, – particularly those of a more Pentecostal bent – is 'mix and match' these approaches. They tend to insist that the narrative is historical – it actually happened. But then in order to support the notion that it simply pre-empts, or anticipates, events in other early Christian writings – in other words, nothings actually happens (my words!) – they invoke the language of a 'Johannine Pentecost', etc. And so, actually *within* the narrative: Jesus does *not* return to the Father (20.18); the disciples do *not* receive the Holy Spirit (20.22); the disciples are *not* sent (20.23).

It is this we take issue with. It is inconceivable that the writer would have written this narrative in the way he did – or the intended hearers would have heard this narrative in the way they did – without seeing all the above. Within the narrative (irrespective of actual history): Jesus *does* return to the Father (20.18); the disciples *do* receive the Holy Spirit (20.22); and the disciples *are* sent (20.23).

To conclude, whether or not one sees the events recorded in Jn 20.19-23 as 'historical' is one matter. But this should not be confused with how one reads the narrative. *Within the narrative*, the disciples receive the Holy Spirit, etc. Of course, for those of us that do see these events as historical, they do not just happen at a *narrative* level – they happen at an *historical* level too. Jesus actually breathes on the disciples; and the disciples actually receive the Holy Spirit!

2.3 What happens after the disciples receive the Holy Spirit?
Some people object to the notion that the disciples receive the Holy Spirit in Jn 20.22 on the grounds that nothing much happens afterwards. The disciples do not do much. Of course, this thinking itself is somewhat 'Lukan'. What people really mean is that the disciples do not appear particularly 'empowered' *in the Lukan sense of the word*. Nonetheless, it is worth spending a little more time on this objection.

First, it is perfectly true that at one level there seems to be little response on the part of the disciples to receiving the Holy Spirit in Jn 20.22. Despite the fact that Jesus commissions them in the very next verse (v. 23) they do nothing worthy of note during the next week, except recount their experience to Thomas (Jn 20.24-26). Furthermore, after Jesus' second appearance a week later, all Simon Peter can think to do is go (back?) fishing – and six other disciples decide to join him (Jn 21.1-14). After an ensuing conversation between Jesus and Peter, John's Gospel ends (Jn 21.15-23).

Let us, however, take a closer look at this. First, let us return for a moment to the Lukan corpus. The popular reading of the reception of the Holy Spirit as recounted in Acts 2.1-4 is that it is immediately followed by successful and empowered missionary activity on the part of the disciples. This is not a fair reading. It is true that the disciples enjoy a period of 'empowered growth' in Jerusalem itself (see Acts 3 – 7.) But in terms of the commission to 'go' – 'to Judea, Samaria and the ends of the earth' (Acts 1.8; compare Lk. 24.47-49) – this does not *begin* until the persecution of the disciples as spearheaded by Saul at the start of Acts 8 (see especially Acts 8.1, 4; compare 8.25).[27]

Why is this significant? Simply because the objection that the disciples are not seen to do much after they receive the Holy Spirit in John's Gospel overlooks the fact that, within the Lukan corpus, the missionary activity of the disciples based in Jerusalem immediately after Pentecost is hardly impressive either!

Second – and this is a more fundamental matter – we need to deal with the nature of John 21. The scholarly consensus is that this chapter is an appendix to the Gospel, written by later (Johannine) disciples.[28] That is to say, John 1- 20 traces its authorship back to the Beloved Disciple in a way that John 21 does not (see Jn 21.24.) This means that John's Gospel as written by the Beloved Disciple finishes at the end of John 20. Indeed, the final two verses of this chapter (vv. 30-31) form his concluding words. It is noticeable how the final words of the next chapter (21.25) distinctly echo them.

In fact, then, that the disciples' receiving of the Holy Spirit *does* mark the end of John's Gospel – as written by the main author. It really *is* the climax and the finale to the words of the Beloved Disciple. Apart from Jesus' subsequent appearance to Thomas (which we will deal with next), there is nothing between the disciples being

---

[27] Only now do we have the account of the first gentile convert – the Ethiopian eunuch (Acts 8.26-39).

[28] For an overview of scholarly views on John's Gospel, see A.T. Lincoln, *The Gospel According to Saint John* (BNTC; London: Continuum, 2005), pp. 1-89.

commanded to receive the Holy Spirit, being sent out to forgive sins, and the Beloved Disciple's conclusion. What a way to finish!

So, the argument that the disciples are not seen to do much after they receive the Holy Spirit in John's Gospel is both unfair and pre-critical. The words of the Beloved Disciple effectively finish with this event.

2.4 Jesus' appearance to Thomas (John 20.24-29)

Finally, some people get concerned by the ensuing appearance of Jesus to the disciples involving Thomas (Jn 20.24-29). The usual question asked is: when does Thomas receive the Holy Spirit? This too deserves some attention, since it reveals some interesting answers.

First, we should bear in mind that this is the only event mentioned between the climax of John's Gospel (the disciples receiving the Holy Spirit and being sent) and the Beloved Disciple's own, 'original' conclusion (Jn 20.30-31). The fact, then, that it appears here at all suggests that the writer is making a clear point by including it. Let us explore this a little more, by asking ourselves a few more questions.

Assume for a moment that Jesus' command for the disciples to receive the Holy Spirit really does mark the 'baton passing' moment from Jesus Christ to the (other) Paraclete, the Holy Spirit. What is the real *point* behind this? It is to indicate that from now on the Holy Spirit takes over from Jesus Christ as the 'one called alongside' – the Paraclete.[29] So, *from this point on*, when does the (new) disciple of Jesus receive the Holy Spirit? When do *we* receive the Holy Spirit, so to speak? Surely it is when we believe (compare Jn 3.9; 7.39; 14.15-21, etc.)

This is the thrust behind the Beloved Disciple's conclusion in a few verses time (20.31): 'These things have been written so that *you may believe* that Jesus is the Christ, the Son of God, and so that by believing *you may have life* in his name'.[30] That is to say, *believing* in Jesus Christ intrinsically produces '*life*' (ἡ ζωή) – 'eternal life', 'salvation'. In light of everything we have read so far in John's Gospel, that 'life'

---

[29] We must be careful not to think in terms of Jesus as no longer being the Paraclete. The whole point of this 'baton passing' moment is to ensure that both Jesus and the Father remain in the disciples forever.

[30] The textual evidence may support the more continuous, 'so that you may continue to believe'. The thrust remains the same – it is the believing that intrinsically produces the 'life'.

is surely the necessary corollary of the indwelling Holy Spirit (see Jn 3.9; 4.10; 7.39; 14.6, 20, etc.)

How, then, does Jesus' appearance to Thomas fit into this? The answer is clear. Thomas provides the first instance of this new paradigm.

2.4.1 John 20.24-27

The scene is set in these verses. Thomas happened not to be there for the momentous event a week earlier; so, the other disciples tell him – 'We have seen the Lord!' Thomas replies that he will not believe unless he sees and touches the crucified Lord for himself. A week later[31] the disciples are again all together, inside. This time Thomas is with them. In a very similar way that he did before, Jesus comes – even though the doors are again locked – and stands among them.

He says what he said on the previous occasion – 'Peace be to you.' The repetition here of the same details as in the previous appearance (Jn 20.19-21a) gives extra emphasis to all the themes present there – including the implicit allusion to the Holy Spirit. It is perhaps also worth asking one final time the question we have posed before: 'From where does Jesus appear here?' Our answer is: 'from the Father.'

At this point the conversation takes a different twist to that of the previous appearance. What every reader notices at this point – as well they might – is that Jesus does *not* breathe on Thomas and does *not* command, 'Receive [the] Holy Spirit'. Why, then, does Jesus not do either of these things? Quite simply, Jesus has *already* 'passed the baton' on to the Holy Spirit and does not need to do so again. That is to say, the events of the previous Sunday evening augured in a new era, in which the Holy Spirit enters into the life of the individual through the simple yet profound act of believing in Jesus Christ as God's Son.

Thomas – just like every subsequent disciple of Jesus – receives the Holy Spirit by virtue of the act of believing. This makes Jesus' next words all the more significant – 'Put your finger here; see my hands. Reach out your hand and put it into my side. *Stop being*

---

[31] The Greek specifically says, 'eight days later' (μεθ' ἡμέρας ὀκτὼ). John's Gospel uses the Greek method of counting days – this method counts both the day one is on, and the day one is getting to.

unbelieving but be believing.' In other words, the challenge for Thomas is *to believe* in Jesus Christ.

2.4.2 John 20.28-29

Thomas' response to Jesus has gone down in the history of Christian tradition – 'My Lord and my God' (ὁ κύριός μου καὶ ὁ θεός μου). For all its brevity, this response speaks volumes. It ticks all the right boxes in terms of 'high christology'. From a Jewish perspective, it identifies Jesus with the God of Israel. From a Greco-Roman perspective, it identifies Jesus with the highest echelons of the divine pantheon and may well also tap into the newly emerging language associated with emperor worship.[32] From a Christian perspective, it affirms Jesus using the highest language possible (compare Jn 1.1).

Most importantly in this immediate context, this response demonstrates that Thomas has come to faith in Jesus Christ. Herein lies the answer to our earlier question – it is in this moment of faith that Thomas receives the Holy Spirit. By believing in Jesus, he has 'life' in his name (see Jn 20.31). In this moment Thomas thereby becomes a paradigm for all subsequent believers – by believing that Jesus is the Son of God, we too have 'life in his name'. We too receive the (other) Paraclete – with all that this implies. The significance of this appearance to Thomas right at the end of the Beloved Disciple's words becomes all too apparent.

It just remains for the risen Jesus to say that those who do not have the opportunity to see him are all the more blessed when they believe in him (v. 29). This would be of particular relevance to the Johannine target audience. As a stroke of true irony, moreover, it is the Beloved Disciples himself – who believed without seeing the risen Jesus (Jn 20.8b) – who becomes the ultimate paradigm for all subsequent believers. The irony is not just in the statement, 'he saw and believed' (20.8b). It is also in the fact that in this respect he is the antithesis of Thomas. The Beloved Disciple comes to faith in Jesus when he 'sees'; but it is what he does *not* see that makes him, not Thomas, the ultimate Johannine model for all subsequent generations of believers in Jesus.

Let us unpack this a little more. When Peter and the other disciple whom Jesus loved came to the tomb on that previous Sunday

---

[32] Emperor worship reached its highest expression with the emperor Domitian (81 – 96 CE).

morning (20.3-9), they both looked separately into the tomb. Something unique is stated about the other disciple – 'he saw and believed' (v. 8: εἶδεν καὶ ἐπίστευσεν). There are two questions to ask here: What does the disciple see? What does he believe?

First, what does the disciple see? One could say he sees the grave clothes, and the fact that the tomb is empty; but in itself these observations do not cause faith. Peter has already seen these things, but there is no suggestion that he believes anything at this point (20.6-7). Mary too will see these things, and she certainly does not believe anything as a result. Indeed, she also seems to fail to recognise two angels for what they are (20.11-13). So, the real question becomes: what does the disciple *not* see? The answer to this is clear – Jesus. Second, what does he believe? There really is only one reasonable answer to this – he believes that Jesus is risen from the dead. It is almost as if he sees nothing *and* believes everything.

There is real Johannine irony here. Upon closer inspection this Beloved Disciple, who 'sees and believes', actually is the *antithesis* of Thomas, who will not believe unless he sees (20.25). In so doing he becomes the 'model' for all future believers (20.29). This, of course, includes the intended hearers of this Gospel – who are alive too late to see Christ risen, and alive too early to see Christ returned (compare 21.22-24). No wonder Bultmann call this disciple the 'Ideal Disciple'. That is exactly who he is.

It also says something about the Johannine emphasis on and understanding of faith. This disciple's coming to faith is truly remarkable. It is not merely that he has nothing *visible* to base it on; actually, he has nothing *at all* to base it on. The very next verse, John 20.9 – which is often put in brackets in English editions of the Bible, for some reason – is at pains to make this point. There was no process of scriptural reasoning yet developed to help this disciple believe what he now believed. This is 'naked faith' – faith based on no evidence and no understanding of scripture. This, perhaps, is the writer's point: true faith is based ultimately not on anything *physical* or *mental*; true faith is based ultimately purely on revelation. Faith is a *spiritual* thing.[33]

---

[33] This message about faith forms part of the very core of John's Gospel. E.g. also see 2.11; 3.8; 4.48; 9.39; 20.16 (compare 10.3-4), 29.

With this, the disciple whom Jesus loved finishes his work (Jn 20.30-31). He finishes it by telling the readers that this is why he picked up a quill in the first place – so that the readers might (continue to) believe in Jesus Christ, God's Son. By believing, the readers have 'life' in his name – eternal life (Jn 3.16) – life as a consequence of the indwelling Paraclete.

3. A Final Note for Pentecostals

The Classical Pentecostal position is theologically distinctive in one essential respect. It considers there to be *two distinct types of reception* of the Holy Spirit. One reception is intrinsically *soteriological* and happens at a moment of faith. The other reception is intrinsically *empowering* and happens at a moment of impartation. The Pentecostal position is often understood as stating that the empowerment reception of the Spirit is *subsequent* to the soteriological reception. This is not strictly so. The Pentecostal position is that the empowerment reception is *distinct* from the soteriological reception – and this does not intrinsically require separation or subsequence.[34]

Our proposal offers this position a unique *apologia*. By taking what might appear be a non-Classical Pentecostal approach to John's Gospel, we have, perhaps surprisingly, produced a schema that offers support to the Classical Pentecostal position. We have proposed that there is a reception of the Spirit in Jn 20.19-23. Rather than attempting to homogenise the reception of the Spirit in Acts 2.1-4 with this one, then, they should *both* be given their full and deserved space. That is to say, there is more than one sense in which followers of Jesus can receive the Holy Spirit.

---

[34] E.g. Pawson, *The Normal Christian Birth*, argues that the 'empowerment reception' of the Holy Spirit is an *integral* part of the Christian birth (compare Acts 2.38). Also see R.P. Menzies, *Empowered for Witness: The Spirit in Luke-Acts* (JPTSup 6; Sheffield, SAP, 1994).

6

PNEUMATOLOGY AND THE OLD TESTAMENT

ROBIN ROUTLEDGE[*]

Introduction

Pentecostal Pneumatology tends to focus on texts from the NT. There are no passages from the OT listed in relation to the Spirit in the most recent Statement of Fundamental Truths from the American Assemblies of God, or in the UK Assemblies of God Statement of Faith. Longer treatments by Pentecostal and Charismatic writers usually contain some reference to the Spirit before Pentecost, including references to the role of the Spirit of God in the OT.[1] However,

---

[*] Robin Routledge (PhD, University of Sheffield) was before his retirement the Academic Dean and Director of Research at Mattersey Hall Bible College in Mattersey, England.

[1] John Rea, *The Holy Spirit in the Bible* (London: Marshall Pickering, 1994), pp. 27-116 gives one of the more thorough treatments of the Spirit in the OT; see also, e.g. Michael Green, *I Believe in the Holy Spirit* (London: Hodder and Stoughton, 1975), pp. 18-31; Stanley M. Horton, *What the Bible Says about the Holy Spirit* (Springfield: Gospel Publishing House, 1976), pp. 17-78; Stanley M. Horton, 'Old Testament Foundations of Pentecostal Faith', *Pneuma*, 1.1 (1979), pp. 21-30; David Petts, *The Holy Spirit: An Introduction* (Mattersey: Mattersey Hall, 1998), pp. 17-24; Roger Stronstad, 'The influence of the Old Testament on the charismatic theology of St Luke', *Pneuma* 2.1 (1980), pp. 32-50. For a more specific discussion of the work of the Spirit in the OT see Christopher J.H. Wright, *Knowing the Holy Spirit through the Old Testament* (Downers Grove: IVP Academic, 2006); see also John Goldingay, 'Was the Holy Spirit Active in Old Testament Times? What Was New About The

the events of the Day of Pentecost recorded in Acts 2 are seen as a watershed; and treatments of earlier passages, and in particular passages from the OT, often seem intended, either to note key differences between pre- and post-Pentecost understandings of the work and ministry of the Spirit; or to point to things generally associated with the later work of the Spirit that appear to be foreshadowed in the OT material, in order to draw out their fuller implications.

These are important considerations. However, both tend to view the OT through a charismatic, post-Pentecost lens, and so do not engage fully with the text as Scripture, in its own right. There is the possibility of overplaying the differences in order to emphasise the uniqueness of the post-Pentecost ministry of the Spirit. And there is the opposite danger of reading back ideas from the NT or from Christian theology and, either of attaching more significance to them in OT texts than is warranted, or of interpreting texts, which may be more naturally interpreted in other ways, in the light of them. This tendency to use the NT and Christian theology to inform (and maybe determine) the interpretation of OT references to the Spirit undermines the contribution of the OT to a truly biblical Pneumatology. The purpose of this paper is to reverse that order and to look at ways in which the OT may (and should) inform the Christian doctrine of the Spirit.

In my view it is important to recognise that the OT as canonical Scripture is divine revelation and, when properly interpreted, taking account of cultural differences and theological development, is relevant and authoritative for the life of Christian believers.[2] This is true of many theological themes in the OT, though the emphasis here is on the understanding of the Spirit. It is my intention to consider some of the key aspects of the work and ministry of the Spirit of God that we find in the OT and relate them to our present understanding of the Holy Spirit. There are certainly differences between pre- and post-Pentecost views of the Spirit, though these may not be as stark as is sometimes proposed. There are also considerable points

Christian Experience Of God', *Ex Auditu* 12 (1996), pp. 14-28; G. Henton Davies, 'The Holy Spirit in the Old Testament', *Review and Expositor* 63.2 (1966), pp. 129-34; James Dunn, 'Spirit, Holy Spirit', in J.D. Douglas, N. Hillyer *et al.* (eds.), *The Illustrated Bible Dictionary* 3 vols. (Leicester: IVP, 1980), 3, pp. 1478-83; Robin Routledge, *Old Testament Theology: A Thematic Approach* (Nottingham: Apollos, 2008; Downers Grove: IVP Academic, 2009), pp. 112-17.
    [2] For further discussion of this see Routledge, *Old Testament Theology*, pp. 17-80.

of contact that will enhance our appreciation of the work and ministry of the Spirit.

The Spirit and God

One important area of Christian Pneumatology is to demonstrate that the Holy Spirit is God, and so one of the Persons of the Trinity. The OT, with its emphasis on Israel's one God, contains little that can be taken as directly Trinitarian (which is essentially a category of Christian dogmatic theology).[3] However, within the OT, the work of the Spirit is viewed as the work of God. John Goldingay suggests that 'talk of the activity of God's Spirit is a First Testament way of describing God's activity in the world';[4] and Norman Snaith describes the Spirit in the OT as 'the manifestation in human experience of the life-giving, energy creating power of God'.[5]

This close link between God's presence and his Spirit is seen, for example, in Ps. 139.7 where the Spirit (רוּחַ) of God is parallel with the divine presence:

Where can I go from your Spirit?
Where can I flee from your presence?

There is a similar parallel in Ps. 51.11. The psalmist, overwhelmed by his sin and its possible effect on his relationship with God, prays:

Do not cast me from your presence,
Or take your Holy Spirit from me.

Another example of the close relationship between God and the Spirit is seen in Isa. 63.7-14. This appears to recall God's words in Exod. 33.14 which focus on God's presence and activity: 'my presence will go with you, and I will give you rest'. In the Isaiah passage, it is the Spirit who accompanies the people – 'where is he who set his

---

[3] Trinitarian ideas are sometimes read back into OT passages, such as Gen. 1.26 – *God said: 'Let us make man in our image …'* This is more widely thought to refer to a conversation within the heavenly assembly; though it is not impossible that it is between God and the Spirit. However, the idea of one God in three persons would be wholly alien to the theology of the OT.

[4] John Goldingay, *Old Testament Theology* 3 vols. (Downers Grove: IVP; Milton Keynes: Paternoster, 2003-2009), 1, p. 794.

[5] Norman H. Snaith, *Distinctive Ideas of the Old Testament* (London: Epworth, 1953), p. 153.

Holy Spirit among them?' (v. 11) – again emphasising that it is by his Spirit that God is present among his people.[6] We also see here that God's action on behalf of his people in giving them 'rest', is also associated with the Spirit – 'they were given rest by the Spirit of the LORD' (v. 14). This link between God's activity and the activity of the Spirit is reinforced by the parallel between the Spirit that God has set among his people (v. 11) and God's 'glorious arm of power' (v. 12). It is thus by his Spirit that God is with his people, and through the Spirit that his power is at work in their lives.

In addition to the identification of the Spirit as God, post-Pentecost, Trinitarian Pneumatology wants, too, to emphasise the Personhood of the Spirit, over against the idea of the Spirit as an impersonal force. This is evident in the frequent designation of the Spirit as 'he' and not 'it' (e.g. Jn 14.26; 15.26).[7] In the OT, the Spirit's close link with the presence and activity of God means that he is not viewed in personal terms; he is the power of God at work in the world. Whilst God is viewed as personal, seen both in anthropomorphisms and in his description as husband and father,[8] the Spirit in the OT is not described in a similar way. Though the reference in Isa. 63.10 to the Spirit being 'grieved' by the people of Israel (cf. Eph. 4.30) maybe moving towards a more personal view. It is necessary, though, to nuance our understanding of the Holy Spirit as a 'person'. The term is used in the statement of the doctrine of the Trinity: God is of one substance, while existing in three persons. Those three persons are mentioned together on several occasions (e.g. Mt. 28.19; 2 Cor. 13.13; 1 Pet. 1.2), suggesting that if the Father and Son are personal then the Spirit should be seen in the same way. Nonetheless, in practice, there does seem to be a difference, even in Christian theology, in the way the Spirit is regarded in comparison with the Father and the Son. The Father and Son are described in language that points to the possibility of relationship; whereas the Holy Spirit is viewed less in terms of relationship and more as the enabling and empowering divine presence. The idea of the Spirit as Counsellor (Jn 14.16, 26; 15.26; 16.7) and as one who intercedes in prayer (Rom. 8.26-27) does move

---

[6] See also, e.g., Hag. 2.4-5, 'I [God] am with you … and my Spirit remains among you'.

[7] See, e.g. Wayne Grudem, *Systematic Theology: An Introduction to Biblical Doctrine* (Leicester: IVP; Grand Rapids: Zondervan, 1994), p. 232.

[8] Routledge, *Old Testament Theology*, pp. 102-103.

morc towards relationship – but even here the main emphasis is on the activity of the Spirit in mediating divine help. Clearly these passages do indicate a development in the personal view of the Spirit from the OT to the NT; however, even after Pentecost, the description of the Spirit as 'the manifestation in human experience of the life-giving, energy creating power of God' continues to reflect one very significant, even dominant, aspect of the Spirit's role.

The Spirit Imparts Physical and Spiritual Life

The Spirit and Creation

One of the OT roles of the Spirit frequently commented upon in post-Pentecost discussion is in relation to creation. In Gen. 1.2, the 'Spirit of God' (רוח אלהים) was hovering over the pre-creation waters;[9] and in Ps. 33.6 the 'breath (רוח) of his mouth' parallels the 'word of Yahweh' by which the heavens were created.[10]

Psalm 104.29-30 also links God's Spirit with creation:

When you hide your face, they are terrified;
    When you take away their breath (רוח), they die and return to
    the dust.
When you send your Spirit (רוח), they are created,
    and you renew the face of the Earth.

The emphasis here, though, is more on ongoing dependence of his creation on God's provision – including the provision of the breath that is required to create and sustain life. Significantly, that giving of breath is associated with the work of the Spirit. In the OT understanding of human personality, human beings are made up of flesh animated by divine breath. We see this, for example, in Gen. 2.7 – 'the LORD God formed man from the dust of the ground and breathed into his nostrils the breath of life; and the man became a living being'. The word translated 'breath' here is נשמה rather than

---

[9] The expression רוח אלהים is sometimes translated 'a mighty wind' (NRSVmg), though 'spirit of God' is the more usual translation, and in this context seems more likely; see, e.g. Victor P. Hamilton, *Genesis 1-17* (NICOT; Grand Rapids: Eerdmans, 1990), pp. 111-17; Gordon Wenham, *Genesis 1-15* (WBC 1; Milton Keynes: Word, 1991), pp. 16-17.

[10] Rea takes this link between Spirit and Word (Son) to indicate the activity of the Trinity in creation (*Holy Spirit*, pp. 29-30). However, it is unlikely that that is what the OT writers have in mind.

רוּחַ. However, these two terms overlap in meaning;[11] and רוּחַ is used when the expression 'breath of life' occurs elsewhere, (Gen. 1.30; 6.17). The two words appear in parallel in a similar context in Job 33.3:

> The spirit (רוּחַ) of God has made me,
> And the breath (נְשָׁמָה) of the Almighty gives me life.

Here again we see the role of the Spirit in imparting the divine breath that enables human existence. This, though, is a general activity relating to all flesh, and must not be confused with other more specific endowments of the Spirit. The presence of the divine רוּחַ within human beings might possibly indicate a spiritual dimension to human life which enables relationship with God.[12] The primary emphasis, though, is on enabling physical life; and when the רוּחַ is withdrawn the result (unlike, for example, the prospect faced by the psalmist in Ps. 51.11) is physical death (Job 34.14-15; Ps. 104.29). It is important to note, too, that this רוּחַ which animates flesh is not an intrinsic part of human personality. It belongs to God: it comes from him and when it is withdrawn, bringing human life to an end, it returns to him. The situation is complicated in that רוּחַ may also be used to refer to the human 'spirit' in the sense of a human being's inward motivating disposition,[13] but this needs to be distinguished from the divine רוּחַ that enables physical existence.[14]

---

[11] נְשָׁמָה also refers to God's breath, and to the breath that gives life to human beings and occurs in parallel with רוּחַ in Job 27.3; 32.8; 33.4; 34.14; Isa. 42.5; 57.16. Eichrodt suggests that נְשָׁמָה may be a poetic synonym for רוּחַ; see Walther Eichrodt, *Theology of the Old Testament* 2 vols. (London: SCM, 1961-1967), 2, p. 142.

[12] Although the 'breath (רוּחַ) of life' is also shared by animals (e.g. Gen. 1.30; 6.17), it is only into human beings that God is said to breathe the breath of life (Gen. 2.7). Christopher Wright suggests that this points to a 'special tender intimacy' and indicates the presence of the Spirit in a way that is not shared by other creatures (*Knowing the Holy Spirit*, p. 28). The main distinction between human beings and the rest of the created order is that human beings are made in the image of God (Gen. 1.26-27) – which, in its OT context, is not directly related to the Spirit of God.

[13] רוּחַ denotes human disposition and feelings is, e.g. Gen. 26.35; 45.27; Num. 14.24; 1 Sam. 1.15; Ps. 51.10; Isa. 29.24; see Routledge, *Old Testament Theology*, pp. 144-45

[14] Contra Rea (*Holy Spirit*, pp. 31-37). Rea links Gen. 2.7 with the origin of the human spirit, which comes from God and has capacity to know God; and as such it is 'the very essence of human nature' (p. 34). He goes on to suggest that the

The dependence of human beings on God's Spirit to maintain life may also be indicated in Gen. 6.3, 'my spirit shall not abide in mortals forever,[15] for they are flesh' (NRSV).[16] This is part of the introduction to the flood narrative, and points to the limitation of human life by the withdrawal of God's Spirit.[17] As 'flesh' human beings are mortal; human life depends on the presence of God's Spirit. When God's Spirit no longer remains, human life comes to an end.

The Spirit and Renewal

The activity of the Spirit in imparting physical life is also seen in Ezekiel's vision of the 'valley of dry bones' (37.1-10); and again, we see that the divine רוּחַ is needed to bring life to lifeless flesh (vv. 8-10). Here, though, the breathing of new life into dry bones becomes a metaphor for the spiritual rebirth and renewal of Israel following the exile:

> Then he said to me: 'Son of man, these bones are the whole house of Israel. They say, "Our bones are dried up and our hope is gone; we are cut off." Therefore, prophesy and say to them: "This is what the Sovereign Lord says: O my people, I am going to open your graves and bring you up from them; I will bring you back to the land of Israel … I will put my Spirit in you, and you will live."'
> (Ezek. 37.11-14)

---

entrance of sin brought spiritual death: 'the spirit of the unsaved person is dead to God' (p. 36). This seems to be reading a bipartite view of human personality (body and spirit) back into the OT, where the emphasis is on human beings as a unity, with death bringing an end to the life of the entire person.

[15] In the traditional translation of this verse, God's Spirit will not *contend with*, rather than *remain in*, human beings. The problem is the Hebrew word יָדוֹן, which is uncertain; 'remain' is based on the LXX, and seems to be preferred by most recent commentators; see, e.g. Walter Brueggemann, *Genesis* (Interpretation; Louisville: Westminster John Knox, 1982), p. 72; Hamilton, *Genesis 1-17*, pp. 267-68; Wenham, *Genesis 1-15*, p. 142; Claus Westermann, *Genesis 1-11* (London: SPCK, 1984; Minneapolis: Fortress, 1994), pp. 364-65, 375; see also Wright, *Knowing the Holy Spirit*, p. 29.

[16] The traditional translation – 'my Spirit will not contend with man forever' – suggests that the Spirit plays a role in challenging and convicting human beings in the period leading up to the flood (cf. Jn 16.8-10). This view is reflected by, e.g Horton, *Holy Spirit*, pp. 22-23; Petts, *Holy Spirit*, p. 20; Rea, *Holy Spirit*, pp. 37-39; however, it is questionable in the light of the more widely accepted translation.

[17] The reference to 120 years in Gen. 6.3 may point to the reduction of the human lifespan after the flood, or to a period of grace before the flood will destroy human life. Both indicate human mortality – which is linked with the withdrawal of God's Spirit.

Earlier in Ezekiel's prophecy the renewal of God's people is also associated with the activity of the Spirit: I will give you a new heart and
put a new spirit in you; I will remove from you your heart of stone
and give you a heart of flesh. And I will put my Spirit in you and
move you to follow my decrees and be careful to keep my laws (Ezek.
36.24-25). The exile was the result of disobedience: the people failed
to live up to the demands of their covenant relationship with God.
However, God's ongoing commitment to his people results in the
promise not only of forgiveness and restoration, but of the renewal
that is necessary to enable them to be obedient in the future.

In Jeremiah's vision of the future this renewal is linked with the
promise of the New Covenant (Jer. 31.31-34), which will be accompanied by putting God's law within his people, and thereby creating
new people with the ability to be obedient (cf. Jer. 24.7).[18] Ezekiel
does not specifically mention a new covenant in chapter 36;[19] however his use of the covenant formula, 'you will be my people and I
will be your God' (v. 29),[20] sets the promise within a covenantal
framework, and it is reasonable to suppose that the transformation
of God's people associated with the New Covenant is also the work
of God's Spirit. The Sinaitic covenant marked the birth of Israel as a
nation. During that time the Spirit was present among the people (Isa.
63.11-14, cf. Neh 9.20);[21] though the relationship was marred by rebellion, which grieved the Spirit. Nevertheless, on the basis of his
commitment to his covenant promises,[22] God's Spirit will remain
among his people (e.g., Hag. 2.5) to bring about the inward renewal
which will overcome their rebellion and enable them to fulfil their
covenant obligations. The result will be a new covenant relationship

---

[18] On the New Covenant see, e.g., Routledge, *Old Testament Theology*, pp. 269-72.

[19] Ezekiel does, though, refer to a new covenant relationship in 16.60; 34.25;
37.26.

[20] This expression occurs in relation to the Sinaitic covenant in Exod. 6.7; cf.
Lev. 26.12; Jer. 7.23; 11.4; 30.22. See further, Rolf Rendtorff, *The Covenant Formula:
An Exegetical and Theological Investigation* (OTS; Edinburgh: T. and T. Clark, 1998).

[21] We can note, too, the presence of the Spirit on Moses and Israel's elders
(Num. 11.17, 25) and Joshua (Num. 27.18; Deut. 34.9).

[22] See, e.g., Routledge, *Old Testament Theology*, pp. 269-70. God's commitment to
his people is closely linked with his חסד, which expresses love and faithfulness
within the context of a (covenant) relationship. It is on the basis of his חסד that
God preserves the relationship with his people and so promises a new covenant;
see further, Robin Routledge, '*Hesed* as Obligation: A Re-Examination', *TynBul* 46.1
(1995), pp. 179-96; Routledge, *Old Testament Theology*, pp. 108-10.

which will not be broken by the people's sin and which, therefore, may be described as *everlasting* (e.g., Jer. 32.38; Ezek. 16.60; Isa. 55.3).[23]

The promise of a new covenant is one of the themes that link the return from exile with the exodus.[24] Just as God brought Israel out of Egypt and, through the Sinaitic covenant, established them as his own people, so he will act again to bring his people out of Babylon. In describing the return from exile, exodus imagery sometimes appears alongside imagery associated with creation.[25] Thus the exodus is seen as a creative act by which God brought Israel into being as a nation; and the return from exile is set within the context of a new creation. The exile represents a return to the chaos described in Gen. 1.2,[26] but as then God will act both creatively and redemptively to restore his people and his world. It is through the Spirit, who hovered over the chaotic waters in the beginning, that God will transform the chaos of exile.

As well as describing the restoration of the nation in terms of a second exodus, Isaiah 40-55 also points to the role of the Servant of the LORD in bringing renewal. As already noted, the Servant will be endowed with the Spirit (Isa. 42.1, cf. 61.1) in order to fulfil his task, which includes both restoring Israel and bringing light and salvation to the nations (Isa. 49.5-6, cf. 42.6). In Isaiah 40-55 Israel, too, is

---

[23] In the inter-Testamental period the feast of Pentecost came to be regarded as the anniversary of the Sinaitic covenant, and this provides a link with the coming of the Spirit at Pentecost – which marks the birth of the Church. There may also be a parallel between the three thousand people killed when the people rebelled against God and worshipped the golden calf (Exod. 32.28) and the three thousand added to the Church after Peter's sermon on the Day of Pentecost (Acts 2.41).

[24] The view of the return as a second exodus is seen primarily in Isaiah 40-55 (e.g. Isa. 43.16; 48.20-21; 51.9-11), though exodus imagery also occurs in Jeremiah 31 in the context of the new covenant.

[25] E.g. in Isa. 51.9-11, which relates the coming deliverance from exile to what God has done in the past, references to drying up the sea and making a road for the redeemed to cross over (v. 10) allude to crossing the Red Sea at the time of the exodus; however, references to cutting Rahab into pieces and piercing the dragon (v. 9) and the 'waters of the great deep' appear to allude to mythological imagery that depicts creation as God's victory over the waters of chaos. For further discussion of this theme see Routledge, *Old Testament Theology*, pp. 137-38; Routledge, 'Mission and Covenant in the OT', in Grams, Marshall, Penner, Routledge (eds.), *Bible and Mission*, pp. 17-20.

[26] In describing the effects of divine judgment, Jeremiah refers to the earth as *formless and empty* (תהו ובהו), the same expression that describes pre-creation chaos in Gen. 1.2. Zeph 1.2-4 also appears to present God's judgment on Judah as the reversal of creation.

described as God's servant (e.g. Isa. 41.8; 43.10; 49.3); with a role in relation to the non-Israelite nations – as a witness to what God in has done in her history (e.g. Isa. 43.10; 44.8). However, the people have failed; they seem oblivious to God's saving activity (Isa. 42.19-20; 43.7-8). As a result, God has appointed another Servant who 'is the embodiment of what Israel was intended to be',[27] and will also be the means by which Israel may be restored and able, again, to fulfil her divine calling.[28] In my view the task of equipping Israel to be a witness to the nations is an important part of what it means for the Servant to be described as 'a light for the Gentiles' (Isa. 42.6; 49.6).

Future restoration and renewal are also the central themes of Joel 2, which contains probably the best known OT text associated with the Spirit: God's promise to pour out his Spirit on all flesh (Joel 2.28-29), which, according to Peter, was fulfilled on the day of Pentecost (Acts 2.17-18). God's coming judgment on Judah is prefigured by the devastation caused by a locust swarm (Joel 2.1-11). This leads to a call to repentance (vv. 12-17), which is followed by the promise of an outpouring of divine blessing (vv. 18-32). This will include material prosperity seen in the coming of rain (v. 23) and the abundant harvest that will accompany it. Here, as in other OT passages, the rain that brings life and fruitfulness points towards the nation's spiritual renewal through the outpouring of God's Spirit (vv. 28-29; cf. Isa. 32.15; 44.3-4).

All this, though, relates to the future renewal of the nation. What about the role of the Spirit in bringing renewal to individuals now? This is not a major theme in the OT, where the main emphasis is on the corporate life of God's people; but there may be an indication of it in Ps. 51.10-12.[29] We have already noted the parallel between God's Spirit (רוּחַ) and his presence in v. 11. The term רוּחַ also occurs in the immediately adjacent verses; though there it appears to refer to the

---

[27] Routledge, *Old Testament Theology*, p. 292. This seems the most likely explanation of Isa. 49.3, 5-6, where the Servant seems both to be identified with Israel and to have a ministry to Israel.

[28] For further discussion of Israel's calling, failure, and renewal through the Servant see Robin Routledge, 'Is There a Narrative Sub-structure Underlying the Book of Isaiah', *TynBul* 55.2 (2004), pp. 183-204.

[29] Goldingay links these verses with Ezek. 36.26; see John Goldingay, *Psalms* 3 vols. (Grand Rapids: Baker Academic, 2007), 1, p. 132; see also Lloyd Neve, 'Realized Eschatology in Psalm 51', *Expository Times* 80 (1969), pp. 264-66.

psalmist's inward disposition, rather than to the Spirit of God.[30] Whilst praying that God will not remove his Spirit (and so his presence), the psalmist also recognises his need of renewal, which involves inner transformation through the creation of a 'steadfast spirit' (v. 10) and the granting of a 'willing spirit' (v. 12). The structural link between these verses,[31] together with the repetition of רוח suggests an association between the renewed spirit that the psalmist prays he may receive (vv. 10, 12), and the continuing presence of the divine spirit (v. 11); as Goldingay suggests, in these verses 'we should think of the activity of the divine spirit on the human spirit'.[32] The reference to 'create' in v. 10 is significant in this context. The Hebrew word is ברא, the same word used of the creation of the world and of human beings (Gen. 1.1, 27); and also, of the continuing creative activity of God through his Spirit in Ps. 104.29. Thus, the psalmist's appeal in Ps. 51.10 appears to be that the divine Spirit who brings physical life to lifeless flesh, will again act creatively to bring about the spiritual transformation he needs to maintain his relationship with God (cf. Ezek. 37.1-14).

The creative activity of the Spirit finds echoes in the NT. John's Gospel appears to present the coming of Christ as a new creation;[33] and so it is not surprising that he also emphasises the activity of the Spirit in bringing new life (Jn 3.1-10). It is not surprising, either, to

---

[30] Tate argues that 'spirit' in all of these verses probably refers to the Spirit of God; see Marvin Tate, *Psalms 51-100* (WBC 20; Dallas: Word Books, 1990), pp. 22-25; see also Goldingay, 'Was the Holy Spirit Active?', pp. 16, 21; Goldingay, *Psalms*, 2, pp. 132-35. However, see, e.g. A.A. Anderson, *Psalms* 2 vols. (NCB; London: Marshall, Morgan and Scott, 1972), 1, pp. 398-99; Derek Kidner, *Psalms* 2 vols. (TOTC; Leicester: IVP, 1973), 1, p. 192; Artur Weiser, *Psalms* (OTL; London: SCM, 1962), pp. 406-408. The parallel of 'spirit' with 'heart' in v. 10 indicates that both refer to aspects of human personality, though the reference in v. 12 is less clear.

[31] In particular, the second part of each verse is constructed in the same way: רוח, followed by an adjective (vv. 11, 12) or adjectives (v. 10), followed by the verb, which in v. 14 has a pronominal suffix, and in vv. 11, 12 is followed by a preposition with pronominal suffix.

[32] Goldingay, *Psalms*, 1, p. 135

[33] This seems evident from a comparison of Jn 1.1 with Gen. 1.1; see, e.g. Raymond E. Brown, *The Gospel According to John I-XII* (2nd edn; Anchor Bible 29; Garden City, NY: 1966), and R.E. Brown, *The Gospel of John and the Epistles of John A Concise Commentary* (Collegeville, MN: Liturgical Press, 1988), pp. 21-28; F.F. Bruce, *The Gospel of John* (Cambridge: Pickering and Inglis; Grand Rapids: Eerdmans, 1983), pp. 28-29; D.A. Carson, *The Gospel According to John* (Leicester: Apollos; Grand Rapids: Eerdmans, 1991), pp. 113-14; Leon Morris, *The Gospel According to John* (rev. edn; Grand Rapids: Eerdmans, 1995), pp. 64-65.

see the role of the Spirit in renewal (e.g. 2 Cor. 3.17-18; Gal. 5.16-26). It is through the Spirit that we are transformed to become what God intends us to be. It is through the Spirit that we are enabled to be obedient (1 Pet. 1.2). It is surprising, however, that, despite its direct relevance and the important insights that it offers, many post-Pentecost treatments of the role of the Spirit in sanctification make few if any references to this significant aspect of the Spirit's work in the OT.[34] In my view this is one area in which the OT emphasis could be usefully pursued and applied corporately and individually to the life of the Church.

We have noted, too, that the renewal of Israel in the OT includes its enabling to fulfil its role as a witness to the nations. The general renewal of Israel is linked with the activity of the Spirit; and this specific goal will be accomplished through the Servant, who is also endowed with the Spirit. Thus, even in the OT, the Spirit plays an important part in empowering God's people for ministry to the nations. In the NT the importance of the Holy Spirit in empowering the Church for mission is significantly developed;[35] though the essential task of equipping the people of God to be 'witnesses' (Acts 1.8) remains.

Within the OT, the spiritual renewal of the nation remains future; it is associated with a coming era of salvation in which God will restore the fortunes of his people and establish his kingdom. The coming age may thus, rightly, be referred to as the age of the Spirit. This has two implications for Christian Pneumatology. First, the coming of the Spirit at Pentecost may be seen as the fulfilment of the OT hope (e.g. Acts 2.16, 21; cf. Joel 2.28-3.1). However, that hope has not been fully realised, and so we see, second, that there is still a looking forward to the age to come, which will be consummated when Christ returns. In the meantime, the Holy Spirit is a guarantee of what is to come (2 Cor. 1.22; 5.5; Eph. 1.13-14); and through the

---

[34] Grudem does not mention the OT in relation to the Spirit's role in purification (*Systematic Theology*, pp. 639-40); see also Green, *I Believe in the Holy Spirit*, pp. 88-91; Petts, *Holy Spirit*, pp. 55-62. Horton and Rea note the role of the Spirit in renewal in the OT; but make no reference to it when discussing sanctification; see Horton, *Holy Spirit*, pp. 69-72, cf. pp. 175-85, 243-45; Rea, *Holy Spirit*, pp. 101-104, cf. pp. 233-38, 275-77, 280-84.

[35] Michael Green suggests that 'the prime purpose of the coming of the Spirit of God upon the disciples was to equip them for mission' (*Holy Spirit*, p. 58)

Spirit the power of that coming age may break through into the present age.

Something that is not generally developed in Christian Pneumatology is the role of God's Spirit in giving and sustaining physical life. That is also unsurprising; but it is important. This aspect of the Spirit's work emphasises the total dependence of human beings on God; it emphasises God's continuing interest in, and commitment to, all that he has made; and it points, too, to the ongoing activity of the Spirit in relation to all human life. In the flood, God did cut off the breath of human beings. Even then, though, it was not a total destruction; and after the flood God made a covenant with Noah and with every living creature and renewed his commitment to the world he had made. It is this divine commitment to the whole of creation that provides the basis for mission.[36] The continuing activity of the Spirit in bringing physical life to the inhabitants of the earth reinforces that ongoing divine commitment. God's choice of Israel was also part of his commitment to the whole world. Through Israel God would make his glory known to all nations;[37] and Israel's life in relation to God may thus be seen as a 'microcosm of what God intends for all peoples'.[38] In Israel, as we have seen, the physical life that resulted from breathing divine רוּחַ into the nostrils of the first human pair is a pattern for the spiritual life and renewal that comes from the indwelling Spirit. However, just as the activity of the Spirit in bringing physical life is not limited to Israel, nor is his activity in bringing

---

[36] For a discussion of the relationship between the Noahic covenant and mission see, e.g. Robin Routledge, 'Mission and Covenant in the Old Testament', in Rollin G. Grams, Peter F. Penner, I. Howard Marshall, and Robin Routledge (eds.), *Bible and Mission: A Conversation between Biblical Studies and Missiology* (Schwarzenwald: Neufeld Verlag, 2008), pp. 8-41 [16-20].

[37] I have argued elsewhere that God's purpose reflected in the OT is to reveal his glory to the whole world (cf. Isa. 6.3); see Routledge, 'Is There a Narrative Substructure Underlying the Book of Isaiah?', pp. 183–204; Routledge, *Old Testament Theology*, pp. 311-15.

[38] See Routledge, 'Mission and Covenant', in Grams, Penner, Marshal, Routledge, *Bible and Mission*, pp. 18-21 [19]; Routledge, *Old Testament Theology*, p. 322. Goldingay describes Israel as a 'microcosm of humanity' (*OT Theology* II, p. 517) and suggests that Israel's commission is to provide a working model of what it means to be in covenant with Yhwh and a promise of what Yhwh intends for all peoples' (*OT Theology* II, p. 226); see also James Chukwuma Okoye, *Israel and the Nations: A Mission Theology of the Old Testament* (Maryknoll: Orbis, 2006), pp. 31-32.

spiritual life. This is something intended for, and one day to be experienced by, the whole world.[39]

The Spirit Empowers for Service.

The role of the Spirit in empowering the people of God for service is a main theme both in the OT and in post-Pentecost treatments of the ministry of the Holy Spirit.

In the OT the Spirit of God is associated with skill and ability of various kinds. The artistic skills of Bezalel, who worked with others on the construction of the tabernacle, are attributed to the Spirit of God (Exod. 31.3-4; 35.31 cf. 28.3). There is no suggestion that these abilities were spontaneously endowed just for this occasion. These were what we might describe as 'natural' gifts; nevertheless, they are recognised as coming from God, through his Spirit. The Spirit is also associated with clearly supernatural ability, such as the great feats of strength performed by Samson (Judg. 14.6; 15.14).

The Spirit in the OT is also seen to empower for leadership. Moses was endowed with the Spirit, and when some of his responsibility was delegated to Israel's elders, the Spirit also came upon them (Num. 11.17, 25). After Moses' death it is noted that his successor, Joshua, was also filled with the Spirit (Deut. 34.9). In both of these cases there is the sense of continuity of leadership and therefore of authority: the elders of Israel are endowed with some of the same Spirit that was on Moses; and Joshua was filled with the Spirit as a result of Moses laying hands on him.

Israel's judges also had the Spirit come upon them. This is specifically mentioned in the cases of Othniel (Judg. 3.9-10), Gideon (Judg. 6.34), Jephthah (Judg. 11.29), and Samson (Judg. 13.25); though it is assumed for other judges too. The oil with which kings were anointed also indicated the presence of God's Spirit. This connection is clear in relation to Saul (1 Sam. 10.1, 6; 11.6) and David (1 Sam. 16.13);[40]

---

[39] Goldingay extends this in relation to the Church. The activity of the Spirit in believers in producing fruit and releasing gifts 'are not essentially novel enlargements of this human nature, but the fulfilment of what created human beings are intended to be and have the inherent potential to be … Thus, the renewing of the Church is the shaping of a microcosm of creation' (Goldingay, 'Was the Holy Spirit Active?', p. 16).

[40] The reference to the Spirit coming upon David and at the same time being taken from Saul (1 Sam. 16.13-14) again indicates continuity of leadership.

and though it is not explicit in relation to subsequent kings, again, it may be assumed.[41] The Spirit is associated, explicitly, with the coming Messianic king (e.g. Isa. 11.1-3), and with the Servant, who is sometimes identified with the Messiah (e.g. Isa. 42.1 cf. 61.1).[42] Aaron and his sons were also formally anointed when they were ordained as priests (e.g. Exod. 29.21; 30.30; Num. 3.3). This, too, suggests equipping and empowering by the Spirit; though, again, the connection is not made directly.

A further key role of the Spirit in the OT is in relation to prophecy.[43] Prophesying is seen as the outward sign of the Spirit coming upon a person – including the elders of Israel (Num. 11.25-29), Saul (1 Sam. 10.6, 10; 19.23), Saul's men (1 Sam. 19.20-21) and, ultimately, all people (Joel 2.28; cf. Isa. 59.21). In the case of the elders of Israel it is specifically noted that they prophesied only on this occasion – suggesting that this was only a sign to indicate the presence of the Spirit.[44] It seems probable that with Saul's men this was also a one-off experience; and even in the case of Saul, the surprise implicit in the exclamation, 'is Saul also amongst the prophets' (1 Sam. 10.11-12 19.24) indicates that Saul's behaviour was unusual, if not unique. In each of these cases, too, there is no mention of what was said – suggesting that the actual content of the prophecy was less important than the evidence it gave of the Spirit's presence. It has been suggested that the verb usually translated 'prophesy' – which also refers to Saul's fitful outburst as a result of an 'evil spirit from God' (1 Sam. 18.10-11), and the frenzy of the prophets of Baal (1 Kgs 18.29) – might sometimes indicate ecstatic behaviour that is not directly related to prophetic speech.[45] If so, and the matter is by no means

---

[41] Omitting to mention the Spirit after David may be intentional on the part of OT writers in order to emphasise the general failure of the monarchy in contrast to the Davidic ideal.

[42] See, e.g. Routledge, *Old Testament Theology*, pp. 293-94

[43] See, e.g. Green, *Holy Spirit*, pp. 21-23; Horton, *Holy Spirit*, pp. 55-58; Rea, *Holy Spirit*, pp. 71-83; Wright, *Knowing the Holy Spirit*, pp. 63-86; see also Johannes Lindblom, *Prophecy in Ancient Israel* (Oxford: Blackwell, 1962), pp. 174-79

[44] See, e.g. Eryl W. Davies, *Numbers* (NCB; London: Marshall Pickering, 1995), pp. 109-10; Lindblom, *Prophecy*, p. 101.

[45] See, e.g. Simon B. Parker, 'Possession Trance and Prophecy in Pre-exilic Israel', *VT* 28.3 (1978), pp. 271-85. Parker argues that in the case of Saul, the verb means 'to fall into a possession trance' and has 'nothing to do with prophecy or divination' (p. 274). Ecstatic behaviour is often associated with the hithpael form

certain, this offers the possibility that the 'prophesying' that signifies the presence of the Spirit may not necessarily include intelligible words.

On other occasions the Spirit is associated with prophets whose words are recorded. Ezekiel attributed his inspiration to the direct activity of the Spirit (Ezek. 2.2; 3.24; 8.3; 11.1; 37.1; 43.5). Micah, too, pointed to the Spirit as the one who empowered him to deliver an uncomfortable message to Israel, and in so doing distinguished his words from the empty words of false prophets:

> But as for me, I am filled with power,
>   with the Spirit of the Lord,
>   and with justice and might,
> to declare to Jacob his transgression,
>   to Israel his sin. (Mic. 3.8 cf. vv. 6-7).

Many other passages also point to the Spirit of God as the one through whom prophets are inspired to bring their message (e.g. Num. 24.2-3; 2 Chr. 15.1-7; 20.14-17; 24.20; Neh. 9.30; Isa. 61.1; Zech. 7.12); and in Hos. 9.7, 'prophet' is parallel to 'inspired man' (literally 'man of the spirit').

Some pre-exilic prophets seem to express a reluctance to attribute their prophecies to the inspiration of the Spirit. Jeremiah, for example, does not refer to the Spirit at all in connection with his prophecy, emphasising instead the 'word of the LORD' (e.g., Jer. 1.2, 4; 11.1; 18.1),[46] and his access to the divine council where he hears that word declared (Jer. 23.18, 21-22). Not mentioning the Spirit may be intended to distance true prophets from the ecstatic ravings that were

---

(as in the cases mentioned). Rendtorff contrasts these occurrences of the verb with 'prophetic speech'; see Rolf Rendtorff, *Canonical Hebrew Bible: A Theology of the Old Testament* (Leiden: Deo, 2005), pp. 653-54. On prophetic ecstasy, see also, e.g. John R. Levison, 'Prophecy in Ancient Israel: The Case of the Ecstatic Elders', *CBQ* 65.4 (2003), pp. 503-21; Robert L. Alden, 'Ecstasy and the Prophets', *BETS* 9.3 (1966), pp. 149-56; *CBQ* 65.4 (2003), pp. 503-21; Lindblom, *Prophecy*, pp. 47-65; 'Robert R. Wilson, 'Prophecy and Ecstasy: a Re-examination', *JBL* 98.3 (1979), pp. 321-37; Leon J. Wood, 'Ecstasy and Israel's Early Prophets', *BETS* 9.3 (1966), pp. 125-37.

[46] This is not an uncommon way to speak about a prophet receiving his message; Ezekiel also frequently refers to 'the word of the LORD' coming to him (e.g. 3.16; 6.1; 7.1); the difference, though, is in the lack of reference in the book of Jeremiah to the Spirit in connection with prophetic inspiration.

characteristic of prophets of other religions, and from false prophets in Israel who may have tried to emulate them.[47]

In several OT passages the Spirit is also linked with the impartation of *wisdom*. After Joseph has interpreted Pharaoh's dreams and set out plans to preserve Egypt's food supplies through years of plenty in order to sustain the nation during years of famine, Pharaoh acknowledges Joseph's God-given wisdom and insight (Gen. 41.39), which is associated with his description of Joseph as 'one in whom is the spirit of God' (Gen. 41.38, cf. Dan. 4.8).[48] Joshua's wisdom is also linked with the Spirit (Deut. 34.9). Moses had, previously, transferred some of his authority to his protégé by laying his hands on him (Num. 27.18-23). There Joshua is described as 'a man in whom is the Spirit' (v. 18). Following Moses' death, Joshua is described as having received the Spirit from Moses (Deut. 34.9) and so is presented as Moses' legitimate successor. In the context of Joshua's new responsibility, the Spirit is specifically designated as 'the spirit of wisdom', indicating the importance of wisdom as a leadership quality. We see this link between wisdom and the Spirit also in relation to the Messianic king (Isa. 11.2).

In the OT, wisdom is closely related to insight and understanding; but it is also practical. In the case of Joseph, it includes both knowledge, gained through interpreting Pharaoh's dreams, and the application of that knowledge to produce credible plans. Wisdom also includes technical and artistic ability – such as Bezalel's craftsmanship (Exod. 31.3-4; 35.31) which, as we have noted, is also attributed to the Spirit.[49] In its more general OT context, wisdom may be seen as insight into the way the world works; and includes the application of that understanding and of specialist knowledge or

---

[47] For further discussion, see e.g J.D.G. Dunn, 'Spirit, Holy Spirit', in Douglas, Hillyer (eds.), *Illustrated Bible Dictionary*, III, p. 1480; Lindblom, *Prophecy*, pp. 177-78; Goldingay, 'Was the Holy Spirit Active?', p. 17; Rea, *Holy Spirit*, pp. 76-77.

[48] רוח אלהים might be translated 'spirit of (the) gods' (NIVmg), and this might seem to be a more appropriate expression on the lips of Pharaoh. However, Joseph has already made it clear that the interpretation of dreams comes from God (Gen. 40.8; 41.25, 28), and it is possible that Pharaoh was prepared to acknowledge the help of Joseph's God. Even if that is not the case, it is likely that the narrator's use of the expression רוח אלהים, which is usually translated 'Spirit of God', is intended to indicate that God is the true source of the revelation, whatever Pharaoh might have thought.

[49] Practical aspects of wisdom in various walks of life are also seen in, e.g. Exod. 8.3; Isa. 10.13; Jer. 9.17; Ezek. 27.8-9; Esth. 1.13.

skill, to achieve success in life. True wisdom is, however, also theological; it comes from God, and may be received only by those who know God (Prov. 9.10, cf. Job 32.8).[50] It could be said that through wisdom God's people may be successful in achieving his purpose for their lives; and the impartation of that wisdom is associated with the activity of the Spirit.

The NT writers also emphasise the role of the Spirit in empowering the people of God for service. There are some clear areas of overlap. The Spirit equips for ministry and leadership (e.g. Acts 6.3, 10; 11.23-24; cf. 1 Cor. 12.28; Eph. 4.11); there is a link between the Spirit and wisdom (e.g. Acts 6.3, 10; 1 Cor. 2.6; 12.8; Col. 1.9; cf. 3.16 however see 1 Cor. 2.4-5); and the Spirit in the NT as in the OT inspires prophets and prophecy (e.g. Lk. 1.67; 1 Cor. 12.10; cf. 2 Pet. 1.21). This is not the place for a detailed discussion of the gifts of the Spirit in the NT. However, it is important both to be aware (as the NT writers undoubtedly were) of the OT background of these aspects of the Spirit's work; and whilst recognising differences and development between the testaments, to allow the OT to inform our understanding of the role and activity of the Spirit.

Some of the other gifts and ministries linked with the Holy Spirit in the NT also have OT equivalents, though ones that are, may not be directly linked with the Spirit, including healing, working miracles, faith, supernatural knowledge (1 Cor. 12.8-11), and gifts of administration (1 Cor. 12.28). One gift that does not feature explicitly in the OT is 'speaking in different kinds of tongues'.[51] However, it might be possible to see a link between this, particularly when it is a sign of presence of the Spirit (e.g. Acts 2.4; 19.6; 10.46), and the prophesying that also seems, primarily, to provide evidence of the Spirit's presence, and which, as noted above, may include unintelligible speech.

---

[50] For further discussion of wisdom in the OT, see, e.g. Routledge, *Old Testament Theology*, pp. 215-24

[51] When discussing speaking in tongues Paul refers to Isa. 28.11 (1 Cor. 14.21). This is not an OT example of the spiritual gift, but points to the judgment reflected in the foreign tongues of (Assyrian) invaders. The people have not listened to the prophets so God will speak to them in a different way. Paul uses this analogy to indicate how 'tongues' can be a sign of judgment, leading to conviction of sin.

A significant difference between the Old and New Testaments is the universal availability of the Spirit.[52] Joel's prophecy looks forward to a general outpouring of the Spirit – 'I will pour out my Spirit on all people' (Joel 2.28), and this stands in contrast to the view of the OT, where only a relatively few, selected people appear to have been so endowed. It is certainly true that the OT writers link the Spirit directly with only a small number of individuals and say little about the activity of the Spirit in the lives of ordinary people. But does that mean there was no such activity?

Commenting on the phrase 'the spirit was not yet [given]' (Jn 7.39), Goldingay suggests that this might refer to occasions where the Spirit was active in the OT but not specifically named.[53] It only became common to emphasise the role of the Spirit after Jesus had died, risen, and ascended; before that referring to the Spirit might be one way among many of indicating God's activity.[54] This legitimates reading back what we see of the role of the Spirit in the NT into the OT. So, for example, in the NT the Spirit is closely linked with worship; and, though the OT writers do not say so explicitly, there is no reason to suppose that worship in the OT is any less inspired by the Spirit. Similarly, in the OT there are many who display the same qualities that, in the NT, would be described in terms of the fruit of the Spirit; thus, according to Goldingay, 'the Spirit was evidently active on an ongoing basis in the lives of ordinary individuals in the OT'.[55] On the basis of this discussion he then concludes that 'the

---

[52] It is sometimes suggested that another key difference is that the empowering of the Spirit in the OT was temporary. Rea takes the fact that the seventy elders prophesied but 'did not do so again' (Num. 11.25) as an indication that the Spirit's manifestation was 'occasional, sporadic, temporary' (Rea, *Holy Spirit*, p. 47). However, the purpose of the Spirit's presence was to enable the elders to assist Moses to lead the people; and that, we may suppose, continued. Samson seems to receive a series of temporary empowerings, when 'the Spirit of the LORD came upon him in power' (Judg. 14.6, 19; 15.14). However, there is no reference to the Spirit leaving Samson; and the expression might point to the suddenness of the manifestation. The Spirit did leave Saul (1 Sam. 16.14), but that was as a result of his sin (cf. Ps. 51.11) and does not indicate that the initial anointing was intended to be temporary. In other cases, too, there is no reason to suppose that the activity of the Spirit was temporary.

[53] Goldingay, 'Was the Holy Spirit Active?', pp. 16-19.

[54] So, for example, Ezekiel talks about God's *hand* (e.g. Ezek. 8.1; 33.22) in much the same way as he talks about the Spirit.

[55] Goldingay, 'Was the Holy Spirit Active?', p. 19.

relationship between OT believers and God was essentially like that of NT believers rather than essentially unlike it'.[56]

I agree with Goldingay's general conclusion. I, too, would want to emphasise the essential continuity, rather than discontinuity, between the life of God's people in the OT and the life of the Church. The scope of the Spirit's activity in the OT may well be wider than the specific references suggest. However, there is a danger of reading back too much from the later understanding of the Spirit; particularly in relation to his ongoing activity in the lives of ordinary individuals. Even when the OT writers use other expressions to indicate God's activity, this is set in the context of specific areas of service, rather than within the general life of the people. Joel's prophecy appears to indicate a universalising of the Spirit that is more than a matter of terminology. The promise of a future inward transformation also must point beyond what is currently available. After the Day of Pentecost that changes: all believers may know the presence and power of the Spirit to live out the new life that is theirs in Christ. That also brings responsibility. Believers in the OT could look forward to the inward renewal that God would bring through his Spirit; today, that power is already present leaving believers without excuse!

Conclusion

It is a truism that for Christian believers the OT is incomplete without the NT. However, the NT writers were rooted in the OT scriptures, and built on them; consequently, a proper understanding of the NT is also incomplete without an appreciation of the OT.[57] That is true in relation to the Spirit. In this discussion I have tried to highlight the many points of contact between the role of the Spirit in the OT and in the NT. There are, of course, differences, particularly in the part played by the Spirit in the lives of *all* believers: both in enabling for service and in bringing the renewal that the OT can only look forward to (though even here the future work of the Spirit is anticipated). However, there is also an essential continuity between the activity of the Spirit in the lives of OT and NT believers. And in the light of that continuity, it is important, and necessary, to allow the

---

[56] Goldingay, 'Was the Holy Spirit Active?', p. 19.
[57] See Routledge, *Old Testament Theology*, p. 26.

OT view of the Spirit to inform our wider understanding of Pneumatology.

7

THE THOUSAND-YEAR REIGN (REVELATION 20.1-10)

JOHN CHRISTOPHER THOMAS*

It is a delight for me to offer a contribution in honour of my friend and colleague Professor William K. Kay, with whom it has been my pleasure to work for the last several years. William is a first-class scholar, visionary, and pioneer especially in his work in Pentecostal studies. His generous spirit, indefatigable optimism, and deep love for God are all models for his colleagues as well as the coming generation of Pentecostal scholars. I thank God for every remembrance of him. May this *Festschrift* bring a small token of honour to one who is richly deserving of it and much more indeed.

Whilst millennial thought is a well-documented part of the Pentecostal theological worldview, surprisingly little attention has been given to a detailed reading of the primary text upon which an understanding of the millennium is based. This study seeks to provide such a reading and thus make a small contribution toward filling this lacuna. Although Rev. 20.11-15 is properly a part of this section, owing to limitations of space, this study will be confined to Rev. 20.1-10.[1]

* John Christopher Thomas (PhD, University of Sheffield; DD, Bangor University) is Clarence J. Abbott Professor of Biblical Studies at the Pentecostal Theological Seminary in Cleveland, TN, USA and Director of the Centre for Pentecostal Charismatic Studies at Bangor University, Bangor, Wales, UK.

[1] Even Huibert Zegwaart devotes only four pages of his study ['Apocalyptic Eschatology and Pentecostalism: The Relevance of John's Millennium for Today', *Pneuma* 10.1 (Spring, 1988), pp. 3-25] to a reading of this text. The primary exception to this oversight is the work R. Hollis Gause, whose treatment of Revelation 20 stands as part of his fine commentary on the Apocalypse; R.H. Gause, *Revelation:*

As Revelation 20 opens, the hearers are allowed very little time to reflect upon the truly extraordinary eschatological events described in chapter 19 for their attention is immediately directed to yet another aspect of John's vision, 'And I saw an angel coming down out of heaven having the key for the Abyss and a great chain in his hand'. The words 'and I saw' indicates to the hearers that John's visionary experience continues with attention now given to a new detail, a detail that stands in continuity with the previous frequent occurrences of the phrase 'and I saw', beginning in 19.11 and continuing in strategic locations throughout this section of the Apocalypse (19.11, 17, 19). Despite contemporary claims to the contrary, it is difficult to imagine that Johannine hearers would not take these words in continuity with what precedes and in some sense of chronological development. It might strike the hearers as a bit odd that after the detailed description of the rider on the white horse and his disposing of the beast, the false prophet, and all those who stood with them in opposition to this rider, that attention is suddenly shifted to an angel. Such a shift in focus, in and of itself, would create within the hearers a great sense of expectancy, for not only does this angel remind them of other significant angelic figures who have appeared throughout the book doing the work of God, but the physical description of what this angel bears is quite intriguing on its own. The origin of this angel, 'coming down out of heaven', indicates that he comes with divine authority and a sense of divine commission, which the instruments in his hands reveal. The fact that he has the key to the Abyss would remind the hearers of the star that was given the key to the shaft of the Abyss at the time the fifth angel trumpeted (9.1), whose actions released an army of locusts who torment the inhabitants of the earth. In fact, the hearers might well believe that the angel introduced in 20.1 is the same angel as the one described as the angel of the Abyss mentioned in 9.11, where he is given the names 'Destruction' and 'Destroyer', in Hebrew and Greek respectively, names reminiscent of the Destroyer of Exod. 12.23. If so, the hearers would recognize the instruments in his hands as indicating his authority over the Abyss, on the one hand, and his ability to subdue any opponent with the great chain he possesses, on the other hand. Whilst in the Apocalypse

God's Stamp of Sovereignty on History (Cleveland, TN: Pathway Press, 1983), pp. 250-62.

the Abyss is the place of origin of the tormenting locusts (9.1, 2, 11) and the beast (11.7; 17.8), it is clear that God himself controls the Abyss and that God himself has authority over it. Owing to the fact that the rider on the white horse has apparently destroyed all his opponents but one, perhaps the hearers anticipate that the appearance of this angel is connected to the judgment of the final cosmic opponent, the Dragon.

If so, the hearers would not be surprised by the next words they encounter, 'And he seized the Dragon, the Ancient Serpent, who is Devil and Satan, and he bound him for a thousand years'. For a second time in the Apocalypse the Dragon's full identity occurs with the names, the Dragon, the Ancient Serpent, Devil, and Satan standing together. In 20.2, as in 12.9, the occurrence of these names together underscores his identity in all its intensity. The appearance of the name 'the Dragon' would remind the hearers of his role as the persecutor of the woman clothed with the sun (12.3), his attempt to kill her child (12.4), the loss of his place in heaven (12.7-9), his persecution of the rest of the woman's seed (12.13), his giving power to the beast (13.2), receiving idolatrous worship (13.4), and out of whom unclean spirits emerge (16.13). Mention of the Ancient Serpent, as in 12.9, would remind the hearers of the Genesis story (Gen. 3.1-7), where the serpent tempts Adam and Eve with eating from the fruit of the Tree, fruit which was forbidden to them by God. Thus, the serpent of which the hearers would think when hearing the words 'the ancient serpent' would likely be the serpent of Genesis 3. Nor would the correlation between the dragon's intention to devour the woman's child at birth and the enmity between the serpent and Eve's seed be lost on the hearers (12.14). He is the ancient serpent, the liar and murderer from of old. With the mention of the name Devil, Johannine hearers would be reminded that he is a murderer from the beginning and one of whom it is said lying is his native tongue (Jn 8.44). They would also be reminded that 'the one who commits sin is of the Devil, for the Devil sins from the beginning' (1 Jn 3.8) and that the Son of God was manifested in order that he might destroy the works of the latter (1 Jn 3.9). Earlier in the Apocalypse (Rev. 2.10) they learned that '... the Devil is about to cast some of you into prison in order that he might test you. Be faithful unto death and I will give you the crown of life.' Joined to the name Devil in 20.2 is the name Satan, with whom Johannine hearers would be well-acquainted owing to the fact that in the Fourth Gospel, Satan entered Judas just before this disciple goes out into the night (Jn 13.27). In the Apocalypse, this sinister figure is especially associated with Jewish opposition to the church, the synagogue of Satan (Rev. 2.9; 3.9), the powerful presence of Satan (2.13), and the ominous nature of his 'deep things' (2.24). For the great dragon to be identified as identical to Satan concretizes further for the hearers the nature of the dragon's activity and power. But in 20.2, as in 12.9, the remarkable convergence of this impressive cacophony of titles and names does not overwhelm the hearers, for they remember that this very creature, this very opponent has earlier been 'cast down'. In 20.2, the hearers learn that this very creature, with pretensions to deity, is not seized and bound by God directly, but by an unnamed angelic creature![2] In point of fact, the authority of this unnamed angel in 20.2 becomes clear to the hearers, not only by his actions, but also from the structure of this sentence in the Greek text, for in ways reminiscent of his description in 12.9, the Dragon's full identity is surrounded by verbs that describe his impotence. In 12.9 his full identity was surrounded by the words, 'was cast down', whereas in 20.2 his identity is surrounded by the words, 'seized' and 'bound'.

This angel seized him and bound him (apparently with the great chain in his hand). Neither would the length of this binding be without significance for the hearers, for the Dragon is bound for a thousand years, an extraordinarily long period of time. Though numerous periods of time have been encountered throughout the Apocalypse, nothing to this point compares with the thousand years of binding. The hearers might well be impressed by the fact that this period of binding dwarfs all other periods of binding and persecution of the saints in the book. All such times of persecution would now appear different to the hearers in the light of this monumental binding. For while Satan may indeed throw some of the saints in Smyrna into prison for ten days (2.10), Satan himself is to be bound for a thousand years – a ratio of one hundred years of being bound for each day he has imprisoned the saints. While the temple will be trampled underfoot and the beast will speak blasphemy for forty-two months (11.2; 13.5, respectively), the Dragon will be bound for a thousand years – a ratio of some two hundred eighty years of binding for each

---

[2] Gause, *Revelation*, p. 251.

year of persecution. While the bodies of the two prophetic witnesses will lie in the streets of the Great City for all the world to see for three and a half days (11.9), Satan will be bound a thousand years – a ratio of some two hundred eighty years of binding per day of humiliation. While the ten kings who serve the beast will rule for one hour (17.12), Satan will be bound for a thousand years – a ratio of a thousand years of being bound for each hour of reign. Whilst such mathematical ratios may mean little to modern interpreters, their meaning for discerning Johannine hearers would be hard to overestimate. For in the light of this binding of Satan, the saints' periods of persecution, imprisonment, and humiliation lose some of their potency and are seen from a different perspective. For the saints may indeed suffer unto death, but Satan will be bound a thousand years!

The hearers, however, are not allowed to reflect further on this detail for the actions of this unnamed angel continue at almost breakneck speed, 'And he cast him into the Abyss, and he shut/locked it and sealed over it in order that he might not deceive the nations until the thousand years are completed: after these things it is necessary for him to be loosed for a short time'. The next action of the angel is reminiscent of Michael's action (12.9), for on this occasion as well the Dragon is cast down. The hearers might well detect progression in this cosmic story for whereas Michael's activity resulted in the Dragon being cast down out of heaven unto the earth, the unnamed angel's activity results in the Dragon being cast down (from the earth?) into the Abyss. And whereas the earth and sea were warned about the great wrath of the devil, who has little time to carry out his persecution of the rest of the Woman's offspring, the unnamed angel binds and imprisons the Dragon for a thousand years, after which he is to be loosed a short time. No doubt the hearers would find poetic justice in the fact that the Devil, who would cast some of those in the church in Smyrna into jail for ten days (2.10), is now being cast into the Abyss, a place in the Apocalypse over which God and his agents have authority and from which some of his redemptive agents arise (9.1, 2, 11), as well as one of the enemies of God and his people, the Beast (11.7; 17.8).

The hearers next learn more about the unnamed angel's authority over the Dragon, when the unnamed angel both shuts/locks and places a seal upon the Abyss where the Dragon has been cast. The hearers might well discern in the shutting and/or locking of the

Abyss by the angel the same kind of divine activity they encountered in Jesus' words to the church in Philadelphia, 'I have the key of David, the One who opens, and no one can close, and closes and no one can open' (3.7), and the prophetic powers of the two witnesses who have the authority to shut the heavens (11.6). Thus, the shutting and/or locking of the Abyss would be understood as divine activity on the angel's part. The hearers would also understand that when the angel seals over the Abyss he not only ensures that the prisoner cannot escape unobserved,[3] but also that this action is in keeping with the previous sealing vocabulary in the Apocalypse (7.3, 4, 5, 8; 10.4 and 5.1, 2, 5, 9; 6.1, 3, 5, 7, 9, 12; 7.2; 8.1; 9.4; cf. also Jn 3.33; 6.27); indicating divine authorization of this action, ensuring that God's will is to be done in the matter, and serving as an authentication that this activity is indeed God's doing. It is not insignificant that to this point in the Apocalypse all sealing takes place through divine initiative; this sealing would be no different. The purpose of this angelic activity is expressed by means of a *hina* (ἵνα, 'in order that') clause, 'in order that he might not deceive the nations until the thousand years have been completed'.

Several aspects of these words would be of significance to the hearers. First, the relationship between deception and the Dragon would surprise none of the hearers, for as they learned in Rev. 12.9, he is 'the one who deceives the whole inhabited world'. In point of fact, the Dragon is the one who stands behind all human agents of deception (Jn 7.12, 47; 1 Jn 1.8; 2.26; 3.7; Rev. 2.20), as well as the false prophet (13.14; 19.20) and Babylon (18.23).[4] However, unlike the current situation where the church faces daily the Deceiver and his agents, when the Dragon is locked in the Abyss, there will be a thousand year period in which the nations will not be subjected to his deception! Second, the hearers might well be startled to learn that those who are to be protected from the Dragon's deceptive activity are the nations, for apparently all opponents of the Rider on the White Horse were slain by the sword of his mouth in the preceding passage (19.21). Thus, the hearers might well wonder as to the identity and origin of these nations mentioned in 20.3. Would they be understood as the remnants of the nations as a whole that opposed

---

[3] G.R. Beasley-Murray, *Revelation* (Grand Rapids: Eerdmans, 1981), p. 285.
[4] P. Prigent, *L'Apocalypse de saint Jean* (Genève: Labor et Fides, 2000), p. 436.

God, but for some reason were not completely destroyed?[5] Or would they be thought of as representative of the nations?[6] Would they be thought of as nations that did not join in the war of opposition against the Rider on the White Horse? Or would they be thought to be the ghosts of the nations that had earlier been described as slain by the Rider?[7]

While it is possible that any number of these ideas might be rumbling around in the minds of the hearers, their previous pneumatic discernment might lead them to suspect that just as a variety of things in the Apocalypse have disappeared only to reappear later, in ways that push beyond mere cyclical repetition to suggest a certain linear progression, so the (re)appearance of the nations serves a similar function, suggesting that there is even more to the linear development of the nations. At the same time, the major theme of the conversion of the nations, one of the things in the Apocalypse to which the witness of the pneumatic church is called, continues in a somewhat unexpected way. For despite the fact that the nations have apparently been completely destroyed by the Rider on the White Horse, they (re)appear here, and in a context suggesting that at long last they may be able to respond to the witness of the church without the deceptive influence of the Dragon. Just as the detail about the iron rod with which the Rider would shepherd the nations (19.15) suggests a role for the nations still, so their (re)appearance here confirms that they have not yet been completely forgotten! Third, a second mention of the thousand years, in the span of two verses, would reinforce the fact for the hearers that this extraordinary period of time, during which the Dragon is to be bound, serves a specific function. It is a period in which the nations are not to be deceived by the Dragon[8] and a period of time that must run its course for the divine will to be accomplished, as the theologically significant Johannine word translated 'has been completed' (τελεσθῇ) indicates (Jn 19.28, 30; Rev. 10.7; 11.7; 15.1, 8; 17.17). The hearers quickly learn that just as the

---

[5] R.H. Mounce, *The Book of Revelation* (Grand Rapids: Eerdmans, 1977), p. 353. G.B. Caird, *A Commentary on the Revelation of Saint John the Divine* (London: A. and C. Black, 1966), p. 251.

[6] G.E. Ladd, *Revelation* (Grand Rapids: Eerdmans, 1972), p. 263.

[7] M. Rissi, *Die Zukunft der Welt: Eine exgetische Studie über Johannesoffenbarung 19, 11 bis 22, 15* (Basel: Verlag Friedrich Reinhardt, 1966), pp. 34-36 and W. Mealy, *After the Thousand Years* (JSNTSup 70; Sheffield: JSOT Press, 1992), pp. 181-86.

[8] Gause, *Revelation*, p. 252.

thousand years fulfills a divine function so does its conclusion, for 'after these things it is necessary for him to be loosed for a short time'. The word translated 'it is necessary' (δεῖ) would not only convey to the hearers the idea that the conclusion of the period serves a divine necessity,[9] but also indicates that Satan's release is no escape but is itself part of the divine plan.[10] As incredulous as this detail might at first appear, after all, who would release the Dragon after he has been captured(?) perhaps the hearers would suspect that if the nations are being given an opportunity to respond to the witness of the church without the deceptive influence of Satan during this thousand year period, then perhaps they would not be surprised that any such positive response on the nations' part must of necessity be tested by the deception of the Dragon.

As the hearers ponder such a remarkable turn of events, they encounter even more astounding words,

> And I saw thrones, and they were seated upon them, and judgment was given to them, and the souls of those beheaded on account of the witness of Jesus and on account of the word of God, and those who did not worship the Beast nor his image and did not receive his mark upon their forehead and upon their hand. And they came to life and they reigned with Christ a thousand years.

The words 'and I saw' would alert the hearers to the fact that new details of the various visionary reports are to be revealed. On this occasion John sees thrones, a detail that would perhaps speak to the hearers at a couple of different levels. For, on the one hand, they would by this point be quite familiar with the throne of God (and the One who sits upon it), owing to the frequent reference made to it throughout the book (1.4; 3.21; 4.2, 3, 4, 5, 6, 9, 10; 5. 1, 6, 7, 11, 13; 6.16; 7.9, 10, 11, 15, 17; 8.3; 12.5; 14.3; 16.17; 19.4, 5). They would also by this point be aware of the throne of Jesus that he will share with the one who overcomes (3.21) and the thrones of 24 elders (4.4; 11.16). On the other hand, the hearers would have encountered reference to the throne of Satan (2.13), as well as the throne of the Beast (13.2; 16.10). While the throne of God and those of the

---

[9] J.P.M. Sweet, *Revelation* (London: SCM Press, 1979), p. 288.
[10] Gause, *Revelation*, p. 252.

twenty-four elders are located in heaven, the throne of Satan and the Beast appear to be contextualized on earth. Owing to the earthly orientation beginning in 19.11 and extending through 20.10, the hearers might well suspect at this point that the throne of Satan and the Beast have given way to other thrones, perhaps in keeping with the promise of Jesus to those who overcome (3.21), an idea supported by the fact that the verb 'sit' (καθίζω) occurs only in 3.21, where the promise is made, and here in 20.4 in the entire book.

As the vision progresses it may become clear to the hearers that the things seen (by John and described to them) take on a kaleidoscopic form with a variety of images described one after the other, images that appear to converge as they pile one on top of the other. For in addition to the thrones, the hearers learn that there were those seated upon them, yet another somewhat ambiguous individual detail that could set the hearers' minds to wondering as to the identity of such throne sitters, perhaps the twenty-four elders or the overcomers themselves? But before they can contemplate this aspect of the vision in any detail, they encounter yet another somewhat ambiguous individual detail, 'and judgment was given to them'. While it is possible that the hearers might take these words to imply that those who sit on the thrones are involved in the dispensing of judgment,[11] owing in part to the meaning of the term 'judgment' (κρίμα) in its other occurrences in the Apocalypse (17.1; 18.20; cf. also Jn 9.39) it is more likely that the hearers would understand that those who sit on the thrones have received judgment in the sense of vindication.[12] But again, before they can devote much reflection to this aspect of the vision yet another somewhat ambiguous individual detail is encountered, 'and the souls of those beheaded on account of the witness of Jesus and on account of the word of God'. Reference to 'the souls of those beheaded' would be both familiar and unfamiliar to the hearers at one and the same time. For on the one hand, mention of 'the souls' could hardly help but remind them of the souls under the altar who had been slaughtered owing to the word of God and the testimony which they have, who cry out to God for him to judge and vindicate their blood (6.9). It appears that it is they who have now

[11] Mealy, *After the Thousand Years*, p. 109.

[12] S. Pattemore, *The People of God in the Apocalypse: Discourse, Structure, and Exegesis* (SNTSM 128; Cambridge: Cambridge University Press, 2004), p. 108 and S.S. Smalley, *The Revelation to John* (Downers Grove, IL: IVP, 2005), p. 506.

been given judgment. On the other hand, the hearers may be quite unprepared to discover that these are the souls of those who have been beheaded, as here for the first (and only) time (in the whole of Scripture) they encounter the verb 'behead' (πελεκίζω). While it is not altogether clear exactly how the hearers would understand this unexpected detail, it is clear that if reference to the souls in 20.4 is taken in continuity with reference to the souls under the altar of those slaughtered, then the manner of death by beheading stands in direct continuity with the previous description of their death as slaughtered. It would also be clear that the death of these respective souls is owing to their relationship with the witness of Jesus and the word of God. The hearers of course would be well aware by this time of the close relationship that exists between the witness of Jesus and death, not only for Jesus, the faithful witness, but for all those who would follow the Lamb wherever he goes (14.4), a point emphasized as recently as 19.10. The fact that the death of these souls is also directly tied to the word of God would not only remind the hearers of John's own suffering owing to the prophetic activity of God (1.9) but would perhaps, by now, be seen to reinforce the tie to Jesus him-self who has recently been called 'the Word of God'. The connection between the death of these souls and the person of Jesus would be difficult to miss. But the question remains, what would the idea of beheading convey to the hearers? The word itself is a perfect partici-ple indicating that their beheading had taken place in the past, but its effects are still felt. It would seem to be self-evident that reference to this graphic manner of execution would intensify the visceral nature of the description of their death from the more generic 'slaughtered' (a visceral term itself!) to the more specific beheaded. But the hearers might discern even more in the introduction of this detail at this point.

Coming fast on the heels of the observation that those who were seated on the throne had received judgment, perhaps the hearers would be reminded of the contrast between the fate of these be-headed ones, on the one hand, and that of the Beast who had suf-fered a mortal wound to one of his heads, the healing of which re-sulted in his near universal worship, on the other hand. That is to say, while both the Beast and these souls suffered mortal head wounds, the latter being much more severe as the head itself has been re-moved, it is they and not he who in fact have received the judgment

of life! And with this, yet another somewhat ambiguous detail is encountered, 'and those who did not worship the Beast nor his image
and did not receive his mark upon their forehead and upon their
hand'. While the previous phrase seems to have reference to the martyrs exclusively, the latter phrase appears to be inclusive enough to
include all those who offer faithful witness to Jesus by worshipping
God not the Beast in any form, whether their faithful witness results
in a martyr's death or not. However, the paradoxical ambiguity of
these phrases, standing side by side, reinforces to the hearers yet again
the importance of being faithful unto death.[13] It is only with the next
words that the seemingly disparate individual somewhat ambiguous
pieces of this verse converge for the hearers, 'And they came to life
and reigned with Christ a thousand years'. With these words the hearers discover that the souls of the beheaded ones, those who did not
worship the Beast in any form, to whom the verdict of judgment was
given, who are seated upon the thrones themselves experience resurrection, just as had their Lord (1.18; 2.8) and the two prophetic witnesses (11.11),[14] and reign with Christ in accord with his promises to
those who overcome (2.26; 3.21; 5.10) for a thousand years.[15] How
would Johannine hearers understand such words about these overcomers coming to life?

While ambiguities abound, it would appear to be certain that the
hearers would understand this coming to life as similar to and standing in continuity with the coming to life of Jesus, owing in part to the
fact that the same word found here appeared earlier in the Apocalypse to describe the resurrection of Jesus (2.8). Such an understanding would be at home with the idea found in 1 Jn 3.2 that despite the
fact that the nature of such a resurrected existence is not yet evident,
it is enough to know that 'we shall be like him, because we will see
him as he is', and would be at home with the descriptions of the
resurrected Jesus in John 20 and 21. Thus, while modern interpreters
may be fascinated with the idea that this coming to life is not a physical resurrection, but a spiritual one,[16] such an idea would likely be
quite foreign to Johannine hearers. Rather, this is the moment at

13 Mealy, *After the Thousand Years*, pp. 109-19.
14 Sweet, *Revelation*, p. 289.
15 Ladd, *Revelation*, p. 264.
16 P. Gaechter, 'The Original Sequence of Apocalypse 20-22', *Theological Studies*
10 (1949), p. 491 [pp. 485-521].

which the souls of those who had been beheaded, those who have not worshipped the Beast, are resurrected in bodily form, as had been their Lord. Thus, the judgment that is rendered to them is integrally connected to their being brought to life. For in their being brought to life in resurrected form they experience more fully the eternal life with which Johannine hearers are quite familiar and share more immediately in their identification with God who is often described in the Apocalypse as the one who lives forever and ever (4.9, 10; 7.2; 10.6; 15.7). Not only do such ones come to life, but they also reign with Christ for a thousand years.

The sheer temporal magnitude of this period of reigning would serve to dwarf all other reigns mentioned in the Apocalypse to this point, whether it be the forty-two month reign of the Beast (13.5) or the one-hour reign of the ten kings (17.12). The thousand-year reign of these overcomers simply cannot be compared to any reign of the enemies of God upon the earth. Thus, the hearers learn that the entire time that the Dragon is bound in the Abyss, those who have been faithful witnesses experience a different reality altogether – they reign with Christ.

It might strike the hearers as remarkable that after the numerous OT intertexts they have encountered throughout the book, at this point there is a stark absence of OT references, despite the fact that so many appropriate intertexts could be included and perhaps are in the minds of the hearers! Yet, the description of this thousand-year reign is extraordinarily restrained and sparse in its description. In point of fact, the hearers discover that the focus of attention is placed not upon a description of its contents or other characteristics but upon the relational nature of the thousand-year period.[17] Specifically, they will be with Christ for the thousand years. Thus, not only will the deceptive influence of Satan be absent during this period, the overcomers will be with Christ for this entire period; they will be with the same resurrected Lord that they experience even now via the Spirit's prophetic witness. The resurrected Lord whom they know in their worship and faithful witness, whom they follow wherever he goes, whose return is imminent, is the same Lord with whom they will reign. All that Christ is as redeemer, they will now be as

---

[17] C.R. Koester, *Revelation and the End of All Things* (Grand Rapids: Eerdmans, 2001), pp. 184-85.

redeemed.[18] These resurrected overcomers will be with their resurrected Lord for longer than any of the hearers could imagine or fathom – for a thousand years (!) – the exact amount of time for which Satan is bound in the Abyss.

Owing to the relational nature of this reign, the issue about over whom or over what they reign with Christ would not appear to be of primary concern for the hearers. However, if reflection were devoted to this issue it is likely that the hearers would suspect that two things may be involved. Since Satan is unable to deceive the nations during this period, perhaps their reign would be connected to the nations in some way. If one of the purposes of this extraordinarily long period is to give the nations yet another chance to respond in faith, perhaps their reign involves a continuation of bearing their prophetic, faithful witness, not unlike that borne by the two witnesses whom the Spirit of life from God raised up (11.11-14)! At the same time, the idyllic conditions of this thousand year reign might well remind the hearers of the conditions at the beginning in the Garden of Eden, where the human being was given charge over the creation and creatures within it (Gen 1.26-28).[19] On this view, the thousand-year reign with Christ would be designed in part to be a visible sign of the redemption of creation itself, with resurrected human agents reigning with Christ in a way that fulfils that initial command and commission.

The hearers' attention continues to be focused upon resurrection as they encounter the next words, 'The rest of the dead did not come to life until the thousand years were complete. This is the first resurrection.' If the faithful witnesses who overcome come to life and reign with Christ for a thousand years then the rest of the dead would likely be thought to consist of the opponents of the Rider on the White Horse (19.21),[20] as well as all those who do not believe in him.[21] Again, owing in part to the vocabulary, a physical resurrection of the dead appears to be in view.[22] While modern interpreters are sometimes troubled by the idea of two separate resurrections, it does not appear that discerning Johannine hearers would have the same concerns, for they might well understand these two resurrections as in

---

[18] Gause, *Revelation*, p. 254.
[19] Mealy, *After the Thousand Years*, p. 116.
[20] Mealy, *After the Thousand Years*, p. 115.
[21] Ladd, *Revelation*, p. 265.
[22] D. Aune, *Revelation 17-22* (WBC 52c; Nashville, TN: Nelson, 1998), p. 1090.

accord with the teaching of Jesus himself who says in the FG, 'Do not be astonished at this, because an hour comes in which all those who are in their graves will hear his voice and will come out, the ones who have done good into resurrection of life, but the ones who practice evil into resurrection of judgment' (Jn 5.28-29). But unlike those overcomers who come to life and reign with Christ for a thousand years, the rest of the dead do not come to life until after the thousand years. Rather, they are in their graves for this entire period, just as Satan is bound in the Abyss for the period the overcomers reign with Christ. The theologically significant term translated 'were complete' (τελεσθῇ) might well convey to the hearers the idea that just as the binding of Satan in the Abyss until the thousand years is complete is theologically significant, so it is with those who are not resurrected until the thousand years is complete. Mention of the extraordinarily long thousand-year period, the fourth such mention in a five verse span, again underscores the magnitude of the loss for the rest of the dead who lie in their graves while the overcomers reign with Christ. The next words encountered, 'This is the first resurrection', appear to direct the hearers' attention back to the description of those who came to life and reign with Christ for the thousand years. It is these who experience the first resurrection! Clearly in this context, the first resurrection is so named owing to its chronological and theological precedence over the resurrection of the rest of the dead. Though a 'second resurrection' is nowhere named as such in the Johannine literature,[23] the fact that the first resurrection identifies the resurrection of the overcomers who reign with Christ a thousand years and precedes the resurrection of the rest of the dead, confirming that the hearers would understand that two resurrections, separated by a thousand years, are indeed here described,[24] and would be in keeping with the teaching of Jesus as well (Jn 5.28-29).

The hearers' reflection upon the significance of this first resurrection is reinforced by the next words they encounter,

> Blessed and holy is the one who has a part in the first resurrection; over these the second death has no authority, but they will be

---

[23] R.W. Wall, *Revelation* (Peabody, MA: Hendrickson, 1991), p. 239 and Prigent, *L'Apocalypse de saint Jean*, p. 429.

[24] Aune, *Revelation 17-22*, p. 1091.

priests of God and of Christ, and they will reign with him a thousand years.

For a fifth time in the book the hearers encounter a beatitude and for the first time the beatitude contains a compound predicate, for in addition to the characteristic 'blessed' is added 'and holy'.[25] Not only would the beatitude speak directly to the hearers owing to its form, as have the preceding ones (1.3; 14.13; 16.15; 19.9), but the unique addition of 'holy' would also have special significance, for it reinforces the idea of those who overcome as faithful witnesses who have stayed awake and kept their garments, not walking around naked (16.15), and have been deemed worthy of invitation to the marriage supper of the Lamb, having prepared themselves through righteous acts (19.8-9). At the same time, the hearers would know that the word here translated as holy, (ἅγιος), is the same Greek word for 'saint' – 'holy one', perhaps reinforcing for them that all the saints will have part in the first resurrection. Discerning Johannine hearers would not only be sensitive to the significance of the beatitude form, but would also pick up on the theologically significant word 'share' or 'part' (μέρος), which in Jn 13.8 is closely identified with eternal life, solidarity with Jesus' destiny, mission, martyrdom, and resurrection.[26] Thus, the vocabulary itself emphasizes the depth of identification and solidarity between Jesus the faithful witness and the faithful witnesses that participate in the first resurrection. Actually, 'over these the second death has no authority'! Such words would no doubt remind the hearers of the promise of the resurrected Jesus to the church in Smyrna, 'the one who overcomes will not be harmed at all by the second death' (Rev. 2.11), making even clearer that the one who participates in the first resurrection has no fear of the second death, a death that has not yet been fully identified in the text but which the hearers might at this point suspect is tied to some form of eternal death. However, rather than being susceptible to the second death, those who participate in the first resurrection will be in the very presence of God and Christ, serving as priests[27] and reigning with Christ for the thousand years.

---

[25] F.J. Murphy, *Fallen Is Babylon: The Revelation to John* (Harrisburg, PA: Trinity Press International, 1998), p. 399.

[26] J.C. Thomas, *Footwashing in John 13 and the Johannine Community* (JSNTS 61; Sheffield: JSOT Press, 1991), pp. 92-95.

[27] Smalley, *The Revelation to John*, p. 510.

The mention of the word priests would no doubt remind the hearers of the fact that it is through Jesus, the one with whom they will reign for a thousand years, that they have been made into a kingdom – priests to God (1.6; 5.10). It is by his death that they gain admission to the divine presence[28] and minister to God and Christ. Such language may well suggest to the hearers that the overcomers have an active role to play still in the conversion of the nations and that their reigning with Christ may well involve such a priestly dimension as they continue to act as faithful witnesses to the witness of Jesus and the Word of God – for a thousand years![29] The fifth mention of the thousand years in the span of five verses would not likely be taken by the hearers as insignificant repetition, but rather would underscore for them the fact that they shall serve as priests to God and Christ and reign with Christ for an unimaginably long period of time, unquestionably longer than their time of persecution.[30] It will be a reign in which they may enjoy their time with Christ, seek the conversion of the nations, and fulfill the command given to Adam and Eve in the Garden. They will reign with him for a thousand years – a thousand years indeed!

No sooner than these words about the activity of the thousand years are spoken do the hearers encounter words about its completion, 'And when the thousand years were completed, Satan will be loosed out of his prison'. Several aspects of these words would be of significance for the hearers. First, the theologically significant term translated 'were complete' (τελεσθῇ) would not only indicate that the thousand years (and its purposes) have now come to completion,[31] but the occurrence of the verb in the passive form would also remind the hearers that this period did not come to an end on it own but was brought to its completion by God himself. Second, Satan's confinement in the Abyss is now revealed to have been an imprisonment for after the thousand years he will be loosed from his prison. Third, the passive form 'will be loosed' (λυθήσεται), indicates that just as God is active in bringing the thousand years to completion, so the loosing of Satan is no escape but is in accord with the divine purpose and is indeed God's own activity.

---

[28] Gause, *Revelation*, p. 254.
[29] Caird, *Revelation*, pp. 255-56.
[30] B.M. Metzger, *Cracking the Code* (Nashville, TN: Abingdon, 1993), p. 93.
[31] Gause, *Revelation*, p. 255.

If the hearers have been wondering as to Satan's plans upon his release from the Abyss, they find out in the next words they encounter,

> And he will go out to deceive the nations those in the four corners of the earth, Gog and Magog, to gather them together into war, the number of them being as the sand of the sea.

The first words of this verse reveal immediately that the Satan, who was bound for a thousand years so he could no longer deceive the nations in 20.3, is the same Satan who emerges from his prison to deceive the nations in 20.8. For the first word the hearers encounter in this verse after 'and', translated 'he will go out' (ἐξελεύσεται), would be known to discerning Johannine hearers as a term closely associated with deception and betrayal, as it appears to describe Judas' departure to betray Jesus in Jn 13.30 and is used to describe the missionary activity of the many deceivers who have gone out into the world in 2 Jn 7.[32] Thus, even before the hearers are told explicitly that Satan goes out to deceive, they would well suspect that such activity is his intention. But there is no mistake about it, for despite his long imprisonment in the Abyss, Satan emerges as ready as ever to deceive the nations and is prepared to do so in as comprehensive a fashion as possible.[33] The extent of his intended deception is conveyed to the hearers in two ways. First, they learn that Satan goes out to deceive the nations who are at the four corners of the earth, the proverbial furthest points of the earth. Second, these nations are also called by the names Gog and Magog. Gog would be known to the hearers as the chief prince of Meshech and Tubal (Ezek. 38.2), while Magog would be known as the son of Japheth (Gen. 10.2) and becomes identified as the territory located in the uttermost parts of north (Ezek. 38.6).[34] As with other names in the book, the hearers would likely suspect that these two names have a deeper meaning still as it appears that by this point these names would be thought of as the eschatological enemies of the North[35] that attack the people of God

---

[32] J.C. Thomas, *1 John, 2 John, 3 John* (London: T & T Clark, 2004), p. 45 and Smalley, *The Revelation to John*, p. 511.

[33] Koester, *Revelation and the End of All Things*, p. 187.

[34] Mounce, *The Book of Revelation*, p. 362.

[35] E.-B. Allo, *Saint Jean: L'Apocalypse* (Paris: Lecoffe, 1921), p. 288.

after a period of peace.[36] The purpose of Satan's going out to deceive is 'to gather them together into war', a phrase similar to one encountered earlier by the hearers in Rev. 16.14.[37] Such similarity would remind the hearers not only of similar hostile intentions of the nations, but also of their ultimate demise on that occasion as well.

The success of Satan's deception is revealed by the fact that the nations gathered together for war are numbered as the sand of the sea, a phrase that not only indicates something of the overwhelming success of his deceptive work, but one that also would draw upon the ominous associations this phrase has from its earlier appearance, where the Dragon stands upon the sand of the sea looking for the emergence of the Beast (12.18).[38] This detail too would perhaps encourage the hearers with regard to the outcome of this looming conflict as they reflect on the outcome of the conflict championed by the Beast that emerges from the sea. Such language stands in stark contrast to the promise given to Abraham in reference to the number of his descendants,[39] indicating something of the diametric opposition of the purposes of God and those of Satan. If the hearers had wondered as to the outcome of this final opportunity for the nations to convert, the words of this verse suggest that despite the thousand-year period in which Satan is kept from deceiving the nations and despite the fact that Christ himself reigns with those faithful to him, the nations are as susceptible as ever as to the deception of Satan and, despite these ideal circumstances, refuse to repent and worship God and the Lamb.[40]

Little space stands between the description of Satan's desires and their effects as the next words reveal, 'and they went up upon the breadth of the earth and circled the camp of the saints and the beloved city'. The actions of these deceived nations, whose number is as the sand of the sea, is no less significant than their numbers, for they traverse the face of the earth, and encircle their intended targets, a strategy well known in ancient warfare, where cities are circled to cut their inhabitants off from the outside world.[41] While the hearers

---

[36] Caird, *Revelation*, p. 257.
[37] Aune, *Revelation 17-22*, p. 1095.
[38] Sweet, *Revelation*, p. 292.
[39] Aune, *Revelation 17-22*, p. 1096.
[40] Cf. the esp. perceptive comments of Mealy, *After the Thousand Years*, pp. 186 and 189.
[41] Aune, *Revelation 17-22*, p. 1097.

know that the nations have been deceived by Satan to gather together for war, and while they may suspect that Christ and those who reign with him are the intended targets, they learn that the nations intend to make war upon 'the camp of the saints' and 'the beloved city'. Mention of the camp of the saints would not only reveal the intended target of the nations' planned attack as consisting of the saints, those holy ones who have a part in the first resurrection and reign with Christ for a thousand years, but it would also remind the hearers yet again of the tight connection that exists between the Johannine believers and the heritage of Israel, especially in a book where they have already been described as part of a transformed Israel (cf. esp. 7.1-8). Specifically, the phrase 'the camp of the saints' would remind the hearers of Israel's dependency upon God as he led them through the wilderness via a cloud by day and a pillar of fire by night (9.15-22),[42] imagery that would likely remind Johannine hearers of the pneumatic activity that is an essential part of their life together. At the same time, mention of 'the beloved city' would have special significance for the hearers as well, for it would call up memories of Yahweh's special love for Zion, the city of Jerusalem (Pss. 87.2; 132.13; cf. also Jer. 11.15; 12.7), the place where Yahweh chose to dwell,[43] and as such could well be taken as an anticipation of the New Jerusalem that the hearers know is to come down out of heaven (Rev. 3.12), thus, affirming the continuity that exists between the people of God at the end of the thousand years and the New Jerusalem that is to come. To learn that even at the end of the thousand years the people of God face attacks inspired by Satan would also remind the hearers that they are from start to finish always dependent upon God for their protection, security, and defense. But at the very moment of attack the hearers learn, 'and fire came down out of heaven and consumed them'. Even though the hearers might be poised for details of a great battle, a final battle if you will, as with previous war scenes no battle takes place.[44] Rather, the fire of judgment comes from heaven and consumes the nations gathered together for war, reminiscent of the way fire comes from the mouths of the two witnesses and consumes their enemies (11.5). The fact that the fire comes from heaven makes

---

[42] Sweet, *Revelation*, p. 292.
[43] Sweet, *Revelation*, p. 292.
[44] Ladd, *Revelation*, p. 270.

the origin of this victory unmistakable,[45] and reminds of the fire of judgment that falls upon Gog (Ezek. 38.22) and Magog (Ezek. 39.6).[46] Yet again, the people of God stand vindicated. They will be as secure at the end as they are during the present times of distress.

If the vindication of the saints were not enough, the hearers learn even more, 'And Satan, the one who deceives them, was cast into the lake of fire and sulfur, where both the Beast and the false prophet (were cast), and they will be tormented day and night for ever and ever'. Now, at long last, the archenemy of God and his people receive his final judgment. Several things are said about Satan in this verse that would be of significance to the hearers. First, he is identified as 'the one who deceives them', reminding the hearers of 12.9 where he is called 'the one who deceives the whole inhabited world'. This description would tie his fate directly to his activity of deceiving the nations. Second, this marks the third occasion in the book where Satan is described as cast down (ἐβλήθη). This occasion joins his full description in 12.9 where the word stands on either side of his names and the description of the action of the unnamed angel in 20.3 who cast Satan down into the Abyss. This most recent reference to Satan being cast down in 20.10 would remind the hearers that despite his power and opposition he is from start to finish one who has been cast down. But whereas Satan had earlier been cast down to earth (12.9) and into the Abyss (20.3), he is now described as having been cast into the lake of fire and sulfur! Third, if the hearers have not already made this association they learn that Satan goes to the same place of judgement and death to which his accomplices, the Beast and the false prophet (19.20), have preceded him and would understand this as the most ominous of places.[47] Not only would this reveal the final destiny of this triumvirate of evil to the hearers, but their appearance together here makes very clear that all opponents and opposition to God, his Lamb, his Spirit, and his people have no future but judgment and eternal punishment, regardless of the strength they may currently exhibit in their persecution of the faithful witnesses of the prophetic community. They are doomed to judgment! Fourth, the hearers learn that just as they had acted together to deceive the nations and the inhabitants of the whole earth, so they are

---

[45] Gause, *Revelation*, p. 257.
[46] Mounce, *The Book of Revelation*, p. 363.
[47] Beasley-Murray, *Revelation*, p. 298.

judged together and are to be tormented together. The appearance
of the passive verb to be tormented (βασανισθήσόνται) would indicate to the hearers that the torment that awaits, comes from the
hand of God, as the appearance of the divine passive often indicates
in the Apocalypse. The third person plural form of the verb also
makes clear that the torment that awaits includes all three opponents:
Satan, the Beast, and the false prophet. This verb also confirms to
the hearers the fact that the time that awaits the triumvirate in the
lake of fire and sulfur is not only a time of confinement, but a time
of punishment in the form of torment as well. Fifth, the time of
their torment is unfathomably constant and long, a detail the hearers
learn from the two temporal indicators with which these words conclude. The constancy of torment is conveyed by the phrase 'day and
night',[48] indicating something of the unrelenting nature of the torment that awaits. Perhaps the hearers would understand such constancy of torment to be an appropriate judgment for 'the one who
accuses the brothers day and night before our God' (12.10). At the
same time, it is difficult to believe that the hearers would not pick up
on the contrast between the torment of this triumvirate of evil and
the four living creatures who do not cease praising God day and night
(4.8) and those who are coming out of the great tribulation who are
before the throne of God serving him day and night (7.15). The duration of their torment is conveyed by the words 'for ever and ever'.
Perhaps the first thing the hearers would think of when encountering
this temporal designation is how small the thousand-year period
seems next to 'for ever and ever'. But as with the phrase 'day and
night' it is likely that the hearers would pick up other details in the
narrative to this point. On the one hand, they may well see some
continuity between the smoke of destruction of God's enemies that
goes up forever and ever (14.11; 19.3) and the torment of this triumvirate. On the other hand, the hearers may well think of the reign of
God that lasts forever and ever (11.15) and the worship rendered to
God and/or the Lamb by every creature in the universe (5.13) and
the angels and four living creatures and twenty-four elders (7.11-12).
It would be quite clear to the hearers that both the constancy of the

---

[48] Smalley labels these words a hendiadys generating the meaning 'without in-
terruption', *The Revelation to John*, p. 515.

torment and its duration point to an eternal death for Satan, the
Beast, and the false prophet rather than to their annihilation.[49]

Conclusions and Implications

A few conclusions and implications may now be offered from this
reading of Rev. 20.1-10.

First, it would appear that Pentecostals have done well to follow
the lead of this text as they have sought to understand the thousand-
year reign of which it speaks. Whilst some interpreters, troubled by
its challenging contents, have sought to interpret it as a symbol of
the church's life in the world, owing to its context and placement in
the broader narrative, such an interpretive move seems unsatisfying
at the literary, theological, intellectual, and spiritual levels, minimizing
the way in which this period of time functions as a reward for those
who overcome after an incredibly long struggle in their faithful witness to the world.

Second, whilst debate may abound with regard to whether or not
the thousand-year reign is to be understood as a literal thousand
years, this reading suggests that its extraordinary, almost unimagina-
ble, length can only be understood in contrast to and in comparison,
with the other reigns described within the book. As such, it dwarfs
all other reigns, while anticipating the reign that is forever and ever!
Attempts to dismiss its length out of hand, without regard for the
other reigns found in the book, would appear to be illegitimate.

Third, one of the primary characteristics of the thousand-year
reign is its relational quality. The absence of expected OT intertexts,
along with the sparse description of its contents, serve to underscore
the fact that reigning *with Christ* for the entire period is of primary
importance. Many of the questions modern interpreters bring to the
text do not seem to be of interest to it.

Fourth, one of the theological functions of the thousand-year
reign is to fulfill the commission humanity received in Eden to care
for the earth. As such, the thousand-year reign redeems part of the
divine plan for humankind and creation.

Fifth, another primary theological function of the thousand-year
reign underscores the wideness in God's mercy. For despite the

---

[49] Murphy, *Fallen Is Babylon*, p. 403.

repeated refusal of the nations to repent of their evil works and their incessant making of war with God and his people, God's grace and desire for all to repent manifests itself in a thousand-year period devoid of the deceptive influence of Satan during which Christ himself reigns, with those who overcome offering their faithful witness, in order that the nations might even at this late date repent. However, despite this near ideal environment in which to respond in faith, when Satan is released and goes out to deceive the nations he appears to meet with complete success, for even after this period they are open to his entreaties and deception!

While numerous other conclusions and implications could be offered here, perhaps enough have been raised to encourage additional prayerful reflection on this text and this topic for those interested in Pentecostal theology and ministry.

8

Ideology and 'Objective' Biblical Scholarship[1]

Eryl W. Davies[*]

Until comparatively recently the term 'ideology' was seldom heard in the discourse of biblical scholars;[2] however, the last three decades or so have witnessed a veritable plethora of books and articles examining the ideological presuppositions of the biblical texts, some focussing on large tracts of biblical material such as the Deuteronomistic History, while others have focussed on particular books or passages.[3]

---

[1] This chapter is a revised version of my Presidential address to the Society for Old Testament Study delivered at Fitzwilliam College, Cambridge, in January 2013. It is a pleasure to present it in this volume as a tribute to Professor William Kay, my erstwhile colleague at Bangor University, whose scholarship has always been stimulating and whose friendship I have much appreciated over the years.

[*] Eryl W. Davies (PhD, University of Cambridge; DD, Bangor University) is Professor Emeritus of Old Testament at Bangor University, Bangor, Wales UK.

[2] One of the first scholars to emphasise the significance of ideology in the OT was P.D. Miller, Jr., 'Faith and Ideology in the Old Testament', in F.M. Cross, W.E. Lemke, and P.D. Miller, Jr. (eds.), *Magnalia Dei: The Mighty Acts of God* (New York: Doubleday, 1976), pp. 464-79.

[3] See P.A. Ash, 'Jeroboam I and the Deuteronomistic Historian's Ideology of the Founder', *Catholic Biblical Quarterly* 60 (1998), pp. 16-24; S. Japhet, *The Ideology of the Book of Chronicles and its Place in Biblical Thought* (Frankfurt: Peter Lang, 1989); W.P. Brown, *Structure, Role and Ideology in the Hebrew and Greek Texts of Genesis 1:1-2:3* (SBL Dissertation Series 132; Atlanta, GA: Scholars Press, 1993); D. Jobling and T. Pippin (eds.), *Ideological Criticism of Biblical Texts* (*Semeia* 59; Atlanta, GA: Scholars Press, 1992). For a discussion of the importance of ideological criticism in relation to the OT, see Eryl W. Davies, *Biblical Criticism: A Guide for the Perplexed* (London and New York: Bloomsbury T. and T. Clark, 2013), pp. 61-80.

The introduction of the term 'ideology' into biblical discourse, however, has not been universally welcomed. James Barr, for example, has argued that, with a few notable exceptions, the entry of the concept of ideology into biblical scholarship cannot be said to have been a particularly happy event.[4] Barr does not, of course, deny that there is such a thing as ideology in the Bible and that the term may potentially be useful for biblical inquiry, but he argues that the way the term has been used by biblical scholars has been little short of chaotic, for the concept has not always been properly analysed or clearly explained.

Barr's criticism is not entirely unjustified, for ideology is very much a word in search of a definition. There is no uniform or generally accepted understanding of the term, and even a cursory perusal of the relevant literature indicates that it is used in a bewildering variety of ways. Some have defined it in a neutral way as referring merely to a set of ideas or a coherent system of beliefs (not necessarily true or false in themselves) which are characteristic of the values or worldview of a particular group, class or milieu. Others, drawing heavily on Marxist theorists such as Fredrik Jameson and Terry Eagleton, have tended to define ideology in a negative, pejorative sense as referring either to a false or mistaken assemblage of ideas (often designated 'false consciousness') or to a system of illusory beliefs created by a social or economic system with the aim of presenting a distorted or deceptive view of reality. In common parlance the term is usually invested with a negative, pejorative connotation: it is often used, for example, in political debates to discredit opposing views by implying that they represent a narrow or doctrinaire position (as in the oft-repeated phrase 'he/she is just repeating the usual party ideology'). Now it may well be that it is on account of the negative connotations of the term that biblical scholars in the past have been loath to admit that their own interpretations are 'ideological', preferring, instead, to give the impression that they were writing under the guise of a studied neutrality.

Now ideological criticism is charged with the task not only of making the ideological opacities of the text transparent – an enterprise which is still very much in its infancy – but with the equally

---

[4] James Barr, *History and Ideology in the Old Testament: Biblical Studies at the End of a Millennium* (Oxford: Oxford University Press, 2000), p. 139.

daunting job of exposing the ideological position embraced (whether consciously or not) by the biblical interpreter.[5] In this regard, feminist biblical critics have been particularly anxious to raise awareness of the subjective nature of biblical scholarship, encouraging us to reflect self-consciously about the process of interpretation, and to consider the extent to which our own interests, presuppositions and predispositions have shaped and influenced our reading of the biblical text. Scholars are thus challenged to unlearn the habits of a lifetime by coming clean about their ideological positions and confessing unashamedly their vested interests. Elisabeth Schüssler Fiorenza, for example, has argued that scholars can never free themselves from their own prejudices and presuppositions, and nor should they attempt to do so, for what makes their work valuable and interesting is precisely the questions, concerns, and perspectives they bring to the text.[6]

Scholars who steadfastly refuse to acknowledge their own presuppositions succeed only in concealing from themselves the ideologies on which their work is based. Such emphasis on the importance of open self-disclosure is often accompanied in feminist biblical criticism by an attack on the historical-critical approach because of its supposed claim to be objective, neutral, and value-free. Feminist biblical critics argue that historical-critical scholarship generally has been disappointingly unreflective about its own assumptions, and as if to emphasise the subjectivity of their own approach and distance themselves from what they regard as the objective, disinterested posture of traditional biblical scholarship, they often insist on making their own personal background and their own religious, social, political, and ideological interests clear and transparent at the outset of their work. Thus, for example, towards the beginning of her chapter, 'The Feminist and the Bible: Hermeneutical Alternatives', Carolyn Osiek notes that –

I belong to a large institutional church with an amazing amount of diversity in its membership and a firmly entrenched patriarchal

---

[5] See, in particular, D.J.A. Clines, *Interested Parties: The Ideology of Writers and Readers of the Hebrew Bible* (JSOTSup 205; Sheffield: Sheffield Academic Press, 1995).

[6] Elisabeth Schüssler Fiorenza, 'Remembering the Past in Creating the Future: Historical-Critical Scholarship and Feminist Biblical Interpretation', in A.Y. Collins (ed.), *Feminist Perspectives on Biblical Scholarship* (Atlanta, GA: Scholars Press, 1985), pp. 43-63. For a discussion of the views of feminist biblical critics, see Eryl W. Davies, *The Dissenting Reader: Feminist Approaches to the Hebrew Bible* (Aldershot: Burlington, USA: Ashgate Publishing Company, 2003).

leadership. Although that should not determine the direction of my critical scholarship, it inevitably affects my experience; and the two cannot be totally separated.[7]

The implication behind such statements is that as long as we all exchange information openly and honestly about our presuppositions, we will desist from any pretence that our research is objective, and refrain from a misplaced striving after objectivity.

Feminist biblical critics have undoubtedly contributed some valuable insights to mainstream – or what Schüssler Fiorenza insists on calling 'malestream' – biblical criticism; however, two aspects of their work are, perhaps, open to question. First, it seems appropriate to consider the value and purpose of their insistence on personal self-disclosure. Second, their repeated assertion that historical-critical scholarship is a purely objective enterprise needs to be subjected to critical examination.

To begin, then, with the open self-disclosures which now appear to be almost *de rigueur* in the writings of feminist biblical scholars. Its rationale is based on the premise that we should never read a scholarly book or article while immune to the circumstances of its production. But does this mean that we, as readers of the said books or articles, are expected to indulge in some kind of Freudian psychoanalysis in order to reach the unconscious mind of the authors and try to fathom how their own background and ideology have led them to write as they did? Lest we be overawed at such an expectation, biblical scholarship has kindly bequeathed to us a comparatively new genre, commonly called 'autobiographical criticism' or 'confessional criticism', in which the authors themselves are invited to consider how their own ideology and presuppositions have encouraged them to write in the way they did. Indeed, in the mid-1990s an entire issue of the journal of experimental biblical criticism, *Semeia*, was devoted to this new-fangled criticism. In this issue, six scholars were invited to reflect openly on the relation between the biblical text and their own personal experiences, and two further scholars were invited to respond to such self-reflective biblical criticism. Jeffrey L. Staley (one of the guest editors of the volume) could hardly contain his enthusiasm for the new venture, and rather sheepishly admitted that he had

---

[7] Osiek, 'The Feminist and the Bible: Hermeneutical Alternatives', in A.Y. Collins (ed.), *Feminist Perspectives*, p. 93.

been indulging in such criticism for some time and wondered whether other scholars, unbeknown to him, had surreptitiously been doing likewise: 'Like an adolescent exploring the wonders of human sexuality for the first time, I didn't know exactly what I was doing; I didn't know if anyone else had ever done what I was doing, but I sure was having fun doing whatever it was I was doing'.[8] Clearly, the other contributors to the journal knew precisely what they were doing, for they appeared to have no qualms about revealing details about their own lives and experiences. Unfortunately, however, some of the self-revelations appeared to be tediously self-indulgent and – if truth be told – one sometimes ended up knowing more about the interpreter than about the text that was being interpreted. Indeed, one even got the impression that the two respondents were somewhat embarrassed to be involved in such an exercise, one of whom, the respected NT scholar, Robert Fowler, admitting rather self-consciously that 'it is one thing to criticize another person's scholarship; it is quite another to comment on another person's life' – thereby, of course, missing the entire point of autobiographical criticism that life and scholarship were supposed to be inextricably bound together.[9] It is always difficult to make predictions about how biblical studies will develop in the future, but my instinct is that, in spite of the current fashion to emphasise one's existential involvement with the text, so-called autobiographical criticism will turn out to be something of a passing fad and little more than a quixotic indulgence in an interesting but ultimately harmless hobby-horse.

Autobiographical criticism deliberately obfuscates the boundary between the text and the interpreter, and it is clearly intended as a sustained challenge to the very idea of 'objectivity' in biblical scholarship. It has become something of a standard postmodern allegation that scholars in the historical-critical tradition were intent upon providing an objective, disinterested examination of the biblical text. Such a claim, as has been suggested, is most frequently levelled against historical-criticism by feminist biblical critics. Typical in this regard is Elisabeth Schüssler Fiorenza who insists that, traditionally, historical critical scholarship has misguidedly prided itself on being

---

[8] Janice Capel Anderson and Jeffrey L. Staley (eds.), *Taking it Personally: Autobiographical Biblical Criticism* (*Semeia* 72; Atlanta, GA: Scholars Press, 1995), p. 8.

[9] R.M. Fowler, 'Taking it Personally: A Personal Response', in J.C. Anderson and J.L. Staley (eds.), *Taking it Personally*, p. 231.

impartial, objective, and value-neutral.[10] Now when such statements
are asserted with sufficient confidence and repeated often enough,
they perhaps inevitably come to be accepted as a self-evident truth.
But did historical critics *really* have an objective, uncommitted approach to the biblical text? Did they *really* feel duty-bound to espouse
the ideal of objectivity? In order to try to answer these questions it
may be salutary to consider the work of one who must surely be regarded as the prime example of the historical critic, Julius Wellhausen, and in particular his famous *Prolegomena to the History of Israel.*[11]

As is well-known, Wellhausen divided Israelite religion into three
major stages, each distinct from the other: first, there was the period
of the monarchy, when there was no priestly hierarchy and when a
number of local independent sanctuaries were in use;[12] second came
the reform of Josiah, with the cult centralized in Jerusalem; and this
was followed, third, by the period during and after the Babylonian
exile when the priestly class took power and created a ritualized and
legalized religion. It is clear that Wellhausen was by no means averse
to expressing his own value judgment on the development of Israel's
religion as he saw it, and even the most casual reader of the *Prolegomena* can hardly fail to be struck by the frankness with which Wellhausen passed judgment on the biblical material. He made no secret
of the fact that his sympathies lay with the religious instincts of ancient Israel, and he frequently commended the freedom and spontaneity, the freshness and naturalness, of the nation's early impulses; on
the other hand, Wellhausen could hardly conceal his disdain for the
hide-bound ritualism, organization, and decadence which he found
to be so prominent in later priestly developments. Second Temple
Judaism was characterised by a period of deterioration and degener-
ation, when the spontaneous religion characteristic of Israel's early
epoch had been replaced by a narrow and stultifying legalism. Religion had moved from the simple to the formal, from the natural to

---

[10] Elisabeth Schüssler Fiorenza, 'Feminist Theology and New Testament Interpretation', *Journal for the Study of the Old Testament* 22 (1982), pp. 32-46; see, also, her
volume, *Bread Not Stone: The Challenge of Feminist Biblical Interpretation* (Edinburgh: T.
and T. Clark; Boston: Beacon Press, 1984).

[11] J. Wellhausen, *Prolegomena to the History of Israel* (trans. from the 1883 edition
by J.S. Black and A. Menzies; Edinburgh: Adam and Charles Black, 1885).

[12] Wellhausen regarded the establishment of the monarchy as the most decisive
event in Israelite history and viewed it as 'the soil out of which all the other institutions of Israel grow up' (*Prolegomena*, p. 413).

the ceremonial, as priestly elements had entered the faith and narrowed the prophetic vision. Indeed, it is not without significance that he prefixed the second part of the *Prolegomena* with a motto taken from Hesiod: 'the half is greater than the whole', the clear implication being that the pre-exilic age actually gains in stature when the Priestly tradition and the writings influenced by it (such as Chronicles) were omitted.[13] Wellhausen's depiction of early Judaism as 'degenerate' was clearly a pejorative Christian judgment, and although some scholars have (wrongly in my view) argued that his starkly negative evaluation of this period in Israel's history was an expression of a latent anti-Semitism, there can be little doubt that it was reflective of the widespread disparagement of post-exilic Judaism encountered in nineteenth-century German scholarship in general.[14] This is not the place to examine why Wellhausen should have come to such a conclusion, but what is clear is that he was hardly writing as the disinterested, objective, non-partisan historian;[15] indeed, some of his early critics opposed his conclusions by accusing him of being blatantly subjective and thoroughly prejudiced. The fact is that not only was Wellhausen *not* objective but there is no evidence in his writing that he ever even *claimed* to be objective. Thus, the widespread view that the historical-critical approach – certainly as represented by one of its

---

[13] Wellhausen did, however, grudgingly concede that in the work of the Chronicler 'occasionally a grain of good corn may occur among the chaff' (*Prolegomena*, p. 224).

[14] L.H. Silberman, while denying that Wellhausen was anti-Semitic, does claim that the attitude towards Judaism reflected in the *Prolegomena* was predominantly negative 'like practically everything written by German Protestant theologians of the period' ('Wellhausen and Judaism', in D.A. Knight (ed.), *Julius Wellhausen and his Prolegomena to the History of Israel* (*Semeia* 25; Atlanta, GA: Scholars Press, 1983), p. 75). Wellhausen claimed that 'it is well known that there never have been more audacious history-makers than the Rabbis' and added that 'Chronicles affords evidence sufficient that this evil propensity goes back to a very early time, its root the dominating influence of the Law, being the root of Judaism itself' (*Prolegomena*, p. 161).

[15] D.A. Knight ('Wellhausen and the Interpretation of Israel's Literature', in D.A. Knight [ed.], *Julius Wellhausen*, p. 33) claims that Wellhausen found it 'impossible to take a dispassionate approach' to the biblical material and concludes that he 'addressed this ancient document with all the acumen and personal engagement which the text itself deserves'. P.D. Miller, Jr., similarly comments that one of the startling aspects of Wellhausen's *Prolegomena* was the 'significant amount of value judgment' running through the work; Miller also refers to Wellhausen's 'romantic bias' toward the early stages of Israel's history ('Wellhausen and the History of Israel's Religion', in D.A. Knight [ed.], *Julius Wellhausen*, pp. 63, 71).

main exponents – was a neutral and value-free academic pursuit needs to be reassessed, and there is perhaps more than a scintilla of truth in the claim of James Barr that descriptions of the historical-critical approach are often the creation of its enemies. Imagination and intuition seem to have been far more important for Wellhausen that a striving after objectivity, and it is interesting to note that in a revealing passage in the introduction to his *Prolegomena* he recounts the personal experience which led him to date the Law later than the Prophets and which led in turn to his reconstruction of the development of Israelite and Jewish religion:

> In my early student days, I was attracted by the stories of Saul and David, Ahab and Elijah; the discourses of Amos and Isaiah laid strong hold on me, and I read myself well into the prophetic and historical books of the Old Testament. Thanks to such aids as were accessible to me, I even considered that I understood them tolerably, but at the same time was troubled with a bad conscience, as if I were beginning with the roof instead of the foundation; for I had no thorough acquaintance with the Law, of which I was accustomed to being told that it was the basis and postulate of the whole literature … At last, in the course of a casual visit to Göttingen in the summer of 1867, I learned through Ritschl that Karl Heinrich Graf placed the Law later than the Prophets, and almost without knowing his reasons for the hypothesis, I was prepared to accept it; I readily acknowledged to myself the possibility of understanding Hebrew antiquity without the book of the Torah.[16]

And there we have it: Julius Wellhausen, the great pioneer of the historical-critical study of the OT, indulging in a good piece of autobiographical criticism!

Among the most notable twentieth-century biblical scholars to examine the history of ancient Israel, special mention may be made of W.F. Albright, who outlined his own reflections on the historian's task in his book *History, Archaeology and Christian Humanism*, published in 1964. He believed that Israel's history could be reconstructed in an objective sense provided, of course, that one paid sufficient attention to the biblical and extra-biblical evidence available. He did concede that the biblical scholar had to make a concerted effort to be free

---

[16] Wellhausen, *Prolegomena*, pp. 3-4.

from any bias that might compromise one's apprehension of the past, but he was confident that, in principle, an objective approach to the biblical text was possible. Albright's view was that only when scholars were too close to the culture they were examining were they prone to be biased, prejudiced, and less able to view it in its proper perspective; 'a sympathetic, yet dispassionate, foreign observer of a culture', he wrote, 'could understand ancient Egypt better than a Pharaoh or a learned scribe'. Albright clearly regarded himself as just such a 'dispassionate foreign observer' of ancient Israel and he certainly gives the impression of detached objectivity in his writing. The fact is, however, that his portrait of ancient Israel's history and religion is anything but detached and objective. The Christian orientation of his work is readily apparent, and he clearly had a vested interest in portraying Moses as a monotheist, and in viewing the Israelite nation as a monotheistic Yahweh-worshipping community from the beginning. Indeed, so anxious was he to preserve the tradition of the purity of the religion that was to give rise in time to later Judaism and Christianity that he fully accepted the view of the biblical text that the Canaanites were wicked and depraved and that this degenerate culture had to be replaced by one that was morally superior:

> From the impartial standpoint of a philosopher of history, it often seems necessary that a people of markedly inferior type should vanish before a people of superior potentialities, since there is a point beyond which racial mixture cannot go without disaster.[17]

The fact is, however, that Albright was doing anything but 'writing from the impartial standpoint of a philosopher of history', for it is clear that while claiming to be objective he had in fact aligned himself with the dominant voice of the text and identified himself with the people of Israel as he read the biblical account. Of course, that is precisely what the biblical writers would have wanted him to do, and it is a tribute to their success that they have been able to manipulate scholars into accepting their point of view, for the job of purveyors of ideology in every age has been to persuade people to see the world as *they* see it and not as it is in itself.

The last few decades have witnessed something of a paradigm shift in the way in which the history of Israel has been interpreted.

---

[17] W.F. Albright, *From the Stone Age to Christianity: Monotheism and the Historical Process* (Baltimore: The Johns Hopkins Press, 1940), p. 214.

Various postmodern intellectual currents have contrived to chip away at the very foundation of the objectivist posture, so much so that the old model of historiography as a dispassionate, disinterested, value-free exercise is now often regarded as virtually obsolete, as scholars increasingly recognise that factors such as class, background, location, race, gender, and religious and political ideology have conspired to compromise the objectivity of the historian. The rise of postmodernism, the phenomenon that loudly proclaims that there is no consensus view, that all truth is relative, that any one ideology is as appropriate as any other, has only served to erode the old certainties, and it must be conceded that there are many who have welcomed the challenge posed by this new intellectual climate. As Valentine, a character in Tom Stoppard's play *Arcadia* puts it: 'It's the best possible time to be alive, when almost everything you thought you knew is wrong'. Perhaps nowhere are those words more apt in the discipline of biblical studies than in recent discussions of the historical value of the OT traditions. Those discussions have largely been dominated by the differing views held by the so-called minimalist or revisionist scholars on the one hand and the maximalist scholars on the other. The contretemps between the two groups was perhaps most evident in the rather prickly and acrimonious exchange between Iain Provan on the one hand and Philip Davies and Thomas Thompson on the other, a dispute played out on the pages of the *Journal of Biblical Literature* in the mid-1990s.[18] Since that exchange has sometimes been regarded as generating more heat than light, it may be appropriate at this point to unpack some of the more contentious issues, the primary one being the extent to which the ideology of biblical interpreters has influenced their attempts to reconstruct the 'history of Israel'.

The initial salvo was launched by Provan, who took issue with Davies' claim that misty-eyed theologians had been prevented by their faith from engaging in real historical research, and, in the process, had sold 'their academic inheritance for a mess of religious pottage'.[19] Such scholars, it was implied, were quite unlike hard-nosed

---

[18] Iain W. Provan, 'Ideologies, Literary and Critical: Reflections on Recent Writing on the History of Israel', *JBL* 114 (1995), pp. 585-606; Thomas L. Thompson, 'A Neo-Albrightean School in History and Biblical Scholarship?', *JBL* 114 (1995), 683-705; Philip R. Davies, 'Method and Madness: Some Remarks on doing History with the Bible', *JBL* 114 (1995), pp. 699-705.

[19] Provan, 'Ideologies', p. 588.

historians (such as Davies himself) who, as the true guardians of academic scholarship, were continually striving to achieve critical objective research.[20] But in fact, claimed Provan, Davies was just as subjective in his approach as the scholars whom he opposed; it was simply that he was blissfully unaware of the fact.[21] 'The real division in scholarship', he wrote, 'is not ... between those who have a philosophical system and those who do not. It is between those who realize that they have one, and those who are innocent of the fact.'[22]

Not surprisingly, such an accusation drew an immediate rebuttal from Davies, who insisted that 'I am no more free from subjectivity than any human being',[23] and he accused Provan of an 'outright falsification' of his views, adding – perhaps a touch condescendingly – that he should 'work harder at understanding the issues'.[24] So did Davies claim to be 'objective'? The answer is no – or at least, not in so many words; yet, it is not difficult to see how Provan should have come to such a conclusion, for Davies does say that when method 'declares its presumptions and procedures openly and insists on consistent application' it would be 'our best defense *against* ideology, bias and presupposition'.[25] But that rather begs the question: why would one want to eliminate bias and ideology unless one believed that one's ultimate goal was to achieve some kind of objectivity in one's research? For better or worse, the impression one gains from Davies' writings is that the historian should strive to abandon all personal bias and ideology and examine the available evidence as objectively as possible. In his contribution to the volume edited by Lester Grabbe, *Can a History of Israel be Written?*, Davies, reacting negatively to the label 'minimalist', observes that 'such ridiculous terminology only betrays the extent to which the writing of histories of ancient Israel is still driven by an agenda concerned with the reliability of the biblical sources – an issue in which a historian has to be impartial',[26] and

---

[20] Provan, 'Ideologies', p. 599.

[21] Provan could not quite decide whether Davies was, indeed, unaware of his own ideology or whether his strategy was 'to highlight the ideology of others while concealing one's own' ('Ideologies', p. 600).

[22] Provan, 'Ideologies', p. 591, n. 27.

[23] Davies, 'Method', p. 704.

[24] Davies, 'Method', pp. 704-705.

[25] Davies, 'Method', p. 700.

[26] P.R. Davies, 'Whose History? Whose Israel? Whose Bible? Biblical Histories, Ancient and Modern', in L.L. Grabbe, *Can a 'History of Israel' be Written?* (JSOTSup 245; Sheffield: Sheffield Academic Press, 1997), p. 109.

elsewhere he claims that the modern historian can fulfil the demand of objectivity to some extent by 'not taking sides'.[27] Indeed Thomas Thompson states quite plainly that 'we [i.e. the minimalists] do strive to be objective scholars and are not ideologues'.[28] Now there is nothing wrong with believing that objectivity is an ideal that should guide our scholarly deliberations, for surely a qualified objectivity is better than no objectivity at all – but the irony is that this puts the minimalists in the same camp as older scholars such as Albright, who would have been regarded in today's terms as a 'maximalist', for he similarly shared a certain optimism about the possibility of objectivity in research.

In his response to Provan's article, Davies insisted that it was not ideology *per se* to which he objected; his concern, rather, was that the ideology of scholars such as Provan had interfered with their method. This was apparent in the way that the religious commitment of such scholars had led to a distinct bias in favour of the historicity of the biblical text, almost to the point where they had accepted it without the need for further confirmation.[29] The distorting effect of religious belief had resulted in scholars being captivated by the biblical story-line to such an extent that much of their depiction of Israelite history amounted to little more than a bland paraphrasing of the biblical text. Such scholars were criticised for viewing the Bible 'as a specially privileged source, containing divine truth and not amenable to rationalist(ic) methods of investigation, least of all to the principle that you do not call an unsupported statement a historical fact until or unless you have sufficient evidence or argument to support your claim'.[30] In his volume *In Search of 'Ancient Israel'*, Davies accuses various scholars who had written a 'History of Israel' of having been 'motivated by theology and religious sentiment, not critical scholarship',[31] and his plea in the very last sentence of the volume was that,

---

[27] P.R. Davies, 'This is what happens …', in L.L Grabbe (ed.), *"Like a Bird in a Cage": The Invasion of Sennacherib in 701 BCE* (JSOTSup 363; Sheffield: Sheffield Academic Press, 2003), pp. 114-15.
[28] Thomas L. Thompson, 'A Neo-Albrightean School', p. 693.
[29] Davies, 'Method', p. 702. A similar point was made by G. Garbini, who was deeply critical of those 'for whom an unacknowledged confessional interest now appears to have predominated over a concern for scientific objectivity' in *History and Ideology in Ancient Israel* (London: SCM Press, 1988), p. 55.
[30] Davies, 'Method', p. 700.
[31] P.R. Davies, *In Search of 'Ancient Israel'* (JSOTSup 148 Sheffield: Sheffield Academic Press, 1992), p. 31.

for the sake of the discipline, it would be better if scholars ceased to practice 'a theologically dictated form of historical criticism'.[32]

Now Davies' attack on confessionalism of a religious sort in the name of scholarly inquiry merely invited the obvious counter-accusation that the stance which he adopts is no less ideological than that of the opponents he so vehemently criticises. Indeed, this point was eloquently made by Provan, who observed that 'the noisy ejection of religious commitment through the *front* door of the scholarly house is only a cover for the quieter smuggling in ... of a quite different form of commitment through the *rear*'.[33] If religious interpreters have read their own values into the text – and in Davies' terms, allowed their ideology to interfere with their method – then secular interpreters have done exactly the same by embracing a particular philosophy or world-view which had informed *their* thinking as historians; and if the ideology of the former has resulted in an *a priori* prejudice *in favour* of the historicity of the text, the ideology of the latter has resulted in an *a priori* prejudice *against* the historicity of the text. The bias and personal judgments of scholars such as Davies and their self-consciously secular, anti-theological stance and thinly disguised animus against religious belief had led them to an excessive negativity with regard to the biblical text and to a denial of the historical value of substantial elements contained therein.

Another way in which ideology has interfered with method according to the minimalists is in the way archaeological discoveries have been appropriated by biblical scholars. It is argued that the religious ideology of the maximalists has predisposed them to interpret artefacts and inscriptions in such a way as to support the historical reliability of the Bible. Minimalists, conversely, argue that archaeology should separate itself from biblically influenced presuppositions. Artefacts should be evaluated independently and not simply interpreted in the light of a particular biblical narrative, for the temptation will inevitably be to harmonize biblical texts with the archaeological discoveries. Artefacts provide more objective and reliable

---

[32] Davies, *In Search*, p. 161. Given Davies' attack on the religious ideology of certain scholars, it seems ironical that, in a later publication, he claimed to find 'attacks on ideology as such, from any quarter, to be pointless' (*Memories of Ancient Israel: An Introduction to Biblical History – Ancient and Modern* (Louisville, KY: Westminster John Knox Press, 2008), p. 159.

[33] Provan, 'Ideologies', p. 605.

information than do texts, for while texts can deliberately mislead due to the particular ideology the biblical author wishes to promote, artefacts do not possess an intrinsic ideology and therefore never mislead, or, if they *do* mislead, they never do so 'through their own fault'.[34] Such archaeological data as are available, claim the minimalists, cast serious doubts on the historicity of large swathes of the biblical narrative, and this must inevitably instil in us a measure of caution and scepticism towards the remainder so that 'nothing unverified can be assumed to have occurred'.[35] Of course, the maximalists respond to such excessive negativity by claiming that there are many instances where archaeological evidence confirms the biblical account, and even in cases where it does not, it must be remembered that archaeological data are often unreliable and always open to the vagaries of interpretation. That being so, the biblical text should be regarded as reliable unless it can be proved conclusively to be false. Such a view was vociferously advocated by Provan who asks, 'Why should verification be a prerequisite for our acceptance of a tradition as valuable in respect of historical reality? Why should not ancient historical texts rather be given the benefit of the doubt in regard to their statements about the past unless good reasons exist to conclude them unreliable in these statements?'[36]

Once the blanket assumptions are set to one side, the minimalist and maximalist positions have more in common that is generally recognised, and the gap between them has often seemed unbridgeable only because each side of the debate has – whether wilfully or mistakenly – misrepresented the opponent's view.[37] Perhaps the time has come to move beyond the current stalemate between the two opposing groups and to emphasise the elements that they have in common rather than the elements that separate them. Once we put ideology

---

[34] Davies, 'Method', p. 702.
[35] Davies, *Memories*, p. 148.
[36] See Iain W. Provan, V. Phillips Long, and Tremper Longman III, *A Biblical History of Israel* (Louisville, KY: Westminster John Knox Press, 2003), p. 55.
[37] Thompson claims that Provan 'has been both uncritical and less than accurate in presenting the arguments and statements of those he is criticizing', and that he has 'consistently misrepresented the positions he purports to attack' ('Neo-Albrightean School', p. 683). Conversely, Thompson's claim that Provan is objecting to critical scholarship of every persuasion (p. 688) is a gross caricature of his position, and his claim that Provan represents 'fundamentalism as defined by J. Barr' (p. 694) is nothing less than an uncalled-for slur on the integrity of a scholar who happens to hold a different view from his own.

to one side, the basic methods and procedures employed by both is fairly generally agreed. Even Provan and Davies would probably agree on the following points: that the biblical accounts must first be appreciated as narratives before they can be used as historical sources; that the aims of the individual biblical authors have caused them to slant their presentation of events; that all evidence about the past is inconclusive and can, in principle, be over-ridden or contradicted by subsequently acquired evidence; that there is no single authoritative and objectively correct account of the past; and that different types of evidence (biblical texts, artefacts, inscriptions etc.) offer different types of information about the past. Indeed, both scholars would probably even recognise the importance of the OT as a source of information about the past, except that one would claim that the texts are valuable for recreating the period when the texts were composed, while the other would claim that they are valuable for recreating the actual events which they purport to depict.

Many maximalists now incorporate some of the minimalists' caution into their own scholarship, and some of the minimalists now welcome perspectives from scholars of various persuasions, recognising that they can only improve our understanding of the past. Thanks to the systematic challenge posed by the minimalists to the traditional methods of constructing histories of Israel, the maximalist option is no longer regarded as the default position, for such an approach has to be rigorously defended. Indeed, there seems to be such a variety of positions represented within each group that the distinction between them is often blurred, and one is left wondering whether dividing them into two opposing camps serves any useful purpose. Ironically enough, Provan refuses to accept that he is a 'maximalist', and Davies has nothing but contempt for the term 'minimalist', so perhaps the time has finally come to discard the various labels that are used to designate the two groups, labels which are often regarded as either misleading (such as the use of the term 'Copenhagen School' to describe the minimalists, who are virtually unanimous that they do not form a School,[38] since they are by no means

---

[38] Thompson criticises Provan's use of the term 'school' to refer to the minimalists ('Ideologies', pp. 589, 601), since this group consists of dozens of contemporary scholars who have little in common other than a general European orientation of their scholarship ('Neo-Albrightean School', pp. 694-95). Davies agrees that

in agreement about everything, and apart from Thompson and Lemche are not even associated with Copenhagen!) or pejorative (such as the term 'minimalist' which tends to focus on the tendency of scholars to minimise the importance of the Bible as a historical source or the importance of Israel and Judah as historical subjects). The arguments and counter arguments regarding the historical reliability of the biblical traditions will no doubt continue for years to come, hopefully in a spirit of tolerance and magnanimity; in the meantime, scholars should recognise the relativity of all positions in the debate, while acknowledging that only ideologues are always right; biblical scholars know that everything they say and write is potentially wrong.[39]

---

maximalism and minimalism are not so much schools as 'options, representing two different ways of tackling biblical history, usually (but not always) with the same tools' (*Memories*, p. 146).

[39] Cf. E.A. Knauf, 'From History to Interpretation', in D.V. Edelman (ed.), *The Fabric of History: Text, Artifact and Israel's Past* (JSOTSup 127; Sheffield: JSOT Press, 1991), pp. 30-31.

9

THE LIBERATING SPIRIT: A PENTECOSTAL READING OF ISAIAH

ANDREW DAVIES[*]

William Kay was one of the first lecturers I encountered in my time at Bible College, and one of the brightest stars of a stellar and inspirational faculty. I learned from him that it was possible to be passionate about one's scholarship and one's spiritual life without either being harmed; that the OT was worth reading for more than just a few epic stories; that scholarship isn't always as critical and objective as it claims and is rather more ideologically driven than it admits; and that Pentecostal scholars could make a real contribution in 'secular' scholarship. When – still as a teenager – I began to feel a sense of calling to be an academic, William was my role model, advisor, and mentor, and continues to be such a wise guide and supporter over a quarter of a century later. I owe much of my affection for the OT to his teaching, and so it seemed appropriate to offer here in tribute a study which reads the OT through a distinctively Pentecostal framework.

Pentecostals and the Bible

Whilst Pentecostalism is often imagined as a tradition more focussed upon action than reflection, it seems to me that it does not live up to

* Andrew Davies (PhD, University of Sheffield) is Professor of Public Religion and Director of the Edward Cadbury Centre at the University of Birmingham in Birmingham, UK.

its billing in the field of hermeneutics.[1] As illustrated by Chris Thomas' excellent and helpful survey, over the last three decades or more, Pentecostal theologians and biblical scholars have tried, with a considerable measure of success, to identify some distinctive elements of a Pentecostal reading of Scripture.[2] What, in my assessment at least, we have not yet adequately demonstrated is how the theoretical frameworks we have been able to construct are outworked into distinctively Pentecostal readings of the biblical text (and it seems to me that if they are not *distinctively* Pentecostal, then it is hardly fair to label them Pentecostal at all). Admittedly with some very notable exceptions, Pentecostals have in general been rather better at describing how Pentecostal readings should look and the principles upon which they should be based than at actually delivering actual readings of biblical texts up for critical scrutiny.[3] I want, therefore, to attempt a task which is probably impossible for a short paper and a big book: to offer an ideological reading of the Book of Isaiah which will be coherent and will hold up to mainstream critical scrutiny, but is at the same time distinctively Pentecostal, in accordance with the principles which have been established by recent research in the field of Pentecostal biblical interpretation.[4] Whilst I want to spend as much time as

---

[1] Various versions of some of the content of this paper have been presented to the Centre for Pentecostal and Charismatic Studies at the University of Birmingham, the Society for Pentecostal Studies Biblical Studies Subject Group, and as part of the Montagu Barker lecture series at Oxford Centre for Mission Studies, and I have made a number of alterations and clarifications to the paper in the light of discussions at these presentations.

[2] J.C. Thomas, '"Where the Spirit Leads" – The Development of Pentecostal Hermeneutics', *Journal of Beliefs and Values* 30.3 (Dec 2009), pp. 289-302.

[3] There are indeed quite a few exceptions, mostly recent, but they are certainly rather fewer in number than the theological discussions of hermeneutics, and some of these are intended more as studies in biblical theology than as straightforward readings. For example, cf. in particular Larry R. McQueen, *Joel and the Spirit: The Cry of a Prophetic Hermeneutic* (JPTSup 8; Sheffield: Sheffield Academic Press, 1995); Lee Roy Martin, *The Unheard Voice of God: A Pentecostal Hearing of the Book of Judges* (JPTSup 32; Blandford Forum: Deo, 2008); Robby Waddell, *The Spirit of the Book of Revelation* (JPTSup 30; Blandford Forum: Deo, 2006); J.C. Thomas, *The Spirit of the New Testament* (Blandford Forum: Deo, 2005); and Rick D. Moore, 'Canon and Charisma in the Book of Deuteronomy', *JPT* 1 (1991), pp. 75-92. The volumes of the *Pentecostal Commentary Series* clearly fall into this category too.

[4] Thomas, 'Where the Spirit Leads', describes the state of the field very well; I have also interacted with some of the issues involved in two recent articles, 'What Does It Mean to Read the Bible as a Pentecostal?', *Journal of Pentecostal Theology* 18.2 (2009), pp. 216-29 and 'Reading in the Spirit: Some Brief Observations on

I can dealing with the biblical text itself, and so will leave those theoretical issues largely to one side, there are some foundational remarks
as to the theoretical underpinning of my reading which I really need
to highlight briefly in explanation first.

The consensus that has arisen around Pentecostal hermeneutics
has identified three primary aspects of a Pentecostal reading – the
distinctive roles of the Spirit, the Word, and the Community. The role
of the Word, as the focus of the interpretative task, is reasonably
obvious, except that it is worth noting again that, perhaps contrary to
expectation, Pentecostals are not straightforward 'Evangelicals with
tongues' when it comes to biblical interpretation, and are, in general,
rather less fundamentalist than their reputation might imply, and are
far less concerned with the literal than the anagogic sense of the text.[5]
What 'reading in community' means has been well explored in mainstream biblical scholarship perhaps most extensively by Daniel Patte
and the other authors and editors of the 'Global Bible Commentary',
and in Pentecostal circles in some of the writings of Chris Thomas
and Ken Archer in particular.[6] But what it means to be led by the
Spirit in the exegetical process has never really been thoroughly unpacked (at least not to my satisfaction). The centrality of the Spirit's
involvement in the process of reading the Bible for Pentecostals has
certainly been the topic of theological discussion, but I have not yet
seen a convincing account of how this can be outworked into a practical interpretative methodology for today's world, what difference it
would make if it were, and how Pentecostal interpretation could in
any event earn a seat at the table of academic biblical scholarship, if
it fundamentally depends upon such an indefinable and immeasura-
ble internal spiritual process. Whilst I have considerable sympathy
with Archer's model of the interpretative process, and can both understand and relate to his claim that 'Pentecostals believe that it is in
the context of the believing community that Scripture should be interpreted', it is important, in my estimation, that Pentecostal biblical

---

Pentecostal Interpretation and the Ethical Difficulties of the Old Testament', *Journal of Beliefs and Values* 30.3 (2009), pp. 303-12.

[5] Cf. Davies, 'What Does It Mean?', pp. 220-22.

[6] Daniel M. Patte *et al* (eds.), *Global Bible Commentary* (Nashville: Abingdon,
2004); Kenneth J. Archer, *A Pentecostal Hermeneutic for the 21st Century: Spirit, Scripture
and Community* (JPTSup 28; London: T & T Clark, 2005), e.g. esp. pp. 164-66; John
Christopher Thomas, 'Women, Pentecostals, and the Bible: An Experiment in Pentecostal Hermeneutics', *JPT* 5 (1994), pp. 41-56.

scholarship does not allow itself to meander down its own route to irrelevance and shun any contact with the wider world of biblical interpretation, and that it offers no pretension to secret knowledge or insight which is available to the 'uninitiated'.[7] Some went there nearly two millenia previously. Pentecostal hermeneutics faces two diametrically opposed challenges if it is to be taken seriously within the academy as much of a legitimate approach to reading the Bible as, for instance, feminist or postcolonial ideological interpretation: it has to prove that it is distinctively Pentecostal, and it also has to prove at least that it *can* be genuinely hermeneutical in a scholarly environment.

It says something about how committed Pentecostals are to this belief in the involvement of the Spirit in the interpretative process that they cling to it so passionately despite these challenges. Possibly this is because the emotional, the primal, and the visceral are so deeply valued by this tradition. But whilst that is perfectly understandable and acceptable in the context of the numinous experience of a worshipping community, I still struggle to see what a Spirit-led reading would look like in the field of academic biblical scholarship, where I am determined to see the Pentecostal flag planted. The nearest thing to a rationalisation of this element I can yet offer for theoretical purposes is that, as Paul says in 2 Cor. 3.17, 'Where the Spirit of the Lord is, there is freedom'. To be led by the Spirit is to be freed from tyranny and oppression, in this context the restrictive boundaries of the text and the way it seeks to compel us to read it. A Pentecostal reading, therefore, should be pneumatic, a reading 'given air' as much as it is Spiritual – a reading given space and freedom to develop in ways that seem coherent and meaningful to the interpreter and the community, even if that causes it to cross textual borders and even break hermeneutical taboos in the pursuit of theological significance and purpose.[8] In a worship context, Pentecostal believers would claim to sense the Spirit's interaction with their community. Maybe, just maybe, a Pentecostal interpreter might seek to recognise the Spirit's work in the text by highlighting and drawing out the 'pneumatic', by highlighting the intertextual web which supports the infrastructure of the text under consideration. If there is any truth at all

---

[7] Archer, *Pentecostal Hermeneutic*, p. 185.

[8] I have to be honest and admit that I am not entirely satisfied by this explanation even myself, though I do think it is moving in the right direction.

in that suggestion, it would mean, in my assessment, that Pentecostal interpretation is thoroughly intertextual in its very imagining – which is essentially the perspective of Robby Waddell, but also has its more homiletic and devotional counterpart in the 'Bible reading method' identified by Archer.[9] That intertextual element means that it is essential that the reading gains acceptance from its community for it to have much value, of course. Those engaging with the interpretation need to be convinced by the linkages and – this too is particularly important for Pentecostals – it needs to provoke a response from them.[10] The goal of Pentecostal interpretation of the Bible, after all, is not to explain what the text means, but to determine how it is meaningful, and that is something very different altogether.

Reading Isaiah as a Pentecostal

Let me hope, then, that you find something engaging and inspirational about the reading of Isaiah that I am about to offer you. I started my thinking for this project by asking myself, so, how might Isaiah make sense as a coherent whole to me as a Pentecostal reader? In the process of answering that question, I found an image prompted by the work of Peter Miscall on Isaiah in the early 1990s to be extremely helpful.[11] Miscall suggests that by choosing ourselves the ideas and motifs that we wish to work within a text, we ourselves determine the shape of the text we are reading:

> Reading, as I pursue it, is a process of building and (de)constructing a text, a Labyrinth; it is not a specifically directed procedure, 'the method,' to reach a set entrance, center or exit that can serve as the one meaning or interpretation of the text. It is more a

---

[9] Cf. Waddell, *Spirit of the Book of Revelation*, esp. ch. 2; cf. also Archer, *Pentecostal Hermeneutic*, esp. pp. 72-93.

[10] One interesting aspect of the *Pentecostal Commentary* series is its commitment to being 'confessional-critical' and offering 'periodic opportunities for reflection upon and personal response to the biblical text ... consistent with the tradition's practice of not simply hearing the words of Scripture but responding to them in concrete ways' (John Christopher Thomas, *The Pentecostal Commentary on 1 John, 2 John, and 3 John* (London: T&T Clark, 2004), p. xi.

[11] I believe he introduced the idea in Peter D. Miscall, 'Isaiah and the Labyrinth of Images' (*Semeia*, 54; Atlanta: SBL, 1992) before working it out more fully in respect of Isaiah in its entirety in Peter D. Miscall, *Isaiah: Readings: A New Biblical Commentary* (Sheffield: Sheffield Academic Press, 1993).

reader-directed process, in which the reader decides which textual threads to pick up and follow, how far to follow each one and whether to tie them all together at some end or center or just leave them lying on the page.[12]

By reading his 'labyrinth of images' into existence, Miscall constructs his own Isaiah, which is nevertheless genuinely and completely Isaianic, out of the raw material of the book. I like this idea very much and think it is an incredibly helpful model for dealing with a large-scale text such as this one as a coherent whole. The problem with Miscall's conception of labyrinth, however, as Kathryn Pfisterer Darr has noted, is that it invites us to picture ourselves as desperately trying to survive, and navigate our way out of, a maze of meaning-lessness; accordingly, the text has no directive influence whatsoever but making ourselves its adversary.[13]

I would therefore rather spin the idea a little more positively and envisage my interpretative task as one of finding pathways through the text which allow me to pursue my own journey through Isaiah, in accordance with my own preferences and priorities, but which pause to allow me to view and expound the scenery on the way through. I think such a philosophical approach will be ideally suited to this spe-cific task, and so I will try to identify and follow a couple of pathways or threads of images and ideas which merge together to lead readers into, and through, the scriptures, which have particular resonance for me as a Pentecostal biblical scholar.

The starting point for any journey is of course vitally important. Wilfully resisting one reasonably obvious (albeit important) pathway through Isaiah for Pentecostals, which would have been to look for specific references to the person and work of the Holy Spirit, not least because that road has been more fully and expertly trodden be-fore, not least by Wonsuk Ma, I have chosen an alternative route – a route determined for me principally by the gateway by which I chose to enter the world of this prophetic book.[14] The beginning of the book of Isaiah is not that logical a place to start for my purposes. It

---

[12] Miscall, 'Isaiah and the Labyrinth of Images', p. 107.

[13] Kathryn Pfisterer Darr, *Isaiah's Vision and the Family of God* (Louisville, KY: Westminster John Knox, 1994), p. 21.

[14] Ma's discussion of Isaiah's pneumatology is most extensively outworked in Wonsuk Ma, *Until the Spirit Comes: The Spirit of God in the Book of Isaiah* (JSOTSup 271; Sheffield: Sheffield Academic Press, 1999).

anchors the book in a historical context I do not want to cling to
(1.1); it offers an image of a world that I am not too directly familiar
with and cannot relate to, and, to be frank, I find its metaphor of
abuse which pervades much of the chapter as more than a little eth-
ically troublesome. A better place to enter Isaiah's world for my purposes is through the back door from the NT – a route I would frown
upon as an academic but am completely accustomed to as a Pentecostal – into Isa. 61.1-4 – 'The Spirit of the Lord God is upon me,
because the Lord has anointed me, and sent me to preach the gospel
to the oppressed'. After all, these are the words Jesus chooses to
launch his ministry upon. They form therefore something of a bridge
between the covenants, if you like; and, when read paradigmatically,
they unlock a whole new reading of this greatest of the prophetic
books.

The declaration that the Spirit of Yahweh anoints and empowers
people is hardly a surprising one for any Pentecostal to read. What
the Spirit empowers the prophet to do here, though, is perhaps a little
more unexpected, and choosing to enter Isaiah's world through this
particular gateway provokes me to read the book as a fundamentally
liberationist text. In the prophet's understanding here, the Spirit falls
upon him to equip him for the task of bringing good news to the
oppressed and healing the broken-hearted. Furthermore, since Isaiah
appears to envisage himself, in this context at least, as exemplary of
the people of God in their entirety, the Spirit may fall in correspond-
ing moments upon all servants of the Lord, this empowering is available to any believer, including by his own estimation in Luke's gospel,
Jesus himself (Lk. 4.16-21). Isaiah's calling from this passage onwards
is to bring deliverance through proclamation. Just as the words of
God have creative power in Isa. 55.10-11, so do the prophet's (not
least because they are in themselves God's words!). So, whereas in
6.9-10 Isaiah is instructed to preach with the express intent of dulling
the mind of his listeners and denying them the opportunity of returning for healing, now in 61.1-4, Isaiah's proclamation of liberty
and release is what looses and liberates them. 'Proclaiming the year
of the Lord's favour' both announces its arrival, names it for what it
is, and inaugurates it.

If we begin our reading of Isaiah here, then, the essential message
of the prophet is one of release from oppression and bondage,
whether that be the oppression of Judah's Assyrian or Babylonian

overlords (10.24-25; chs. 36-37; 14.4-6) or arising from the corruption of Israel's wicked and equally inept leaders (10.1-2; 13.11 'I will … lay low the insolence of tyrants'). Isaiah, patrician court prophet though he appears to be, is as decidedly on the side of the poor as his radical socialist colleague Amos, and his message is that God's people have suffered enough and can now experience liberation and freedom because God's Spirit is at work in human history (a key message of 40.1-11, for instance).

Hacking a little more textual foliage away enables us to see quite quickly that this little pathway through the text heads deep into the book, branching in multifarious alternative directions as it does so. Isaiah tells us in 14.4-6 how Yahweh will break the sceptre with which the 'wicked' King of Babylon beat the nations, bringing an end to his oppression (in the broader context of a passage, of course, that is often linked in Pentecostal preaching with the fall of Satan, the ultimate oppressor). He talks in chapter 2 of a day when God's people will throw away their false gods and be free once for all from their power – and here, talk of all humanity being 'humbled' and 'brought low' is surely a clever little *double entendre*. Not only will Yahweh humble his people in judgement, but they are also already choosing to humble themselves by bowing down to artefacts they themselves have shaped. Why any creator would choose to worship their creation is very difficult for Isaiah to grasp (a point he makes in such beautifully vivid imagery in the middle section of the book, chs. 40-47 in particular). Furthermore, I wonder if there is not a little symbolism in Isaiah's reference in 40.19 to the chains shaped by the craftsman to hold the idol in place. Is he perhaps subtly reminding his listeners of the bondage they are putting themselves in by bowing to what, as far as he is concerned at least, is just a worthless lump of wood and metal? And, to take just one example from the sphere of military and political intervention, it is interesting to see how Isaiah suggests that any appeal from the citizens of Jerusalem to the Egyptians for help would be just as damaging and oppressive. Not only is asking for Egypt's assistance against the Assyrians worthless ('Rahab the do-nothing', he vividly labels her [30.7]), but also doing so is 'relying on oppression and deceit' (30.12) and will result in the collapse of the nation.

For Isaiah, Yahweh is the only deliverer and the only one who is able to bring liberation and freedom from oppression. If they turn to him, he will free them even from the effects of their own stupidity and pride (the ground of all sin, according to Luther's famous assertion that *omne peccatum est superbia*). Perhaps if his people return to him, Yahweh will even free them from the constraints that he himself has placed upon them. For now, from this rather more liberationist perspective, we can also make a little more sense for our context out of chapter 1, by reading it as a message of freedom from divine judgement, should God's people choose to accept the opportunity of receiving cleansing from sin and its consequences, and perhaps also of freedom from religious system and ritual. In the first few oracles of his vision, Isaiah questions what he appears to envisage as the oppressive protocols of the priestly caste, and Isaiah's Yahweh denies having had anything to do with their institution (1.10-14).

So, the first thread I would propose for my Pentecostal reading of Isaiah is the message that the empowering Spirit frees the people of God from the bondage in which they find themselves, whatever that might be. God's Spirit is the great liberator; and yet he does his work not visibly and publicly in his own right, but through the hands of those he anoints to do his work. Isaiah's so-called messianic theology is rather more, I suggest, an emphasis on the anointing and equipping of the chosen people of God for their distinctive service (and that is an incredibly Pentecostal theme, of course). So, whilst Isaiah does envisage the rise of at least one, if not a number of great deliverers, 'a king [who] will reign in righteousness' (32.1), his message is that Yahweh has appointed and empowered them. In 45.1-2, Cyrus, for instance, does not rise to prominence because of his own strength. He becomes the epitome of the liberating conqueror precisely because Yahweh has anointed him (Isaiah actually describes him here as 'messiah', of course), and he achieves his successes primarily because Yahweh has gone before him and broken down the bronze doors that, literally, kept him out of the city of Babylon, but figuratively keep the people of God in oppression and subjugation.

Isaiah's two most obviously 'messianic' passages fit comfortably into this paradigm as well. Though the child that is born to us in ch. 9 is not explicitly identified as being Spirit-empowered, he is the means by which Yahweh breaks the rod of the oppressor (deliberately left unidentified here, perhaps to emphasise he is the liberator of all who work in darkness). The new kingdom of righteousness, justice, and peace over which he will rule, however (9.7; unpacked further in 11.5-9) is indeed specifically ascribed to the work of the Spirit. The unity and peace which will characterise the new community arises because of the righteous rulership of the 'shoot from the stump of Jesse', and in particular his wise judgements, which result from a specific pneumatological empowerment. 'The Spirit of the Lord will rest upon him: the Spirit of wisdom and understanding, the Spirit of counsel and might, the Spirit of knowledge and the fear of the Lord' (11.2). This righteous king relies upon the Spirit for the resources he needs for the task of establishing peace in the community; and is the recipient of a specific external outpouring of the Spirit's power: – the Spirit rests upon him, and in doing so empowers him to fulfill the divine commission, and to reach the ultimate goal of seeing all the earth 'full of the knowledge of the Lord' (11.9). This is of course a knowledge which we are told in 11.2 comes from the Spirit himself, and therefore it would not be unreasonable to imagine Isaiah, like Joel (Joel 2.28-32), envisages the eschatological descent of the Spirit upon all humanity (perhaps even literally 'all flesh' in the light of the animal references here).

Until that day, the land as well as the people remains subjugated and oppressed. For the moment, 'the palace is forsaken, the populous city deserted' … but when 'the Spirit is poured upon us from on high', Isaiah reminds his listeners, 'the wilderness becomes a fruitful field, the fruitful field is deemed a forest' (32.14-15). He expands upon this image in the delightful oracle of healing and restoration of ch. 35, where he promises that a day is coming where the desert will blossom as a rose, the discouraged will be strengthened by the promise of God's presence, the blind will see, deaf hear and lame walk, and there will be streams in the desert. This is a pretty much all-inclusive presentation of wholeness and restoration, and envisages not mere survival, but abundance and prosperity, and for Isaiah it all results from the outpouring of the Spirit upon both the righteous King and the people at large. The liberty of the Spirit brings freshness and life, which itself facilitates new birth (66.7-9) and exponential growth (54.1-3). The only appropriate response to this is the one which the people actually do offer – everlasting joy and gladness, and renewed enthusiasm to return to worship at the temple, which itself invites and inspires the nations to follow and join them (35.8-10, 2.1-5).

There is one other important thread that I see as being interwoven here. We have seen how liberation from oppression is possible because of the work of the Spirit, and how healing comes to the land and the nation through the person of the Spirit-empowered righteous king (for whom, for Pentecostals and all Christians, the ultimate referent is Jesus). But I think it is interesting and important to note the element of personal choice and responsibility which is also a common Pentecostal emphasis and is clearly alluded to in a few key texts. There is a strongly invitational aspect to the prophet's message: 'Awake, put on your strength, O Zion … shake yourself from the dust and arise … loose the bonds from your neck', he invites the people (52.1-2). Take responsibility for your own restoration and renewal, if you like – refuse the chains of oppression and choose the freedom of the Spirit. Ironically, however, this personal choice is only made possible because the Servant of the Lord chooses to take upon himself the punishment that the people of God deserve. The fourth servant song (52.13-53.12) offers ultimate example of one who is 'oppressed' and 'afflicted' (53.7), 'crushed with pain' (53.10) and is yet through his suffering a means of ultimate liberation; his suffering and death makes many righteous (53.11), gives them the opportunity of experiencing freedom. Or, to switch to the metaphor the prophet uses in 55.1, it affords the chance to 'everyone who is thirsty' to 'come to the waters' to have their spiritual thirst quenched and enjoy God's abundant provision. That image of living water, of course, neatly brings us back full circle to the NT and the ministry of Jesus. Isaiah 61 is the passage Jesus chooses to cite in Luke 4 as his commission and inspiration at the start of his Galilean ministry, and in John 7, as he begins to enter the end-game, he clearly alludes to Isaiah once again.

This brief 'pneumatological-liberationist'[15] ideological reading of Isaiah as a whole is, I hope, coherent, and I have sought to ensure that it arises from the text rather than being imposed upon the text externally, but I would suggest, it is distinctively Pentecostal in both its approach and its message. It understands Isaiah's great theme as being: – because of the self-sacrifice of God's servant, there is an opportunity for universal liberation from the oppression that God's people are enduring, in whatever context or circumstances they might currently find themselves, and that the means of deliverance is through the people themselves and through their anointed leaders, as

---

[15] A phrase suggested to me by Prof. Allan Anderson in our discussions.

the people rise up under the incitement, guidance and empowerment of God's Spirit. And I have to say that it sounds to me very much like the message I have heard preached in Pentecostal churches, week in, week out, for years. Isaiah, perhaps, is as much a Pentecostal prophet as some of his more self-evidently charismatic colleagues.

10

Personality and Charismatic Orientation: an Empirical Study in Psychological Type Theory

Leslie J. Francis,[*] Keith Littler,[**] and Mandy Robbins[***]

Introduction

Charismatic experiences and charismatic phenomena have long been of interest within both theoretical and empirical approaches to the psychology of religion, leading to a range of disparate theories, insights, and snippets of evidence. During the 1990s William K Kay spotted the potential for some of these disparate insights and theories to be drawn together and integrated within the broad field of personality psychology. In particular, Kay was drawn to the potential within Eysenck's dimensional model of personality. The fruits of this approach were organised in a study of 'the personality characteristics of Pentecostal ministry candidates' by Francis and Kay (1995).

---

[*] Leslie J. Francis (PhD, ScD, University of Cambridge; DD, University of Oxford; DLitt, University of Wales, Bangor) is Professor of Religions and Education at the University of Warwick, in Warwick, England, UK.

[**] Keith Littler † (PhD, Hull University; DMin, University of Wales, Bangor) was Research Fellow within the St Mary's Centre, Wales, UK.

[***] Mandy Robbins (PhD, University of Wales, Bangor) is Associate Dean, Faculty of Social and Life Science at Wrexham Glyndŵr University, in Wrexham, Wales, UK.

Eysenck's dimensional model of personality possesses two main defining principles. First, Eysenck maintains that there is a continuity between normal personality and abnormal personality. It is for this reason that the high scoring poles of two of Eysenck's dimensions of normal personality are defined by terms borrowed from abnormal psychology (neuroticism and psychoticism). Second, Eysenck maintains that the dimensions of normal personality are independent one from another. It is for this reason that the empirical development and refinement of Eysenck's model rests so heavily on factor analysis designed to ensure the orthogonality of the three dimensions (extraversion, neuroticism, and psychoticism). These three dimensions have been operationalised through a series of self-report personality measures: The Eysenck Personality Questionnaire (EPQ: Eysenck and Eysenck,1975) and the Eysenck Personality Questionnaire Revised (EPQR: Eysenck, Eysenck, and Barrett, 1985; Eysenck and Eysenck, 1991). Alongside the three scales of extraversion, neuroticism, and psychoticism, the Eysenck family of personality measures also routinely includes a lie scale.

In their attempt to organise the earlier diverse research on charismatic experiences and charismatic phenomena, Francis and Kay (1995) concentrated specifically on the key component of glossolalia and mapped existing psychological knowledge onto the Eysenckian framework. They addressed each of the Eysenckian dimensions in turn.

The first dimension in Eysenck's model of personality is neuroticism. Eysenck's neuroticism scale measures emotional lability and over-reactivity. The opposite of neuroticism is emotional stability. Francis and Kay (1995) suggest that there is a considerable body of research and theory to promote the hypothesis that glossolalics should score higher on the neuroticism scale, including theories advanced by Mackie (1921) and Cutten (1927), and more recent work by Vivier (1960), Lapsley and Simpson (1964), Pattison (1968) and Kildahl (1972, 1975). Conversely, a contradictory strand of research suggests that glossolalia may function as a tension-reducing device which may promote psychological health (Tappeiner, 1974; Coulson and Johnson, 1977; Neisz and Kronenberger, 1978; Ness and Wintrob, 1980; Smith and Fleck, 1981; Williams, 1981; Castelein, 1984).

The second dimension in Eysenck's model of personality is psychoticism. Eysenck and Eysenck (1976) characterise the adult high scorer on the psychoticism scale as not caring for people, lacking in feeling and empathy, and altogether insensitive. The opposite of psychoticism is normal personality. Francis and Kay (1995) suggest that there is evidence to promote the hypothesis that glossolalics should score lower on the psychoticism scale, on the grounds that individuals who score low on psychoticism condition more readily (Beyts, Frcka, Martin, and Levey, 1983; Francis, 1992) and that glossolalia is learned behaviour (Samarin, 1959; Hine, 1969; Spandos, Cross, Lepage, and Coristine, 1986).

The third dimension in Eysenck's model of personality is extraversion. The test manual characterises the adult high scorer on the extraversion scale as a sociable individual who likes parties, has many friends, needs to have people to talk to, and prefers meeting people to reading or studying alone. The typical extravert craves excitement. The opposite of extraversion is introversion. On the basis of reviewing previous research Francis and Kay (1995) are not able to propose a theoretical basis for linking glossolalia with extraversion.

The fourth measure proposed by Eysenck's personality test is the lie scale. While originally introduced to detect respondents, who wished to present a socially desirable image of themselves, the lie scale has been interpreted as measuring a further aspect of personality, variously characterised as social conforming (Massey, 1980), lack of self-insight (Crookes and Buckley, 1976), or immaturity (Francis, Pearson, and Kay, 1983). Francis and Kay (1995) suggest that there is evidence to promote the hypothesis that glossolalics should score higher on the lie scale, on the grounds that the lie scale measures lack of self-insight and immaturity (Francis, Pearson, and Kay, 1983) and that glossolalia represents regressive behaviour (Lapsley and Simpson, 1964; Oates, 1967; Samarin, 1973).

In their original study, Francis and Kay (1995) tested these hypotheses by comparing the Eysenckian personality profile of 259 male and 105 female Pentecostal ministry candidates (attending the British Assemblies of God and Elim bible colleges) with the population norms published in the test manual by Eysenck and Eysenck (1975). The data demonstrate that both male and female Pentecostal ministry candidates score significantly lower than the population norms for the neuroticism scale. They are more stable than men and women in general. The female Pentecostal ministry candidates did not differ from women in general on the dimensions of extraversion, psychoticism, and the lie scale. The male Pentecostal ministry candidates did not differ from men in general on the dimension of extraversion, but they scored significantly lower on the psychoticism scale and significantly higher on the lie scale.

In a second study, designed to test the hypotheses advanced by Francis and Kay (1995), Francis and Thomas (1997) explored the correlation between Eysenck's scales and scores recorded on a 14-item index of charismatic experience among a sample of 222 male clergy serving within the Church in Wales. In this study charismatic experience was correlated negatively with neuroticism and positively with extraversion but was unrelated to either psychoticism or lie scale scores.

In a third study, Francis and Jones (1997) explored the correlations between Eysenck's scales and scores recorded on a 5-item index of charismatic experience among a sample of 368 committed adult Christians. This study confirmed the findings of Francis and Thomas (1997). Once again charismatic experience was correlated negatively with neuroticism and positively with extraversion, but unrelated to either psychoticism or lie scale scores.

In a fourth study, Robbins, Hair, and Francis (1999) explored the correlations between Eysenck's scales and scores recorded as a 15-item index of charismatic experience among a sample of 172 male clergy serving within the Church of England. In this study charismatic experience was correlated positively with extraversion, but unrelated to the other three measures.

In a fifth study, Louden and Francis (2001) replicated the study reported by Robbins, Hair, and Francis (1999) using the same 15-item index of charismatic experience, this time among a sample of 1,468 Roman Catholic priests serving in England and Wales. In this study charismatic experience was correlated positively with extraversion, but unrelated to the other three measures.

In a sixth study, Francis and Robbins (2003) explored the correlations between Eysenck's scales and self-reported frequency of glossolalia. In this study glossolalia was correlated positively with extraversion, correlated negatively with neuroticism, and unrelated to psychoticism.

Taken together this series of empirical studies has begun to build a relatively consistent picture of the location of charismatic experience within the three-dimensional personality space defined by

Eysenck's model. The data generally agree in associating charismatic experience with higher extraversion scores and in failing to find any evidence to link charismatic experience with higher neuroticism or with higher psychoticism scores. Indeed, some of the data link charismatic experience with lower neuroticism scores.

William K. Kay's decision to focus on the Eysenckian model of personality was particularly astute in light of the connection made by this model with psychopathology and in light of the boarder role that this model of personality has come to play within the British tradition in the psychology of religion. In more recent years, however, a second model of personality has also come into prominence in the psychology of religion, namely the notion of psychological type that has its origins in the pioneering work of Carl Jung (1971) and that has been operationalised in a series of type indicators, temperament sorters or type scales, including the Myers Briggs Type Indicator (Myers and McCaulley, 1985), the Keirsey Temperament Sorter (Keirsey and Bates, 1978), and the Francis Psychological Type Scales (Francis, 2005). An overview of developments in this field has been provided by Francis (2009).

Jungian psychological type theory differs from the Eysenckian dimensional model of personality in two important ways. First, type theory is concerned wholly with normal personality and has no conscious connection with psychopathology. Second, type theory is concerned with the identification of discrete type categories, not with defining gradations along a continuum.

At its heart psychological type theory distinguishes between two core psychological processes. The perceiving process is concerned with how data are gathered; in Jung's terms this is the irrational process. The judging process is concerned with how data are evaluated; in Jung's terms this is the rational process. Within the perceiving process the two perceiving functions are defined as sensing (S) and intuition (N). Sensing types are concerned with facts and with details. They are the practical people who prefer to rely on past experience rather than to look for future possibilities. Intuitive types are concerned with meanings and with associations. They are the imaginative people who prefer to trust their inspirations about future possibilities rather than to rely on past experience. Within the judging process, the two judging functions are defined as thinking (T) and feeling (F). Thinking types are concerned with objectivity and truth. They are the logical people who test the coherence of systems and institutional structures. Feeling types are concerned with interpersonal relationships and human values. They are the humane people who care about the people operating the system and the people whose lives are affected by institutional structures.

Alongside the two processes (perceiving and judging), psychological type theory also distinguishes between the orientations and the attitudes toward the outer world. The orientations are concerned with the sources of psychological energy. The distinction is between introversion (I) and extraversion (E). Introverts are energised by the inner world and by their inner life. Introverts need quiet for reflection and space for themselves. Extraverts are energised by the outer world of people and theory. Extraverts need people and social company. They reflect best with others.

The attitudes are concerned with how people function in the outer world. The distinction is between judging (J) and perceiving (P). Judging types turn their preferred judging function (thinking or feeling) to the outer world. There they are seen to be organised, planned, and structured people. Perceiving types turn their preferred perceiving function (sensing or intuition) to the outer world. There they are seen to be flexible, spontaneous, open people.

In addition to discussing the four binary distinctions (introversion *or* extraversion, sensing *or* intuition, thinking *or* feeling, judging *or* perceiving), psychological type theory draws these distinctions together in various ways to speak of the four dominant types (dominant sensing, dominant intuition, dominant thinking, dominant feeling), the eight dominant and auxiliary pairs (dominant sensing with thinking, dominant sensing with feeling, dominant intuition with thinking, dominant intuition with feeling, dominant thinking with sensing, dominant thinking with intuition, dominant feeling with sensing, and dominant feeling with intuition), and the sixteen complete types (conventionally signified by the initial letters, e.g., INTJ, ESFJ).

To date the connection between charismatic experience and psychological type has been explored by just two studies. In the first study, Francis and Jones (1997) drew on the data provided by 368 committed Christian adults to examine mean scores recorded on a five-item index of charismatic experience according to the four binary distinctions proposed by type theory. These data found significantly higher scores of charismatic experience among thinking types than among feeling types, but no significant differences between introverts and extraverts, between sensing types and intuitive types, or between judging types and perceiving types.

In the second study, Jones, Francis, and Craig (2005) took a very different approach. Drawing on data provided by 925 Christian adults, they divided the sample into three groups: 450 were clear that they had been influenced by the charismatic movement, 366 were clear that they had not been influenced by the charismatic movement, and the remaining 109 were not certain. The analytic strategy compared the psychological type profile of the 450 clearly defined charismatics with the 366 clearly defined non-charismatics. Six main aspects of these data were of particular interest. First, the charismatic sample contains a significantly higher proportion of extraverts, compared with the non-charismatic sample. Thus, 50% of the charismatics express a preference for extraversion, in comparison with 39% of the non-charismatics. Second, there is no significant difference in the proportions of sensing types and intuitive types in the two samples. Thus, 58% of the charismatics express a preference for sensing and so do 59% of the non-charismatics. Third, the charismatic sample contains a significantly higher proportion of thinking types compared with the non-charismatic sample. Thus, 39% of the charismatics express a preference for thinking, compared with 31% of the non-charismatics. Fourth, the charismatic sample contains a significantly higher proportion of perceiving types compared with the non-charismatic sample. Thus, 35% of the charismatics express a preference for perceiving, compared with 28% of the non-charismatics. Fifth, there is a significantly higher proportion of dominant thinkers among the charismatic sample (20%), compared with the non-charismatic sample (12%). Sixth, when the type distributions of the two samples are compared, among the charismatic sample there is a significant over-representation of ESTJ and a significant under-representation of ISFJ.

Research question

Against this background, the aim of the present study is to build on the two pioneering studies reported by Francis and Jones (1997) and by Jones, Francis, and Craig (2005) in order to examine the association between charismatic experience and psychological type among a

sample of Anglican clergymen by using a more highly nuanced measure of charismatic experience and by comparing scores recorded on
this measure both by the four binary distinctions proposed by type
theory and by the eight dominant-auxiliary pairs.

Method

Procedure
A questionnaire was mailed to all full-time stipendiary parochial
clergy serving in the Church in Wales. A total of 593 questionnaires
were successfully delivered, and 391 were returned, generating a response rate of 66%.

Sample
The present analysis is based on the 231 male respondents who provided full data on the relevant scales used in the analysis. The sample
comprised 22 clergymen under the age of forty, 43 in their forties,
108 in their fifties, 56 in their sixties, and 2 in their seventies.

Measures
Psychological type was assessed by the Francis Psychological Type Scales
(FPTS: Francis, 2005). This is a 40-item instrument comprising four
sets of 10 forced-choice items relating to each of the four components of psychological type: the two orientations (extraversion and
introversion), the two perceiving functions (sensing and intuition),
the two judging functions (thinking and feeling), and the two attitudes
toward the outer world (judging and perceiving). Participants were
asked for each pair of characteristics to check 'the box next to that
characteristic, which is closer to the real you, even if you feel both
characteristics apply to you. Tick the characteristic that reflects the
real you, even if other people see you differently'.

   Charismatic orientation was assessed by the 21-item Francis-Littler
Charismatic Orientation Scale (COS) developed by Francis and Littler (2011). Respondents were asked to assess 'how important each
experience is to your own faith', using a five-point scale anchored by:
1 = low importance, 3 = medium importance, 5 = high importance.

Data analysis
The scientific literature concerned with psychological type has developed a highly distinctive way of presenting type-related data, providing information on the 16 complete types, the binary comparisons,

the four dominant types, the Jungian functions, and the main pairs within the data. The conventional format of 'type tables' has been employed in the present investigation (although not all the information will be discussed) in order to allow the findings from this study to be located easily alongside other relevant studies in the literature.

Results

The first step in data analysis concerns examining the properties of the charismatic orientation scale. Table one presents the scale items, together with the correlations between the individual items and the sum of the other 20 items, and the proportions of the respondents who voted the importance of the experience for their own faith four or five on the five-point scale. All the 21 items contributed positively to the homogeneity of the scale, with item rest-of-test correlations ranging between .43 or .79, and generated an alpha coefficient of .96 (Cronbach, 1951).

TABLE 1

Francis-Littler Charismatic Orientation Scale: item rest-of-scale correlations and item endorsement

	r	agree %
Having a conversion experience	.6677	29
Praying in tongues	.7371	12
Experiencing the healing work of the Holy Spirit	.7109	56
Attending charismatic prayer-group meetings	.7888	14
Receiving the Baptism of the Holy Spirit	.6839	39
Hearing God speak through a dream or vision	.6397	18
Feeling God's Spirit within me	.4820	64
Being born again	.7315	32
Prophesying	.6770	14
Interpreting tongues	.7403	9
Giving a public utterance in tongues	.6687	3
Laying hands on someone for healing	.5697	53
Sharing in open and informal worship	.6026	41
Being prayed over	.6155	39
Receiving 'a word of knowledge'	.6764	23
Being 'slain in the Spirit'	.7011	6
Singing in the Spirit	.6753	17
Seeing healings happen	.7059	27
Praying in the Spirit	.7258	34
Singing in tongues	.7308	8
Feeling led by God to perform a specific action	.4253	48

The second step in data analysis concerns examining the psychological type profile of the sample of 231 clergymen who participated in the study. These data are presented in table 2. The clergymen show clear preferences for introversion (69%) over extraversion (31%), for sensing (64%) over intuition (36%), for feeling (55%) over thinking (46%), and for judging (78%) over perceiving (23%). In terms of dominant type preferences, 45% of the clergymen are dominant sensing types, 22% dominant feeling types, 18% dominant intuitive types, and 16% dominant thinking types. Of the 16 complete types, the two most frequently represented among clergymen are ISFJ (21%) and ISTJ (19%).

TABLE 2

Type distribution for Anglican clergymen in Wales

The Sixteen Complete Types				Dichotomous Preferences		
ISTJ	ISFJ	INFJ	INTJ	E	n = 72	(31.2%)
n = 44	n = 48	n = 13	n = 21	I	n = 159	(68.8%)
(19.0%)	(20.8%)	(5.6%)	(9.1%)			
+++++	+++++	+++++	+++++	S	n = 148	(64.1%)
+++++	+++++	+	++++	N	n = 83	(35.9%)
+++++	+++++					
++++	+++++			T	n = 105	(45.5%)
	+			F	n = 126	(54.5%)
				J	n = 179	(77.5%)
				P	n = 52	(22.5%)
ISTP	ISFP	INFP	INTP			
n = 3	n = 7	n = 15	n = 8	**Pairs and Temperaments**		
(1.3%)	(3.0%)	(6.5%)	(3.5%)	IJ	n = 126	(54.5%)
+	+++	+++++	++++	IP	n = 33	(14.3%)
		++		EP	n = 19	(8.2%)
				EJ	n = 53	(22.9%)
				ST	n = 66	(28.6%)
				SF	n = 82	(35.5%)
ESTP	ESFP	ENFP	ENTP	NF	n = 44	(19.0%)
n = 1	n = 10	n = 5	n = 3	NT	n = 39	(16.9%)
(0.4%)	(4.3%)	(2.2%)	(1.3%)			
	++++	++	+	SJ	n = 127	(55.0%)
				SP	n = 21	(9.1%)
				NP	n = 31	(13.4%)
				NJ	n = 52	(22.5%)
ESTJ	ESFJ	ENFJ	ENTJ	TJ	n = 90	(39.0%)
n = 18	n = 17	n = 11	n = 7	TP	n = 15	(6.5%)
(7.8%)	(7.4%)	(4.8%)	(3.0%)	FP	n = 37	(16.0%)
+++++	+++++	+++++	+++	FJ	n = 89	(38.5%)
+++	++					
				IN	n = 57	(24.7%)
				EN	n = 26	(11.3%)
				IS	n = 102	(44.2%)
				ES	n = 46	(19.9%)
				ET	n = 29	(12.6%)
				EF	n = 43	(18.6%)
				IF	n = 83	(35.9%)
				IT	n = 76	(32.9%)

Jungian Types (E)			Jungian Types (I)			Dominant Types			*Anglican clergymen in Wales*
	n	%		n	%		n	%	
E-TJ	25	10.8	I-TP	11	4.8	Dt.T	36	15.6	*L. J. Francis, K. Littler, and M. Robbins*
E-FJ	28	12.1	I-FP	22	9.5	Dt.F	50	21.6	
ES-P	11	4.8	IS-J	92	39.8	Dt.S	103	44.6	
EN-P	8	3.5	IN-J	34	14.7	Dt.N	42	18.2	

Note: N = 231   NB: + = 1% of N

The third step in data analysis concerns examining the association between scores recorded on the measure of charismatic orientation and the four preference pairs. These data are presented in Table 3. On the one hand, no significant differences emerged between the charismatic orientation scores recorded by introverts and by extraverts or between the charismatic orientation scores recorded by thinking types and by feeling types. On the other hand, intuitive types recorded significantly higher charismatic orientation scores than sensing types, and perceiving types recorded significantly higher charismatic orientation scores than judging types.

TABLE 3

Charismatic orientation by preference pairs

	N	mean	SD	t	$p <$
Orientations					
extraversion (E)	72	56.1	19.5		
introversion (I)	159	52.3	17.4	1.5	NS
Perceiving processes					
sensing (S)	148	51.4	17.2		
intuition (N)	83	57.3	19.0	2.4	.05
Judging processes					
thinking (T)	105	52.8	18.6		
feeling (F)	126	54.1	17.7	0.5	NS
Attitudes					
judging (J)	179	51.1	16.1		
perceiving (P)	52	61.7	21.9	3.8	.001

Finally, table 4 completes the picture by examining the association between scores recorded on the measure of charismatic orientation and the eight dominant-auxiliary pairs.

TABLE 4

Charismatic orientation by dominant auxiliary pairs

	N	mean	SD	t	p <
Thinking with intuition	15	66.5	25.0		
Feeling with intuition	26	59.8	20.3		
Feeling with sensing	24	54.2	20.1		
Intuition with feeling	18	53.4	13.5		
Thinking with sensing	21	52.8	17.0		
Sensing with feeling	58	51.7	16.3		
Intuition with thinking	24	51.7	14.8		
Sensing with thinking	45	48.8	17.2	2.2	.05

These data demonstrate that the highest charismatic orientations are recorded by dominant thinking types with auxiliary intuition, and that the lowest charismatic orientation scores are recorded by dominant sensing types with auxiliary thinking.

Conclusion

The present study began by reviewing the series of empirical studies stimulated by William K. Kay's inspirational suggestion to draw together a long history of disparate themes and data (within the psychology of religion) concerned with charismatic experience into the context of Eysenck's dimensional model of personality. This review concluded that the series of studies had provided a secure empirical foundation for locating higher levels of charismatic experiences among extraverts than among introverts (as defined on the Eysenckian model) and for rejecting any link between charismatic experience and psychopathology (as defined by the Eysenckian notions of neuroticism and psychoticism).

This review also led to the challenge to explore the connection between charismatic experience and a second model of personality, namely the model of psychological type originally proposed by Carl Jung and subsequently developed and extended by a series of psychological assessment devices. Building on the two foundational studies reported by Francis and Jones (1997) and by Jones, Francis, and Craig (2005) a new empirical study was undertaken employing the Francis Psychological Type Scales (as a measure of psychological type) and the Francis-Littler Charismatic Orientation Scale as a measure of charismatic experience. Three main conclusions can be drawn from these new data.

The first conclusion concerns the application of the Francis-Littler Charismatic Orientation Scale in the context of research of this nature. This instrument performed with highly satisfactory levels of internal consistency reliability and generated a range of scale scores that were successful in illuminating the connection between psychological type and charismatic orientation. The instrument can be commended for use in future studies.

The second conclusion concerns the absence of connection between charismatic orientation and two component parts of psychological type theory. According to the data, neither the two orientations (introversion and extraversion) nor the two judging functions (thinking or feeling) are associated with individual differences in charismatic orientation. Both of these findings require further reflection. The lack of a connection between extraversion and charismatic experience in a study using psychological type theory may seem strange when the connection between extraversion and charismatic experience has been well established in studies using Eysenckian theory. The answer might well be found in the very different concepts of extraversion employed in the two different personality theories. For Eysenck, extraversion is largely a social construct; for Jung extraversion is largely concerned with energy sources. The lack of a connection between thinking and charismatic experience may seem to contradict the earlier finding by Francis and Jones (1997) that thinking types recorded a significantly higher score than feeling types on their measures of charismatic experience. The answer might well be found in the very different measures employed in the two studies. The measure used by Francis and Jones (1997) placed an emphasis on the doctrinal aspect of charismatic belief (which may be of particular interest to thinking types), while the present study placed a higher emphasis on the experiential dimension.

The third conclusion concerns the significant connection between charismatic orientation and the two other component parts of psychological type theory. According to the data, both the perceiving process and the attitudes toward the outer world are implicated in individual differences in charismatic orientation. Intuitive types are significantly more open than sensing types to charismatic experience and perceiving types are significantly more open than judging types to charismatic orientation. Both of these findings require further reflection.

The link between intuition and charismatic orientation is consistent with the view that intuitive types are open to meanings and to possibilities. Intuitive types stretch out beyond the present realities to broader transcendent possibilities. It is this perspective that may open the heart of intuitive types to the possibilities opened up by such phenomena as praying in tongues, interpreting tongues, and singing in the Spirit. Intuitive types are less likely to be distracted by the outward appearance and more likely to be attracted by the unseen spiritual significance.

The link between perceiving and charismatic orientation is consistent with the view that perceiving types tend to be open, flexible and spontaneous in respect of their attitude toward the outer world. Perceiving types are not hemmed in by their pre-made plans and preconceived notions. It is this perspective that may open the outward lives of perceiving types to the movement, to the workings, to the leadings of the Holy Spirit. Perceiving types are unlikely to come to Sunday worship reluctant to go where the Holy Spirit leads them.

The limitation with the present study is that the conclusions have been based on a small sample restricted to just 231 Anglican clergymen serving in Wales. Both the empirical findings and the theoretical account of these findings, however, are sufficiently interesting and sufficiently intriguing to warrant further reflection and extension among other groups.

If the present findings were to be established more widely, they may begin to carry significant implications for ways in which different branches of the Christian church view each other and for ways in which the challenges and opportunities of ecumenical collaboration are embraced and handled. It may be that some of the obstacles in the path of the ecumenical future need to be reconceptualised less in terms of theological differences and more in terms of psychological differences.

Note

With the publication of this paper comes also a note of sadness. Keith Littler, who collaborated with me on so many publications during his retirement, died before he could see this chapter in print. This chapter is dedicated to his memory.

REFERENCES

Beyts, J., G. Frcka, I. Martin, and A.B. Levey. (1983). 'The influence of psychoticism and extraversion on classical eyelid conditioning using a paraorbital shock UCS', *Personality and Individual Differences*, 4 (1983), pp. 275-83.

Castelein, J.D. (1984). 'Glossolalia and the psychology of the self and narcissism', *Journal of Religion and Health* 23 (1984), pp. 47-62.

Coulson, J.E., and R.W. Johnson. (1977). 'Glossolalia and internal-external locus of control', *Journal of Psychology and Theology* 5 (1977), pp. 312-17.

Cronbach, L.J. (1951). 'Coefficient alpha and the internal structure of tests', *Psychometrika*, 16 (1951), pp. 297-334.

Crookes, T.G., and S.J. Buckley. (1976). 'Lie score and insight', *Irish Journal of Psychology* 3 (1976), pp. 134-36.

Cutten, G.B. (1927). *Speaking with Tongues: Historically and psychologically considered* (Yale: Yale University Press, 1927).

Eysenck, H.J., and S.B.G. Eysenck. (1975). *Manual of the Eysenck Personality Questionnaire (adult and junior)* (London: Hodder and Stoughton, 1975).

Eysenck, H.J., and S.B.G. Eysenck. (1976). *Psychoticism as a dimension of personality* (London: Hodder and Stoughton).

Eysenck, H.J., and S.B.G. Eysenck. (1991). *Manual of the Eysenck Personality Scales* (London: Hodder and Stoughton, 1991).

Eysenck, S.B.G., H.J. Eysenck, and P. Barrett. (1985). 'A revised version of the psychoticism scale', *Personality and Individual Differences* 6 (1985), pp. 21-29.

Francis, L.J. (1992). 'Is psychoticism really a dimension of personality fundamental to religiosity?' *Personality and Individual Differences* 13 (1992), pp. 645-52.

Francis, L.J. (2005). *Faith and psychology: Personality, religion and the individual* (London: Darton, Longman and Todd, 2005).

Francis, L.J. (2009). 'Psychological type theory and religious and spiritual experience', in M. De Souza, L.J. Francis, J. O'Higgins-Norman, and D.G. Scott (eds.), *International Handbook of education for spirituality, care and wellbeing* (Dordrecht: Springer, 2009), pp. 125-46.

Francis, L.J., and S.H. Jones. (1997). 'Personality and charismatic experience among adult Christians', *Pastoral Psychology* 45 (1997), pp. 421-28.

Francis, L.J., and W.K. Kay. (1995). 'The personality characteristics of Pentecostal ministry candidates', *Personality and Individual Differences* 18 (1995), pp. 61-69.

Francis, L.J., and K. Littler. (2011). 'The Francis-Littler Charismatic Orientation Scale: A study in personality theory among Anglican clergymen', *PentecoStudies*, 10 (2011), pp. 72-86.

Francis, L.J., P.R. Pearson, and W.K. Kay. (1983). 'Are religious children bigger liars?' *Psychological Reports* 52 (1983), pp. 551-54.

Francis, L.J., and M. Robbins. (2003). 'Personality and glossolalia: A study among male Evangelical clergy', *Pastoral Psychology* 51 (2003), pp. 391-96.

Francis, L.J., and T.H. Thomas. (1997). 'Are charismatic ministers less stable? A study among male Anglican clergy', *Review of Religious Research* 39 (1997), pp. 61-69.

Hine, V.H. (1969). 'Pentecostal glossolalia: Towards a functional interpretation', *Journal for the Scientific Study of Religion* 8 (1969), pp. 211-26.

Jones, S.H., L.J. Francis, and C.L. Craig. (2005). 'Charismatic experience and psychological type: An empirical enquiry', *Journal of the European Pentecostal Theological Association* 25 (2005), pp. 39-53.

Jung, C.G. (1971). *Psychological types: The collected works*, volume 6 (London: Routledge and Kegan Paul, 1971).

Keirsey, D., and M. Bates. (1978). *Please understand me* (Del Mar, California: Prometheus Nemesis, 1978).

Kildahl, J.P. (1972). *The psychology of speaking in tongues* (London: Hodder and Stoughton, 1972).

Kildahl, J.P. (1975). 'Psychological observations', in M.P. Hamilton (ed.), *The Charismatic Movement* (Grand Rapids: Eerdmans, 1975), pp. 124-42.

Lapsley, J.N., and J.K. Simpson. (1964). 'Speaking in tongues: Infantile babble or song of the self', *Pastoral Psychology* 15 (1964), pp. 16-24, 48-55.

Louden, S.H., and L.J. Francis. (2001). 'Are Catholic priests in England and Wales attracted to the charismatic movement emotionally less stable?', *British Journal of Theological Education* 11 (2001), pp. 65-76.

Mackie, A. (1921). *The Gift of Tongues* (New York: G. H. Doran, 1921).

Massey, A. (1980). 'The Eysenck Personality Inventory lie scale: Lack of insight or …?' *Irish Journal of Psychology* 4 (1980), pp. 172-74.

Myers, I.B., and M.H. McCaulley. (1985). *Manual: A guide to the development and use of the Myers-Briggs Type Indicator* (Palo Alto, California: Consulting Psychologists Press, 1985).

Neisz, N.L., and E.J. Kronenberger. (1978). 'Self-actualization in glossolalic and non-glossolalic Pentecostals', *Sociological Analysis* 39 (1978), pp. 25-56.

Ness, R.C., and R.M. Wintrob. (1980). 'The emotional impact of fundamentalist religious participation: An empirical study of intragroup variation', *American Journal of Orthopsychiatry* 50 (1980), pp. 302-15.

Oates, W.E. (1967). 'A socio-psychological study of glossolalia', in F. Stagg, E.G. Hinson, and W.E. Oates (eds.), *Glossolalia: tongue speaking in biblical, historical, and psychological perspective* (Nashville, Tennessee: Abingdon Press, pp. 20-44).

Pattison, E.M. (1968). 'Behavioral science research on the nature of glossolalia', *Journal of American Scientific Affiliation* 20 (1968), pp. 73-86.

Robbins, M., J. Hair, and L.J. Francis. (1999). 'Personality and attraction to the charismatic movement: A study among Anglican clergy', *Journal of Beliefs and Values* 20 (1999), pp. 239-46.

Samarin, W.J. (1959). 'Glossolalia as learned behaviour', *Canadian Journal of Theology* 15 (1959), pp. 60-64.

Samarin, W.J. (1973). 'Glossolalia as regressive speech', *Language and Speech* 16 (1973), pp. 77-79.

Smith, D.S., and J.R. Fleck. (1981). 'Personality correlates of conventional and unconventional glossolalia', *Journal of Social Psychology* 114 (1981), 209-17.

Spandos, N.P., W.P. Cross, M. Lepage, and M. Coristine. (1986). 'Glossolalia as learned behavior: An experimental demonstration', *Journal of Abnormal Psychology* 95 (1986), pp. 21-23.

Tappeiner, D.A. (1974). 'The function of tongue-speaking for the individual: A psycho-theological model', *Journal of American Scientific Affiliation* 26 (1974), pp. 29-32.

Vivier, L.M. (1960). 'Glossolalia' (Doctoral dissertation: Department of Psychiatry, University of Witwatersrand, 1960).

Williams, C.G. (1981). *Tongues of the Spirit: A study of Pentecostal glossolalia and related phenomena* (Cardiff: University of Wales Press, 1981).

11

Psychological Temperament, Psychological Type, and Attraction to the Charismatic Movement: An Empirical Study among Anglican Clergy in England

Leslie J Francis,[*] Andrew Village,[**]
and David Voas[***]

Introduction

The Church of England occupies a distinctive place within Reformation history in a way that enabled this evolving Church to continue to embrace features both of the Catholic tradition and of the Reformed tradition. The roots of these two traditions re-emerged clearly during the early nineteenth century, with the Reformed tradition finding expression in the Evangelical wing of the Church of England (Saward, 1987; Hylson-Smith, 1989) and with the Catholic tradition finding expression in the Tractarian Movement and in the

[*] Leslie J. Francis (PhD, ScD, University of Cambridge; DD, University of Oxford; DLitt, University of Wales, Bangor) is Professor of Religions and Education at the University of Warwick, in Warwick, England, UK.

[**] Andrew Village (PhD, University of Edinburgh; PhD, University of Bristol) is Professor of Practical and Empirical Theology at York St John University in York, England, UK.

[***] David Voas (PhD, University of Cambridge) is Professor of Social Science and Head of Department at University College, London, UK.

Anglo-Catholic wing of the Church of England (Penhale, 1986; Hylson-Smith, 1993; Nockles, 1994). While these differences can be explored in historical terms and in theological terms, they can also be explored in psychological terms as demonstrated by Francis and Thomas (1997), Randall (2005), and Francis and Littler (2012).

The emergence of the Charismatic Movement added a further dimension to the rich texture of the Church of England and to the diversity experienced among the Anglican clergy. It is precisely here that the research interest pioneered by William K. Kay, drawing on psychological theories to illuminate charismatic experience, helps to focus the research question concerning the extent to which fundamental differences in personality may pre-dispose some Anglican clergy more than others to be attracted to the Charismatic Movement.

Kay's early research on the connection between personality and charismatic experience, as represented by Francis and Kay (1995), drew on the three-dimensional model of personality proposed by Eysenck and Eysenck (1975). This model argues that individual differences in personality can be most adequately and economically summarised in terms of the three orthogonal dimensions characterised by their high scoring pole as extraversion, neuroticism, and psychoticism. The core finding to emerge from Kay's original work using the Eysenckian dimensional model of personality linked charismatic experience with emotional stability (low neuroticism scores). Taking his research interest in the psychology of charismatic experience further, in his more recent work Kay has drawn on psychological type theory, as represented by Kay and Francis (2008), Kay, Francis, and Craig (2008), Kay, Francis, and Robbins (2011), and Robbins and Kay (2015).

Psychological type theory

The basic building blocks of psychological type theory as originally proposed by Jung (1971) and as developed and operationalised by the Myers-Briggs Type Indicator (Myers and McCaulley, 1985) distinguish between two orientations (extraversion and introversion), two perceiving functions (sensing and intuition), two judging functions (thinking and feeling), and two attitudes toward the outer world (judging and perceiving).

The two orientations are concerned with where energy is drawn from; energy can be gathered either from the outside world or from the inner world. Extraverts (E) are orientated toward the outside world; they are energised by the events and people around them. They enjoy communicating and thrive in stimulating and exciting environments. They prefer to act in a situation rather than reflect on it. They may vocalise a problem or an idea, rather than think it through privately. They may be drained by silence and solitude. They tend to focus their attention upon what is happening outside themselves. They are usually open individuals, easy to get to know, and enjoy having many friends. In contrast, introverts (I) are orientated toward their inner world; they are energised by their inner ideas and concepts. They may feel drained by events and people around them. They prefer to reflect on a situation rather than act in it. They enjoy solitude, silence, and contemplation, as they tend to focus their attention on what is happening in their inner life. They may appear reserved and detached, and they may prefer to have a small circle of intimate friends rather than many acquaintances.

The perceiving functions are concerned with the way in which people receive and process information; this can be done through use of sensing or through use of intuition. Sensing types (S) tend to focus on specific details, rather than the overall picture. They are concerned with the actual, the real, and the practical and tend to be down-to-earth and matter-of-fact. They may feel that particular details are more significant than general patterns. They are frequently fond of the traditional and conventional. They may be conservative and tend to prefer what is known and well-established. In contrast, intuitive types (N) focus on the possibilities of a situation, perceiving meanings and relationships. They may feel that perception by the senses is not as valuable as information gained from the unconscious mind; indirect associations and concepts impact their perceptions. They focus on the overall picture, rather than specific facts and data. They follow their inspirations enthusiastically, but not always realistically. They can appear to be up in the air and may be seen as idealistic dreamers. They often aspire to bring innovative change to established conventions.

The judging functions are concerned with the way in which people make decisions and judgements; this can be done through use of objective impersonal logic or subjective interpersonal values. Thinking types (T) make judgements based on objective, impersonal logic. They value integrity and justice. They are known for their truthfulness and for their desire for fairness. They consider conforming to principles to be of more importance than cultivating harmony. They are often good at making difficult decisions as they are able to analyse problems in order to reach an unbiased and reasonable solution. They may consider it to be more important to be honest and correct than to be tactful, when working with others. In contrast, feeling types (F) make judgements based on subjective, personal values. They value compassion and mercy. They are known for their tactfulness and for their desire for peace. They are more concerned to promote harmony, than to adhere to abstract principles. They are able to take into account other people's feelings and values in decision-making and problem-solving, ensuring they reach a solution that satisfies everyone. They are often thought of as 'warm-hearted'. They may find it difficult to criticise others, even when it is necessary. They find it easy to empathise with other people and tend to be trusting and encouraging of others.

The attitudes towards the outside world are concerned with the way in which people respond to the world around them, either by imposing structure and order on that world or by remaining open and adaptable to the world around them. Judging types (J) have a planned, orderly approach to life. They enjoy routine and established patterns. They prefer to follow schedules in order to reach an established goal and may make use of lists, timetables, or diaries. They tend to be punctual, organised, and tidy. They may find it difficult to deal with unexpected disruptions of their plans. Likewise, they are inclined to be resistant to changes to established methods. They prefer to make decisions quickly and to stick to their conclusions once made. In contrast, perceiving types (P) have a flexible, open-ended approach to life. They enjoy change and spontaneity. They prefer to leave projects open in order to adapt and improve them. They may find plans and schedules restrictive and tend to be easy-going about issues such as punctuality, deadlines, and tidiness. Indeed, they may consider last minute pressure to be a necessary motivation in order to complete projects. They are often good at dealing with the unexpected. Indeed, they may welcome change and variety as routine bores them. Their behaviour may often seem impulsive and unplanned.

Psychological type data can be reported and interpreted in a number of different ways, drawing on the four dichotomous type preferences (the two orientations, the two perceiving functions, the two judging functions, and the two attitudes), on the 16 complete types (like ISTJ or ENFP), on the four dominant types (dominant sensing, dominant intuition, dominant feeling, or dominant thinking) or on the eight dominant and auxiliary pairs (like dominant thinking with auxiliary intuition, or dominant intuition with auxiliary thinking).

Psychological temperament theory

Drawing on the basic building blocks of psychological type theory, Keirsey and Bates (1978) distinguished between four temperaments characterised as SJ, SP, NT and NF. In the language shaped by Keirsey and Bates (1978) the Epimethean Temperament characterises the SJ profile, people who long to be dutiful and exist primarily to be useful to the social units to which they belong. The Dionysian Temperament characterises the SP profile, people who want to be engaged, involved, and doing something new. The Promethean Temperament characterises the NT profile, people who want to understand, explain, shape, and predict realties, and who prize their personal competence. The Apollonian Temperament characterises the NF profile, people who quest for authenticity and for self-actualisation, who are idealistic and who have great capacity for empathic listening. Keirsey and Bates'(1978) notion of temperament theory was brought to the forefront of clergy studies by Oswald and Kroeger (1988) who built on the characterisation of the four temperaments to create profiles of how these four temperaments may shape four very different styles of religious leadership.

The Epimethean Temperament (SJ) is styled 'the conserving, serving pastor'. SJ clergy tend to be the most traditional of all clergy temperaments, bringing stability and continuity in whatever situation they are called to serve. They proclaim a simple and straightforward faith, committed to down-to-earth rules for the Christian life. They serve as protectors and conservers of the traditions inherited from the past. If change is to take place, it emerges by evolution, not revolution. They excel at building community, fostering a sense of loyalty and belonging. They bring order and stability to their congregations, creating plans, developing procedures, and formulating policies; and they are keen that these procedures should be followed. They can be trusted for their reliability, punctuality, and efficiency. They are effective pastors, showing particular concern for the young, the elderly, and the weak. They are realists who offer practical and down-to-earth solutions to pastoral problems.

The Dionysian Temperament (SP) is styled 'the action-oriented pastor'. SP clergy tend to be the most fun loving of all clergy temperaments, possessing a compulsive need to be engaged in activity. They have little need for or interest in the abstract, the theoretical, and the non-practical aspects of theology and church life. They are flexible and spontaneous people who welcome the unplanned and unpredictable aspects of church life. They can bring the church to life with activities for everyone from cradle to grave. They have a flare for grasping the moment. They are entertainers and performers at heart. They are at their best in a crisis and are good at handling conflict resolution. They are fun loving and enjoy working with children and young people. They are better at starting initiatives than at seeing things through. SP clergy may be particularly attracted to charismatic worship, responding to the leading of the Holy Spirit, welcoming a free-flowing form that allows for impromptu testimonials, speaking in tongues, and spontaneous singing.

The Promethean Temperament (NT) is styled 'the intellectual, competence-seeking pastor'. NT clergy are the most academically and intellectually grounded of all clergy temperaments, motivated by the search for meaning for truth and for possibilities. They are visionaries who need to excel in all they do, and they tend to push their congregations to excel as well. They enjoy the academic study and analysis of the faith and may try to run their church as an extension of the seminary. They make great teachers, preachers, and advocates for social justice. They look for underlying principles rather than basic applications from their study of scripture. They see the value of opposing views and strive to allow alternative visions to be heard. They are more concerned with finding truth than with engineering harmony and compromise. NT clergy need to be challenged in their ministry and to be able to move from one challenge to the next.

The Apollonian Temperament (NF) is styled 'the authenticity-seeking, relationship-oriented pastor'. NF clergy tend to be the most idealistic and romantic of all clergy temperaments, attracted to helping roles that deal with human suffering. They want to meet the needs of others and to find personal affirmation in so doing. They can be articulate and inspiring communicators, committed to influencing others by touching their hearts. They have good empathic capacity, interpersonal skills, and pastoral counselling techniques. They find themselves listening to other people's problems in the most unlikely contexts, and really caring about them. NF clergy tend to be high on inspiration, but lower on the practical down-to-earth aspects of ministry. They are able to draw the best out of people and work well as the catalyst or facilitator in the congregation as long as others are on hand to work with and to implement their vision. They are at their best when leading in people-related projects, such as starting a project for the elderly or for youth. They are most comfortable in unstructured meetings where they are good at facilitating group decision-making processes.

The strength of Oswald and Kroeger's work (1988) resides in the careful and thoughtful extrapolation from the basic conceptualisations of temperament theory. Careful empirical research is still needed to test and to validate the details of such extrapolation.

Psychological type and charismatic experience

The connection between psychological type and charismatic experience has been explored by three bodies of research, although as yet none of these bodies of research has drawn specifically on temperament theory.

The first body of research to explore the connection between psychological type theory and charismatic experience has concentrated on discussing the psychological type profile of groups identified with Charismatic or Pentecostal traditions. William K. Kay has contributed four studies of this kind. In the first study, Kay and Francis (2008) reported on the psychological type profile of 122 female students attending a Pentecostal Bible College in England. In the second study, Kay, Francis, and Craig (2008) reported on the type profile of 190 male students attending the Assemblies of God Bible College in England. In the third study, Kay, Francis, and Robbins (2011) reported on the type profile of 164 male leaders connected with twelve apostolic networks of churches in the UK. In the fourth study, Robbins and Kay (2015) reported on the type profile of 117 pastors who lead Pentecostal churches in Singapore (59% male and 41% female).

The strength of this body of research is that it allows these specific groups to be set alongside the profiles of participants within other Christian traditions. It remains problematic, however, to construct a unified picture of Pentecostal and charismatic groups from such disparate studies given the diversity of these four samples, in terms of sex (male and female), experience (students and established leaders), and culture (the UK and Singapore).

The second body of research to explore the connection between psychological type theory and charismatic experience employed scales of charismatic orientation and correlated scale scores with psychological type preferences. In the first study of this series, Francis and Jones (1997) drew on the data provided by 368 committed Christian adults to examine mean scores recorded on a five-item index of charismatic experience according to the four binary distinctions proposed by type theory. In the second study of this series, Francis, Littler, and Robbins (see chapter 10 above) drew on the data provided by 231 Anglican clergymen in Wales to examine mean scores recorded on a 21-item Index of Charismatic Orientation according to the four binary distinctions proposed by type theory and according to the eight dominant-auxiliary pairs. The two studies confirm the value of the approach although it may be contentious to compare the findings too closely, given the differences both in the samples studied and in the way in which charismatic experience has been operationalised differently in the two measures employed.

A third approach to exploring the connection between psychological type theory and charismatic experience was employed by Jones, Francis, and Craig (2005). Drawing on data provided by 925 Christian adults, they divided the sample into three groups: 450 were clear that they had been influenced by the charismatic movement, 366 were clear that they had not been influenced by the charismatic movement, and the remaining 109 were not certain. The analytic strategy compared the psychological type profile of the 450 participants clearly defined charismatics with the 366 participants clearly defined non-charismatics. Six main aspects of these data were of particular interest. First, the charismatic sample contains a significantly higher proportion of extraverts, compared with the non-charismatic sample. Thus, 50% of the charismatics express a preference for extraversion, in comparison with 39% of the non-charismatics. Second, there is no significant difference in the proportions of sensing types and intuitive types in the two samples. Thus, 58% of the charismatics express a preference for sensing and so do 59% of the non-charismatics. Third, the charismatic sample contains a significantly higher proportion of thinking types compared with the non-charismatic sample. Thus, 39% of the charismatics express a preference for thinking, compared with 31% of the non-charismatics. Fourth, the charismatic sample contains a significantly higher proportion of perceiving types compared with the non-charismatic sample. Thus, 35% of the charismatics express a preference for perceiving, compared with 28% of the non-charismatics. Fifth, there is a significantly higher proportion of dominant thinkers among the charismatic sample (20%), compared with the non-charismatic sample (12%). Sixth, when the type distributions of the two samples are compared, among the charismatic sample there is a significant over-representation of ESTJ and a significant under-representation of ISFJ.

Research question

Against this background, the aim of the present study is to draw on the unique source of data provided by the Church Growth Research Project, as reported by Voas and Watt (2014), in order to replicate the research method employed by Jones, Francis, and Craig (2005) among a sample of stipendiary Anglican clergy serving in the Church of England. This approach will be employed to explore the significant differences between those clergy who are attracted to the Charismatic Movement and those clergy who are not attracted to the Charismatic Movement. These comparisons will be drawn in light both of psychological type theory and of psychological temperament theory.

Method

Procedure
The data used in this study came from a large online survey administered between April and July 2013 as part of the Church of England's Church Growth Research Programme. Invitations to participate in the survey were sent by email to clergy (mostly with incumbent status) within a large sample of parishes. More detail regarding the sample and overall study can be found in Voas and Watt (2014).

Participants

The present analysis is based on the 1,387 participants who provided full data on the measure of psychological type, who completed the measure of charismatic attraction, who were engaged in stipendiary ministry, and who were not over the age of seventy. The sample comprised 1,107 clergymen and 280 clergywomen, of whom 92 were under the age of forty, 314 were in their forties, 624 were in their fifties, and 357 were aged between sixty and seventy.

Measures

Psychological type was assessed by the Francis Psychological Type Scales (FPTS: Francis, 2005). This is a 40-item instrument comprising four sets of 10 forced-choice items relating to each of the four components of psychological type: the two orientations (extraversion and introversion), the two perceiving functions (sensing and intuition), the two judging functions (thinking and feeling), and the two attitudes toward the outer world (judging and perceiving). Participants were asked for each pair of characteristics to check 'the box next to that characteristic, which is closer to the real you, even if you feel both characteristics apply to you. Tick the characteristic that reflects the real you, even if other people see you differently'.

Charismatic attraction was assessed by a seven-point semantic differential grid anchored by the poles: charismatic and non-charismatic. Following earlier practice (Village and Francis, 2009) this seven-point scale was dichotomised, classifying the two points at the charismatic end as indicative of clear attraction to the Charismatic Movement.

Data analysis

According to the classification proposed by dichotomising the scores recorded on the semantic grid, 326 of the participants were classified as attracted to the Charismatic Movement, and the remaining 1,061 participants were classified as not attracted to the Charismatic Movement. Separate type tables were constructed for these two groups. Within the scientific literature concerned with analysing and presenting psychological type data, the distinctive type tables provide information about the 16 complete types, about the four dichotomous preferences, about the six sets of pairs and temperaments, about the dominant types, and about the introverted and extraverted Jungian types. Commentary on this table will, however, be restricted to those aspects of the data strictly relevant to the research question. In the context of type tables, the statistical significance of the difference between two groups is established by means of the selection ratio index (*I*), an extension of chi-square (McCaulley, 1985).

Results

Table 1 presents the psychological type profile of the 1,061 clergy not attracted to the Charismatic Movement. In terms of dichotomous type preferences these clergy display a clear preference for introversion (59%) over extraversion (41%), a mild preference for intuition (53%) over sensing (47%), a clear preference for feeling (60%) over thinking (40%), and a strong preference for judging (77%) over perceiving (23%). In terms of dominant type preferences, 32% reported dominant intuition, 29% dominant sensing, 25% dominant feeling, and 14% dominant thinking. In terms of temperament theory, 41% reported SJ preference, 32% NF preference, 21% NT preference, and 6% SP preference. In terms of the sixteen complete types, the most frequently occurring type was ISFJ (15%).

TABLE 1

Type distribution for Anglican clergy not attracted to the Charismatic Movement

The Sixteen Complete Types				Dichotomous Preferences		
ISTJ	ISFJ	INFJ	INTJ	E	n = 435	(41.0%)
n = 118	n = 163	n = 119	n = 114	I	n = 626	(59.0%)
(11.1%)	(15.4%)	(11.2%)	(10.7%)			
+++++	+++++	+++++	+++++	S	n = 498	(46.9%)
+++++	+++++	+++++	+++++	N	n = 563	(53.1%)
+	+++++	+	+			
				T	n = 422	(39.8%)
				F	n = 639	(60.2%)
				J	n = 815	(76.8%)
				P	n = 246	(23.2%)
ISTP	ISFP	INFP	INTP	**Pairs and Temperaments**		
n = 8	n = 26	n = 58	n = 20	IJ	n = 514	(48.4%)
(0.8%)	(2.5%)	(5.5%)	(1.9%)	IP	n = 112	(10.6%)
+	+++	+++++	++	EP	n = 134	(12.6%)
		+		EJ	n = 301	(28.4%)
				ST	n = 201	(18.9%)
				SF	n = 297	(28.0%)
				NF	n = 342	(32.2%)
ESTP	ESFP	ENFP	ENTP	NT	n = 221	(20.8%)
n = 10	n = 18	n = 78	n = 28			
(0.9%)	(1.7%)	(7.4%)	(2.6%)	SJ	n = 436	(41.1%)
+	++	+++++	+++	SP	n = 62	(5.8%)
		++		NP	n = 184	(17.3%)
				NJ	n = 379	(35.7%)
				TJ	n = 356	(33.6%)
				TP	n = 66	(6.2%)
				FP	n = 180	(17.0%)
				FJ	n = 459	(43.3%)
ESTJ	ESFJ	ENFJ	ENTJ	IN	n = 311	(29.3%)
n = 65	n = 90	n = 87	n = 59	EN	n = 252	(23.8%)
(6.1%)	(8.5%)	(8.2%)	(5.6%)	IS	n = 315	(29.7%)
+++++	+++++	+++++	+++++	ES	n = 183	(17.2%)
+	++++	+++	+			
				ET	n = 162	(15.3%)
				EF	n = 273	(25.7%)
				IF	n = 366	(34.5%)
				IT	n = 260	(24.5%)

Jungian Types (E)			Jungian Types (I)			Dominant Types		
	n	%		n	%		n	%
E-TJ	124	11.7	I-TP	28	2.6	Dt.T	152	14.3
E-FJ	177	16.7	I-FP	84	7.9	Dt.F	261	24.6
ES-P	28	2.6	IS-J	281	26.5	Dt.S	309	2.1
EN-P	106	10.0	IN-J	233	22.0	Dt.N	339	32.0

Note: N = 1,061 (NB: + = 1% of N)

TABLE 2

Type distribution for Anglican clergy attracted to the Charismatic Movement, compared with those not attracted to the Charismatic Movement

The Sixteen Complete Types

ISTJ	ISFJ	INFJ	INTJ
n = 23	*n* = 28	*n* = 30	*n* = 31
(7.1%)	(8.6%)	(9.2%)	(9.5%)
I = 0.63*	*I* = 0.56**	*I* = 0.82	*I* = 0.89
+++++	+++++	+++++	+++++
++	++++	++++	+++++

ISTP	ISFP	INFP	INTP
n = 2	*n* = 6	*n* = 13	*n* = 14
(0.6%)	(1.8%)	(4.0%)	(4.3%)
I = 0.81	*I* = 0.75	*I* = 0.73	*I* = 2.28*
+	++	++++	++++

ESTP	ESFP	ENFP	ENTP
n = 4	*n* = 8	*n* = 31	*n* = 17
(1.2%)	(2.5%)	(9.5%)	(5.2%)
I = 1.30	*I* = 1.45	*I* = 1.29	*I* = 1.98*
+	+++	+++++	+++++
		+++++	

ESTJ	ESFJ	ENFJ	ENTJ
n = 19	*n* = 32	*n* = 36	*n* = 32
(5.8%)	(9.8%)	(11.0%)	(9.8%)
I = 0.95	*I* = 1.16	*I* = 1.35	*I* = 1.77**
+++++	+++++	+++++	+++++
+	+++++	+++++	+++++
		+	

Dichotomous Preferences

E	*n* = 179	(54.9%) *I* = 1.34***
I	*n* = 147	(45.1%) *I* = 0.76***
S	*n* = 122	(37.4%) *I* = 0.80**
N	*n* = 204	(62.6%) *I* = 1.18**
T	*n* = 142	(43.6%) *I* = 1.10
F	*n* = 184	(56.4%) *I* = 0.94
J	*n* = 231	(70.9%) *I* = 0.92*
P	*n* = 95	(29.1%) *I* = 1.26*

Pairs and Temperaments

IJ	*n* = 112	(34.4%) *I* = 0.71***
IP	*n* = 35	(10.7%) *I* = 1.02
EP	*n* = 60	(18.4%) *I* = 1.46**
EJ	*n* = 119	(36.5%) *I* = 1.29**
ST	*n* = 48	(14.7%) *I* = 0.78
SF	*n* = 74	(22.7%) *I* = 0.81
NF	*n* = 110	(33.7%) *I* = 1.05
NT	*n* = 94	(28.8%) *I* = 1.38**
SJ	*n* = 102	(31.3%) *I* = 0.76***
SP	*n* = 20	(6.1%) *I* = 1.05
NP	*n* = 75	(23.0%) *I* = 1.33*
NJ	*n* = 129	(39.6%) *I* = 1.11
TJ	*n* = 105	(32.2%) *I* = 0.96
TP	*n* = 37	(11.3%) *I* = 1.82**
FP	*n* = 58	(17.8%) *I* = 1.05
FJ	*n* = 126	(38.7%) *I* = 0.89
IN	*n* = 88	(27.0%) *I* = 0.92
EN	*n* = 116	(35.6%) *I* = 1.50***
IS	*n* = 59	(18.1%) *I* = 0.61***
ES	*n* = 63	(19.3%) *I* = 1.12
ET	*n* = 72	(22.1%) *I* = 1.45**
EF	*n* = 107	(32.8%) *I* = 1.28*
IF	*n* = 77	(23.6%) *I* = 0.68***
IT	*n* = 70	(21.5%) *I* = 0.88

Jungian Types (E)

	n	%	*Index*
E-TJ	51	15.6	1.34
E-FJ	68	20.9	1.25
ES-P	12	3.7	1.39
EN-P	48	14.7	1.47*

Jungian Types (I)

	n	%	*Index*
I-TP	16	4.9	1.86*
I-FP	19	5.8	0.74
IS-J	51	15.6	0.59***
IN-J	61	18.7	0.85

Dominant Types

	n	%	*Index*
Dt.T	67	20.6	1.43**
Dt.F	87	26.7	1.08
Dt.S	63	19.3	0.66***
Dt.N	109	33.4	1.05

Note: *N* = 1,061 (NB: + = 1% of *N*)   *p < .05, **p < .01, ***p < .001

Table 2 presents the psychological type profile of the 326 clergy attracted to the Charismatic Movement. In terms of dichotomous type preferences, these clergy display a clear preference for extraversion (55%) over introversion (45%), a clear preference for intuition (63%) over sensing (37%), a clear preference for feeling (56%) over thinking (44%), and a strong preference for judging (71%) over perceiving (29%). In terms of dominant type preferences, 33% reported dominant intuition, 27% dominant feeling, 21% dominant thinking, and 19% dominant sensing. In terms of temperament theory, 34% reported NF preference, 31% SJ preference, 29 NT preference, and 6% SP preference. In terms of the sixteen complete types, the most frequently occurring type was ENFJ (11%).

Table 2 also draws attention to the statistically significant differences between the profile of clergy attracted to the Charismatic Movement and the profile of clergy reported in table 1 not attracted to the Charismatic Movement. In terms of dichotomous preference, clergy attracted to the Charismatic Movement are more inclined to prefer extraversion (55% compared with 41%), more inclined to prefer intuition (63% compared with 53%), and more inclined to prefer perceiving (29% compared with 23%), although there are no significant differences in terms of preferences between thinking and feeling. In terms of dominant type preferences, clergy attracted to the Charismatic Movement are more inclined to prefer dominant thinking (21% compared with 14%) and less inclined to prefer dominant sensing (19% compared with 29%). In terms of temperament theory, clergy attracted to the Charismatic Movement are more inclined to report NT preference (29% compared with 21%) and less inclined to report SJ preference (31% compared with 41%). In terms of the sixteen complete types, among clergy attracted to the Charismatic Movement there is greater representation of ENTJ (10% compared with 6%) and lesser representation of ISFJ (9% compared with 15%).

Conclusion

This study set out to build on a body of research concerned with exploring the connection between charismatic experience and personality theory as shaped by the models of individual differences proposed by psychological type theory (Myers and McCaulley, 1985) and by psychological temperament theory (Keirsey and Bates, 1978). This body of research, stimulated and nurtured by William K. Kay's interest in the psychology of Charismatic and Pentecostal experience, had followed three main trajectories: studies reporting on the psychological type profile of Charismatic or Pentecostal groups (Kay and Francis, 2008; Kay, Francis, and Craig, 2008; Kay, Francis, and Robbins, 2011; Robbins and Kay, 2015), studies correlating scores on indices of charismatic experience or charismatic orientation with psychological type profile (Francis and Jones, 1997; Francis, Littler, and Robbins, see chapter 10 above); and one study comparing the profiles of two groups within one survey, namely Charismatic participants in the survey and non-Charismatic participants in the survey (Jones, Francis, and Craig, 2005).

The present study extended this body of research in two ways: by replicating the approach pioneered by Jones, Francis, and Craig (2005) and extending this approach to a study among Anglican clergy, and by broadening the theoretical framework from psychological type theory to embrace psychological temperament theory. This development of previous research was facilitated by drawing on the unique database assembled by the Church Growth Research project (Voas and Watt, 2014), selecting from this database 1,387 clergy engaged in stipendiary ministry who were not over the age of seventy, who had provided full data on the measure of psychological type, and who had completed the measure of charismatic attraction. Four main conclusions emerged from comparing the profiles of 326 clergy who were attracted to the Charismatic Movement and 1,061 clergy who were not.

The first conclusion concerns the insights into charismatic experience generated by considering the four components of psychological type theory individually. This perspective indicates that among Anglican clergy attraction to the Charismatic Movement is associated with extraversion (rather than introversion), with intuition (rather than sensing), and with perceiving (rather than judging). Within the framework of Anglican ministry within the Church of England, charismatic congregations are more likely to be led by socially outgoing clergy who are energised by engagement with the outer world of people and events (characteristics of extraversion). They are more likely to be led by clergy who are interested in and engaged with exploring new possibilities and new opportunities in church life (characteristics of intuition). They are more likely to be led by clergy who display an open, flexible and spontaneous approach to life lived in the external world (characteristics of perceiving). Looking at the four components of psychological type theory individually fails to implicate the judging process (thinking and feeling) in the defining distinctiveness of attraction to the Charismatic Movement among Anglican clergy.

The second conclusion concerns the insights into charismatic experience generated by considering the four dominant psychological type functions. Consideration of the dominant functions brings an added clarity of perspective by focusing attention on the key function that shapes the individual personality. This perspective indicates that attraction to the Charismatic Movement is positively associated with dominant thinking and negatively associated with dominant sensing. Within the framework of Anglican ministry with the Church of England, charismatic congregations are more likely than non-charismatic congregations to be led by dominant thinking type clergy and less likely to be led by dominant sensing type clergy. This difference in dominant type profile has implications for the style of leadership within charismatic congregations. These congregations are more likely than other congregations to be led by clergy who appear to be strongly analytical and driven by attachment to theological principles. In dealing with conflicts and problems in church life they are likely to place more weight on matters of objectivity, truth and justice (characteristics of the thinking preference) than matters of interpersonal relations, harmony and peace (characteristics of the feeling preference). These congregations are less likely than other congregations to be led by clergy who appear to be strongly practical and driven by attachment to detail. In dealing with church policy and programme, they are less likely to keep a tight grasp on matters of practical concern.

The third conclusion concerns the additional insights into charismatic experience generated by considering the four psychological temperaments. Consideration of temperament theory brings an added texture into play in understanding the dynamics of church leadership, drawing on the insights of Oswald and Kroeger (1988). This perspective indicates that attraction to the Charismatic Movement is positively associated with the Promethean Temperament (NT) and negatively associated with the Epimethean Temperament (SJ). While the theory discussed in the introduction suggested that the Dionysian Temperament (SP) might be especially attracted to the

Charismatic Movement, the data found no significant difference in the proportions of Dionysian clergy leading charismatic congregations and leading non-charismatic congregations. Since within the overall sample only 6% of clergy reported preference for the Dionysian Temperament, it emerged that this style is not well represented among the current generation of Anglican clergy.

Within the framework of Anglican ministry within the Church of England, charismatic congregations are more likely than non-charismatic congregations to be led by Promethean clergy and less likely to be led by Epimethean clergy. This, too, has implications for the style of leadership within charismatic congregations. Promethean clergy, who are more in evidence leading charismatic congregations, are the visionary leaders who need to excel in all they do, and who tend to push their congregations to excel as well. Epimethean clergy, who are less in evidence leading charismatic congregations, are the leaders who are cautious about change and innovation. Such contrasting emphases in leadership styles may suggest grounds for hypothesising distinctive growth patterns in charismatic congregations, but also vulnerabilities to disruption and to unsettling patterns of change.

The fourth conclusion concerns the insights into charismatic experiences generated by considering the sixteen complete types. This perspective indicates that there is a greater representation of ENTJ clergy among those attracted to the Charismatic Movement and a lower representation of ISFJ clergy. The significance of these complete psychological types for style of leadership is well captured by the type vignettes published by Myers (1998, p. 7). Here Myers describes the ENTJ profile as:

> Frank, decisive leaders in activities. Develop and implement comprehensive systems designed to solve organisational problems. Good in anything that requires reasoning and intelligent talk, such as public speaking. Are usually well informed and enjoy adding to their fund of knowledge.

By way of contrast Myers describes the ISFJ profile as:

> Quiet, friendly, responsible and conscientious. Work devotedly to meet their obligations. Lend stability to any project or group. Thorough, painstaking, accurate. Their interests are usually not technical. Can be patient with necessary details. Loyal, considerate, perceptive, concerned with how other people feel.

By replicating the methodology employed by Jones, Francis, and Craig (2005) the present study is able to engage in direct dialogue with the findings of that earlier study. In terms of four dichotomous preferences, both studies reported significant connections between charismatic experience and both extraversion and perceiving. The two studies do not agree, however, on the other two dichotomous components of type theory. In terms of dominant type preferences, both studies reported among the charismatic group higher proportions of dominant thinking types and lower proportions of dominant sensing types. In terms of psychological temperament theory, both studies found a higher proportion of Promethean Temperament (NT) among the charismatic group. In terms of the sixteen complete types, both studies found among the charismatic group greater representation of ENTJs or ESTJs and lower representation of ISFJs.

While the present study was conducted among 1,387 Anglican stipendiary clergy, the earlier study reported by Jones, Francis, and Craig (2005) was conducted among 925 Christian adults attending workshops on personality and spirituality. The difference in the findings between these two studies may also reflect some key difference in the psychological type profiles of Anglican clergy (Francis, Craig, Whinney, Tilley, and Slater, 2007) and Anglican congregations (Francis, Robbins, and Craig, 2011). Given the potential implications of the conclusions drawn from the present study for understanding the distinctive leadership models preferred by Anglican clergy who lead charismatic organisations, there would be advantages in replicating the current analyses among other samples of Anglican clergy.

REFERENCES

Eysenck, H.J., and S.B.G. Eysenck. (1975). *Manual of the Eysenck Personality Questionnaire (adult and junior)* (London: Hodder and Stoughton, 1975).

Francis, L.J. (2005). *Faith and psychology: Personality, religion and the individual* (London: Darton, Longman and Todd, 2005).

Francis, L.J., C.L. Craig, M. Whinney, D. Tilley, and P. Slater. (2007). 'Psychological profiling of Anglican clergy in England: Employing Jungian typology to interpret diversity, strengths, and potential weaknesses in ministry', *International Journal of Practical Theology* 11 (2007), pp. 266-84. doi.org/10.1515/IJPT.2007.17

Francis, L.J., and S.H. Jones. (1997). 'Personality and charismatic experience among adult Christians', *Pastoral Psychology* 45 (1997), pp. 421-28. doi.org/10.1007/BF02310642

Francis, L.J., and W.K. Kay. (1995). 'The personality characteristics of Pentecostal ministry candidates', *Personality and Individual Differences* 18 (1995), pp. 61-69. doi.org/10.1016/0191-8869(94)00210-j

Francis, L.J., and K. Littler. (2012). 'Churchmanship and personality among clergymen in the Church in Wales: are Anglo-Catholic priests more feminine?' *Journal of Empirical Theology* 25 (2012), pp. 236-45.

Francis, L.J., K. Littler, and M. Robbins. (2021). 'Personality and charismatic orientation: An empirical study in psychological type theory', in Andrew Davies and Anne E. Dyer (eds.), *The Spirit and Society: Essays in Honour of William K. Kay* (Cleveland, TN: CPT Press 2021), pp. 155-86.

Francis, L.J., M. Robbins, and C.L. Craig. (2011). 'The psychological type profile of Anglican churchgoers in England: Compatible or incompatible with their clergy?' *International Journal of Practical Theology* 15 (2011), pp. 243-59. doi.org/10.1515/IJPT.2011.036

Francis, L.J., and T.H. Thomas. (1997). 'Are charismatic ministers less stable? A study among male Anglican clergy', *Review of Religious Research* 39 (1997), pp. 61-69. doi.org/10.2307/3512479

Hylson-Smith, K. (1989). *Evangelicals in the Church of England 1734-1984* (Edinburgh: T & T Clark, 1989).

Hylson-Smith, K. (1993). *High churchmanship in the Church of England from the sixteenth century to the late twentieth century* (Edinburgh: T & T Clark, 1993).

Jones, S.H., L.J. Francis, and C.L. Craig. (2005). 'Charismatic experience and psychological type: An empirical enquiry', *Journal of the European Pentecostal Theological Association* 25 (2005), pp. 39-53. doi.org/10.1179/jep.2005.25.1.004

Jung, C.G. (1971). *Psychological types: The collected works* (volume 6) (London: Routledge and Kegan Paul, 1971).

Kay, W.K., and L.J. Francis. (2008). 'Psychological type preferences of female Bible College students in England', *Journal of Beliefs and Values* 29 (2008), pp. 101-105. doi.org/10.1080/13617670801928324

Kay, W.K., L.J. Francis, and C.L. Craig. (2008). 'Psychological type preferences of male British Assemblies of God Bible College students: Tough minded or tender hearted?' *Journal of the European Pentecostal Theological Association* 28 (2008), pp. 6-20. doi.org/10.1179/jep.2008.28.1.002

Kay W.K., L.J. Francis, and M. Robbins. (2011). 'A distinctive leadership for a distinctive network of churches? Psychological type theory and the Apostolic Networks', *Journal of Pentecostal Theology* 20 (2011), pp. 306-22. doi.org/10.1163/174552511X597170

Keirsey, D., and M. Bates. (1978). *Please understand me* (Del Mar, CA: Prometheus Nemesis, 1978).

McCaulley, M.H. (1985). 'The Selection Ratio Type Table: A research strategy for comparing type distributions', *Journal of Psychological Type* 10 (1985), pp. 46-56.

Myers, I.B. (1998). *Introduction to type: A guide to understanding your results on the Myers-Briggs Type Indicator* (fifth edition, European English version; Oxford: Oxford Psychologists Press (1998).

Myers, I.B., and M.H. McCaulley. (1985). *Manual: A guide to the development and use of the Myers-Briggs Type Indicator* (Palo Alto, CA: Consulting Psychologists Press, 1985).

Nockles, P.B. (1994). *The Oxford Movement in context: Anglican high churchmanship, 1760-1857* (Cambridge: Cambridge University Press, 1994). doi.org/10.1017/CBO9780511520570.

Oswald, R.M., and O. Kroeger. (1988). *Personality type and religious leadership* (Washington, DC: The Alban Institute, 1988).

Penhale, F. (1986). *Catholics in crisis* (London: Mowbray, 1986).

Randall, K. (2005). *Evangelicals et cetera: Conflict and conviction in the Church of England's parties* (Aldershot: Ashgate, 2005).

Robbins, M., and W.K. Kay. (2015). 'The psychological type profile of Singaporean Pentecostal Pastors: A research report', *Research in the Social Scientific Study of Religion* 26 (2015), pp. 77-86. doi.org/10.1163/9789004299436_006.

Saward, M. (1987). *Evangelicals on the move* (London: Mowbray, 1987).

Village, A., and L.J. Francis. (2009). *The mind of the Anglican clergy: Assessing attitudes and beliefs in the Church of England* (Lampeter: Mellen, 2009).

Voas, D., and L. Watt. (2014). *Numerical change in church attendance: National, local and individual factors.* Report commissioned by the Church of England. Retrieved from http://www.churchgrowthresearch.org./uk/progress_findingsreports.

12

ORDINARY TRINITARIAN THEOLOGY IN THE ASSEMBLIES OF GOD: A QUALITATIVE STUDY

MARK J. CARTLEDGE[*]

Introduction

This chapter aims to analyse and reflect upon ordinary Pentecostal theology using a qualitative empirical approach to data collection. It seeks to listen to and record the ordinary theology of Pentecostal adherents in order to appreciate the theology on the ground. Therefore, questions were asked in order to tease out beliefs concerning the doctrine of the Trinity. Data from this study are presented in this piece and reflected upon in the light of current research in the field of Pentecostal studies and Trinitarian theology. *Therefore, the aim of the study is to analyse ordinary discourse in order to appreciate the nature of Trinitarian theology in the context of one sector of contemporary British Pentecostalism.* In order to fulfil this aim, I shall explain the nature of ordinary theology, the denominational context of the Assemblies of God and the (anonymous) congregational context before outlining the method of data gathering, sample, analysis, and results. These results are subsequently discussed before conclusions and recommendations for further research are made.

---

[*] Mark J. Cartledge (PhD, University of Wales) is the Principal of London School of Theology and Professor of Practical Theology, England, UK.

Ordinary Theology

This study describes the contours of what Jeff Astley calls 'ordinary' theology of Pentecostals (Astley, 2002; Astley and Christie, 2007; Christie and Astley, 2009), or what some theologians have called 'local' (Schreiter, 1985), 'contextual' (Bevans, 2002), 'non-academic' or indeed 'irregular' theology (Macchia, 2002) located at the 'ground level' (Cruchley-Jones, 2008). Astley defines ordinary theology in the following way:

> Ordinary Christian theology is my phrase for *the theology and theologizing of Christians who have received little or no theological education of a scholarly, academic or systematic kind*. 'Ordinary', in this context, implies *non-scholarly and non-academic*; it fits the dictionary definition that refers to an 'ordinary person' as one who is 'without exceptional experience or expert knowledge'. (Astley, 2002: 56)

This type of theology is grounded in attitudes, values and commitments, experiences and practices of individuals and communities, often categorised as 'folk' or 'common' religion. However, he contends that religious beliefs should not be called 'theology' unless there is evidence of reflection of some kind (Astley, 2002: 139). Pentecostals certainly engage in reflection on their beliefs and have acquired some understanding of theological concepts, even if they have not read tomes in systematic theology. Therefore, it seems appropriate to use Astley's notion of 'ordinary theology' as relevant to this enquiry.

The Assemblies of God

The Assemblies of God of Great Britain is one of the main classical Pentecostal denominations in the UK. Its history is connected to the very early Pentecostal meetings held by Alexander A. Boddy at All Saints' Church, Monkwearmouth between 1908 and 1914. These Whitsuntide conventions enabled Pentecostal identity to be formed as participants were able to hear famous preachers, such as Thomas Ball Barratt from Oslo, worship together and pray for their personal Pentecostal, that is, an overwhelming experience of the Holy Spirit signalled by speaking with other tongues, as on the day of Pentecost (Acts 2.4). It was also sustained by the periodical, *Confidence* magazine, which was the first Pentecostal publication in the UK and continued to be published until 1926.

During the early years of the Pentecostal movement independent assemblies sprang up all around the UK, but it was not until the early 1920s that there was increasing pressure to form an alliance. After an initial meeting in 1922, the inaugural meeting of the Assemblies of God was held at Aston, Birmingham, in February 1924, followed by a conference in May of the same year. At this conference 74 assemblies affiliated with the new denomination and agreed to a statement of Fundamental Truths (*Redemption Tidings*, 1924). It was at this conference that the reasons for the emergence of the denomination became clear. It was because of the need to preserve a distinctly Pentecostal identity, especially the post-conversion experience of baptism in the Spirit as evidenced by speaking with other tongues (or glossolalia), co-ordination of fellowship and witness, especially in the context of social hostility to Pentecostalism, and protection against error and indiscipline, notably inappropriate use of the *charismata* (Massey, 1987: 213-98; 1992: 57-77). The denomination has both waxed and waned over the course of the twentieth century but now has nearly 600 congregations in its membership. It is allied to the Assemblies of God World Fellowship, the Worldwide Pentecostal Fellowship and the Evangelical Alliance (UK); therefore, it has both national and international links within the Evangelical and Pentecostal worlds.

In 2004 the denomination revised its Statement of Faith and changed the wording and positioning of some of the articles of faith. It is worth noting that Scripture is still regarded as normative, orthodox Trinitarian theology is now more explicit, the whole of the ministerial life of Jesus is now affirmed but detached from a premillennial eschatology. Baptism of the Spirit is now explicitly defined in terms of enduement of power for service and the 'initial evidence' of tongues has now become the 'essential biblical evidence'. The wording on 'healing in the atonement' remains largely unchanged. Everlasting punishment for those whose names are not written in the Lamb's Book of Life continues to be affirmed but now with the word 'conscious' added before 'everlasting punishment'. Gifts of the Spirit have now been expanded to include 'gifts of Christ in the Church today', which refer to the ministry gifts of Eph. 4.11.

Empirical Research in Trinitarian Theology

This research can be understood within the context of two previous research projects.

The first study explored the nature and function of glossolalia among ordinary members of the New Church movement on Merseyside (UK) by means of empirical methods (Cartledge, 1999; 2002). It used both qualitative and quantitative data in order to explore theological attitudes and addressed Trinitarian theology in a very preliminary manner. The qualitative data revealed that there was some fluidity regarding which person of the Trinity was addressed through speaking in tongues, with Jesus being more of a focus for some participants because of his role as mediator, while others preferred the Father as the focus of prayer, and others could not distinguish sufficiently and therefore considered that they were addressing all three persons (2002: 56-57). This initial qualitative material was used to conceptualize and operationalize the doctrine of the Trinity in order to explore whether it influenced attitudes towards glossolalia symbols (2002: 137-40). It tested the assertion by Hollenweger (1991: 16-18) that Pentecostal spirituality is fundamentally subordinationist or hierarchical because of its Christological focus and its debt to the *filioque* clause in Western Christianity which subordinates the Spirit to Christ, rather than the social model of the Trinity, which excludes subordination of one person to another. Therefore, these models (as well as modalism) were tested on a survey of Charismatic Christians (N = 633). The main finding of this research was that there was most support for a social doctrine of the Trinity as the dominant model in relation to attitudes towards glossolalia (2002: 169-74).

Further analysis of the same data with respect to the overall spirituality was conducted subsequently (Cartledge, 2004). It discovered that most respondents preferred to think about God as three Persons (62.2%), as equal (87.5%), as community (53.1%), as different (61.8%), and as eternal (83.9%). This supports a social understanding of the doctrine of the Trinity. When respondents address the persons of the Trinity in specific acts, such as worship, prayer, adoration, thanksgiving, and fellowship there are a number of interesting findings. The Father is the most preferred person in terms of worship (39.5%), prayer (50.6%), and thanksgiving (43.4%). Jesus Christ is most preferred addressee for the activities of adoration (40.8%) and fellowship (33.2%), while the Holy Spirit hardly figures as a recipient of worship (0.9%), prayer (1.1%), and thanksgiving (0.9%). Analysis shows that equality, community, and difference are the most common understandings of the persons of the Trinity, with a preference for the person of the Jesus Christ (2004: 81-82). This supports the social understanding of the Trinity rather than the alleged subordination-ism that Hollenweger proposed based upon an almost exclusive Christological focus (2004: 83). It also suggests that there is some fluidity in the focus of worship and prayer between the Father and the Son, if not the Spirit.

The second study built upon the initial project and tested different theoretical models of the Trinity in order to understand which models, if any, were salient for the sample (Cartledge, 2006; 2009a; cf. 2009b). It surveyed theology students in the UK from Adventist, Ecumenical, Evangelical, and Pentecostal educational contexts (N = 244). Starting with the basic tension between the one and the three, unity and plurality categories were used as the basis for the Trinitarian discussion (Brown, 1985). It was suggested that Modalism is based upon the unity category, while Social and Subordinationist models are based upon the plurality category (Cartledge, 2006: 138-44). Therefore, these models were used as initial points of departure in order to explore Trinitarian theology. As a result of the data analysis, five original empirical-theological models were constructed. The Orthodox-exclusivist model contains items that affirm certain Trinitarian beliefs (the three persons constitute the Godhead, are equal and are in communion), together with an exclusivist Christology (Christ is the Son of God, redeemer, only saviour of the world and unique revelation of God). The Pneumatic-social model emphasises the community of the persons of the Godhead together with the work of the Holy Spirit (Spirit of Jesus, God's Spirit and lifegiver). The Modalist model, unsurprisingly, includes the key characteristics of modalism (one God appearing in three ways, the persons being roles for the one God and three modes of being). The Subordinationist model, also as expected, displays an ontological hierarchy between the persons (the Son is 'under' the Father, the Spirit is 'under' the Son). Finally, the Transgender model includes the items of both 'motherly Father' and 'fatherly Mother' to produce a single androgynous construct. The findings indicated that the educational contexts are significant factors in explaining attitudes towards these different models. Compared to other students, Pentecostal students associated most strongly with Orthodox-exclusivist (although this was generally strongly supported) and Subordinationist models (although generally weakly supported); and showed the second strongest affiliation towards Modalism after Adventist students (generally moderately supported). This finding suggests that there is a dominant model in operation with a couple of minor models in use alongside this dominant one.

Analysis of the data with respect to a socialization scale (alpha = .76) suggests that specific variables influence the acquisition of particular empirical-theological models of the Trinity (Cartledge, 2009a). For Pentecostals, the factors of famous preachers (mean 3.4, range 1-5), church leaders (mean 4.0, range 1-5), attendance at conferences (mean 3.4, range 1-5), audio tapes (mean 2.9, range 1-5), and personal Bible study (4.6, range 1-5) are the most significant socialization factors for understanding the nature of God. Of these factors, the item of famous preachers is significantly associated with the Orthodox-exclusivist, Pneumatic-social, and Modalist models; the item of audio tapes is significantly associated with Orthodox-exclusivist, Pneumatic-social, Subordinationist, and Modalist models; and the item of personal Bible study is significantly associated with Orthodox-exclusivist and Pneumatic social models. However, the items of conference attendance and church leaders fail to be associated with any of the empirical-theological models. These findings suggest that Pentecostals are most likely to be influenced in the direction of Orthodox-exclusivist and Pneumatic-social models via famous preachers, audio tapes, and personal Bible study; and they are mostly likely to be influenced in the direction of Subordinationist and Modalist models by audio tapes (2009a: 284).

This research sets the context for this current study and suggests that while there may be some dominant models in operation (Social for ordinary members and Orthodox-exclusivist for students), there is some fluidity in the theology as well. Therefore, it is precisely this fluidity that requires exploration in a more nuanced qualitative manner than has previously been attempted in the empirical studies of Trinitarian theology.

Method

In order to provide original data for discussion, material from a congregational study conducted in 2007-2008 will be presented and reflected upon.

Congregational Study

The project focuses on one Assemblies of God congregation in order to attend to the ordinary theology of the members in a particular context and takes an inductive qualitative approach that treated the congregation as a case study (Yin, 1989; 1993). It is best described as a case study because it is a 'bounded system': bounded by time (eight months data collection) and place (single congregational site), using multiple sources of information (Creswell, 1998: 37). It can also be further described as an 'instrumental case study' because the study focused upon a specific concern, namely the ordinary theology rather than the intrinsic nature of the congregation (Stake, 1995: 3). In this sense the project can be understood as an explicitly theological enterprise and could also be classified in congregational study terms as 'extrinsic-theological' (Woodhead et al, 2004: 8-9). This classification refers to studies that consider a congregation in relation to an external concern, such as 'social capital' or a desire to hear congregational voices for their distinctive contribution (Woodhead et al, 2004: 2). The present study falls within this category, as it aims to take the perspectives uncovered 'on the ground' to another place, namely an engagement with academic discourse in the context of Empirical Theology. But it also seeks to understand the nature of the congregation in its own terms, and in this way also fulfils something of the 'intrinsic' agenda as well (cf. Cameron et al, 2005; Swinton and Mowat, 2006).

The congregation was chosen because I wished to study a classical Pentecostal church that was authentically Pentecostal and reflected the multi-cultural context of where I lived in the West Midlands of England. After considering the lists of churches available on the classical Pentecostal websites, and after a discussion with colleagues and local students it appeared to me that the congregation chosen fitted the type of church I was interested in studying.

The congregation is located in an urban and multi-cultural setting and scores extremely highly on measures of social deprivation.[1] The working population is categorised as: managers and senior officials (6.7%), professional occupations (9.0%), associate professional (12.4%), administrative or secretarial (13.1%), skilled trades (11.4%), personal service (10.2%), sales and customer services (6.0%), plant and machinery operatives (10.6%), or elementary occupation (20.6%).

In terms of stated religious affiliation, the area is 64.0% Christian (compared to 59.0% for Birmingham), 1.0% Buddhist (compared to 0.3% for Birmingham), 1.2% Hindu (compared to 2.0% for Birmingham), 0% Jewish (compared to 0.2% for Birmingham), 5.5% Muslim (compared to 14.3% for Birmingham), 0.9% Sikh (compared to 3.0% for Birmingham), 14.4% for no religion (compared to 12.4% for Birmingham), 0.4% for other religion (compared to 0.4% for Birmingham), and 13% for religion not stated (compared to 8.4% for Birmingham).

In ethnic terms, Birmingham is 67.2% White (compared to 88.7% for England), 3.2% Mixed (compared to 1.6% for England), 20.7% Asian or Asian British (compared to 5.5% for England), 6.6% for Black or Black British (compared to 2.8% for England), and 2.3% Chinese or Other (compared to 1.4% for England). The congregation is attended by mostly Caribbean and African born Christians (approximately 60-70%) integrated within a Pentecostal denomination shaped by the Holiness, Evangelical, and classical Pentecostal traditions of the British context of the twentieth century. It is within this denominational context that the congregation flourishes as a church with approximately 245 regular worshippers and 109 'signed up' members. The majority of these worshippers are women (65%). It is estimated that the majority of the worshippers would be classified as 'working class' (70%) with a minority being classified as 'professional class' (30%). It is estimated that the majority (approximately 80%) live within a two-mile radius of the church building.

Focus groups

The overall research strategy included participant observation, focus groups and documentary analysis of publicly available church

---

[1] Office for National Statistics: www.neighbourhood.statistics.gov.uk, accessed on 7.9.09.

material. In this study, I shall concentrate upon the main source for ordinary theology narratives, namely the focus group material.

In order to understand the ordinary theology of the members, I used the practice of testimony as a way of helping members participate in conversation. Realising that most would be familiar with the giving and receiving of testimony and that this is best done in a group setting, I decided to conduct 'focus groups'. I used this title because most members would have been familiar with this idea through its use in research by commerce and government. It was a way of getting people with a common spirituality to talk together in a non-threatening environment about a theme in depth (Krueger, 1988: 18, 27-30). It was also a means of listening to a conversation between members of the church and noting their interaction as a group (Bryman, 2004: 348). In order to select an appropriate number of participants, the adult membership list was used as a sampling frame and a diverse group of ten people were invited to participate. Therefore, each focus group contained Pentecostal Christians, that is, homogeneous in terms of spirituality, but also stratified so that there was a mixture of people in each group according to gender, age, ethnicity, and lack of close knowledge of each other (Bryman, 2004: 349; Krueger, 1988: 92). In the end, the groups were sufficiently varied so as to suggest that a genuinely stratified sample had been selected from the 100 people who were invited. From those invited, 82% participated in the ten focus groups (N = 82), therefore 18% felt under no compulsion to take part in this project and exercised their freedom not to participate. Ten individuals were invited to participate in each focus group on the assumption that at least two would drop out thereby leaving an ideal size of six to eight people (Krueger, 1988: 18). In the event, the average group size was nine.

The focus groups contained 31 men (38%) and 51 women (62%). The age range for men was 16% in 18-29 years; 19% in 30-39 years; 26% in 40-49 years; 3% in 50-59 years; 16% in 60-69 years; 13% over 70 years; and 7% did not give their ages. The age range for women was 10% in 18-29 years; 16% in 30-39 years; 18% in 40-49 years; 23% in 50-59 years; 14% in 60-69 years; 15% in over 70 years; and 4% did not give their ages.

The church is a very international and multi-cultural church with worshippers from many different countries, although some have now become British citizens. The men originated from Africa: Nigeria

(10%), Togo (3%); Uganda (10%), and Zambia (3%); Asia: India (7%); Europe: Ireland (3%), Macedonia (3%), the UK (Black 7%; Mixed Heritage 3%; White 32%); and the Caribbean: Barbados (3%), Jamaica (10%), Montserrat (3%), and St Kitts (3%). The women originated from Africa: Ghana (2%), Nigeria (10%), Uganda (4%), and Zimbabwe (2%); Europe: Ireland (6%), Germany (2%), and the UK (Black 2%; Mixed Heritage 2%; White 33%); and the Caribbean: Barbados (6%), Dominica (2%), Jamaica (21%); Montserrat (6%), and the Turks and Caicos Islands (2%).

Not everyone specified their occupation, especially if retired. The men gave the following occupations: hospital porter, cleaner, caretaker, crane worker, heavy goods driver, as well as accountant, legal practitioner, college tutor, local government manager, business adviser, teacher, engineer, IT consultant, and student. The women gave the following occupations: homemaker, care assistant, cook, hospital domestic, housekeeper, cleaner, factory worker, support worker, administrative assistant, teaching assistant, administrator, traffic enumerator, sales representative, nurse, PA executive, student, evangelist, and unemployed.

A series of open questions were used to guide the focus group discussion and each group generally used similar questions but addressed to different themes (Bryman 2004: 355; Krueger, 1988: 59). In keeping with Pentecostal spirituality, each discussion began with an invitation for two or three participants to give a testimony of their experience and the subject in question. This usually gave the desired result of helping the participants to relax and engage in a conversation as I gently probed and began to ask subsequent questions. Each focus group recording was subsequently transcribed and analysed using a content analysis technique (Krueger, 1988: 79-80, 106, 118; Robson, 2002: 459-60). After the data had been analysed and reflected upon (Creswell, 1998: 153-54), I conducted a feedback session at which all those who had attended a focus group could be informed of the preliminary findings (Creswell, 1998: 202; Stake, 1995:115-16). This allowed members to check the validity of my findings and to offer any further reflections.

Research questions

In the context of this discussion, four research questions will guide the analysis of the data.

- First, what is the dominant language used in order to describe the doctrine of the Trinity?
- Second, is there a dominant empirical-theological model of the Trinity in operation?
- Third, how is this language reflected in prayer and worship?
- Fourth, given the lack of focus on the person of the Holy Spirit in previous research, is there a particular focus on the person of the Holy Spirit in ordinary Pentecostal discourse?

Results

A number of interesting findings emerged from data analysis of the verbatim transcripts. These can be reported under four categories: (1) three in one; (2) appropriation or modalism?; (3) personhood of the Holy Spirit; and (4) prayer and worship.

Three in One

A good number of participants mentioned the classic formula that the Trinity is 'three persons in one [God]' (Rodney, Joseph, Beverley, Lewis, Jacob, Lisa, Lois, Ellie), or they used slightly different expressions: one God in three persons (Harry), 'all three are one' (Alisa) or 'three being together' (Emily). In order to get a flavour of the kinds of expressions in use, here are three extracts from the focus group conversations.

> I believe in the Godhead: three in one. So, they are all God. I'm so glad that John had the revelation and he said: 'The Word by whom all things were created, took on human form and became flesh'. So, it was God the Word who became Jesus Christ the Son. Now the Holy Spirit and God the Word was in the beginning because John says all things were made by Christ, you see. But then you go down to Genesis, and you get the Spirit of God moved upon the waters. So, [when] you put the Old Testament and New Testament together I'm very convinced that the Godhead is one. And I think we always create problems for ourselves and everybody else when we then start saying but this is this, no, there are three in one. They have their own personality, they have their own

function, and so the Spirit moves in accordance with the wishes of the Father and the Son (Rodney).

Three persons in one. The three persons are different. All of them work in unison together. The Trinity is the powerhouse, for God so loved the world. When Jesus come in the flesh, and he was both man and God. An angel speaks to Mary and says, Jesus would come. When Jesus was going around, they invited him to stay. Jesus said he had to go and 'when I go I pray [to] the Father to send the Holy Spirit' (Jn 16.7-8). So, Jesus was talking about the Father at the same time, and he was talking about the Holy Spirit at the same [time]. Jesus confirmed that he had a Father, and he had the Holy Spirit. Approach, the throne in the Spirit, the Father is in the middle, the Spirit on the left hand and the Son on the right (Joseph).

When I pray, I pray to God […], God is God the Father, the Son and the Holy Spirit. It is not like they are three being[s], it's three in one, Okay. So, when I pray to God I can pray and give my praise to Jesus. Jesus, I praise you, Holy Spirit I praise you, Father I praise you, you know. But the way the Bible explains it is not like that they have […] one's higher than the other. They are all equal, you know, they can be arranged in any order. They are like on a straight line not like a staircase going up, whatever, or something like that. But they are all equal. So, if I say to my living God, I'm addressing the Holy Spirit … I'm addressing Jesus, I'm addressing God the Father, so they are all equal. It's three in one and it's that unity (Jacob).

Appropriation or Modalism?

It is clear that priority is given to the unity of the Godhead, and this naturally led to a comment about how the different roles of the persons related to each other.

I believe the role of the Father, the Holy Spirit, Jesus, they have tasks, I think. They have each a part to play, you know. There's that dedication of work, I think, among the three of them. The Father does this, Jesus this, and the Holy Spirit does this. Like so I was saying, so right now the Holy Spirit here on earth with us just 'cos he's [Jesus] in heaven. And he's interceding to the Father, and the Father gives the answer to Jesus. Jesus speaks to the Holy

Spirit and the Holy Spirit enforces it here on earth. And we have it manifesting here on earth because of the Holy Spirit. So, they are all doing their job, you know. This one does this and this one does the other (Jacob).

In some conversations the desire to differentiate the roles of the persons of the Godhead meant that some of the participants tended to speak in language that is reminiscent of modalism.

Another explanation I've heard is that there is one God, but this one God takes three different offices. One takes the office of the Holy Spirit; I mean in the office of the Holy Spirit he performs specific responsibilities. In the office of the Son, he performs given responsibilities and in the office of God the Father, he [is] given responsibilities but it is like me. One person but my profession is as an accountant, I am an accountant, but at the same time I am a Father to my child, and I am husband to my wife. But it is me. Okay, so that is how I could explain the concept of the Holy Trinity (Abraham).

I think that if you actually see it as the Trinity. It is one. Yea in praying to God the Father, you are conversing with the others. So, I don't necessarily think that, you know, you consciously think, Okay I'm praying to the Holy Spirit now, having a separate kind of conversation as such. It's more, you know, we're speaking to, well we've got this relationship with God and that relationship is in those three forms. And maybe the bit that links directly with God is slightly [...] than the bit that you have with the Spirit. But it's one relationship with God (Samuel).

I suppose I latch on to the phrase triune God quite a lot and I see the Trinity as a three-fold operation of the one God. The Holy Spirit is as much God the Father, Hallelujah, as the Holy Spirit is Jesus. They are all one. They all work in harmony. You can't really separate them and that makes it rather awesome, isn't it? But God the Father and Jesus, through the presence of the Holy Spirit are living is us. It is just incredible. It is just awesome (George).

Prayer and Worship

It is interesting to listen to how participants addressed God in prayer and worship and whether they had preferences and problems with any of the language that was used in the church.

Some people said that they addressed the Father in prayer (Gwynne, Salome, Luke), even if others always prayed in the name of Jesus as well (Harry, Rebekah, Sandra, Lisa) or through Jesus (Samuel, Joseph, Lee). Some stated that they prayed both to the Father and to Jesus (Sharon, Harry), even as they invited the Holy Spirit to assist them in their prayers (Helen). Some only prayed to Jesus (Glenda, Lois, Charlotte, and Hannah), while others were quite content to pray to the Holy Spirit (Jacob). Prayer to Jesus and the Holy Spirit were combined by some participants (Rebekah). A few participants preferred to think simply in terms of God (Oliver), although also acknowledged the Father (Valerie, Oliver, Brian), with Jesus or with God (Lucinda, Chloe). One person felt that you should pray to the Father in the name of Jesus with the help of the Holy Spirit (Elinor), which is echoed by another person:

> It is [in] the Holy Spirit that you pray through Jesus Christ, and you pray to God, you know. Yea, the Holy Spirit leads you to pray and you pray through Jesus, you know, because through Jesus you pray to God, so that your prayer can't be answered without Jesus. You know, you're praying through Jesus […] It's in the Bible. You pray through Jesus. That's why we say in the name of Jesus, you know (Patricia).

Jesus is regarded as the doorway to God with the Holy Spirit as the guide, assisting pray-ers in their choice and use of words (Samuel, Sheila, Dylan). For some this was the difference between praying 'in' rather than 'to' the Holy Spirit (Rachel, Sophie).

For some participants, the instruction of the Lord Jesus regarding prayer was still the most helpful way of considering the matter.

> When I pray, I pray to the Father. I always start my prayer time with Jesus, instruct[ing] us when we pray, 'Our Father who art in heaven'. And I always find myself praying to the Father. When I look in my spirit I go before the Father and I know that the Son is there and the Holy Spirit is there, when I pray to the Father. And when I finish my prayer, I say in Jesus' name. And I feel justified that I pray then because I need all three (Joseph).

> I was just going to say because we are given the prayer example. The fact that Jesus said when you pray, pray 'Our Father'. So, you

direct your prayer to the Father, you're invoking the name of Jesus (Isabel).

One person said that when she worshipped God she concentrated on God as a Trinity and worshipped all three persons (Angela) while another distinguished between prayer and worship. Prayer must be directed to the Father in Jesus' name, while worship can be directed towards all three persons (Ethel).

Personhood of the Holy Spirit
Quite naturally this led to a conversation regarding the role of the Holy Spirit as a person within the Godhead. A number of interesting and contrasting views were expressed. Some people regarded the Holy Spirit very much as a person (Harry, Beverley) while others considered the Holy Spirit in impersonal terms (Glenda, Martin). Another person, while recognising the Holy Spirit's personal qualities, tended to prioritise his role in terms of his work rather than as a recipient of worship (Brian). It is worth noting the language of participants.

> I never thought of it in that way, to tell you the truth. I've always felt that I have a relationship with God and God has given me the Holy Spirit. I don't always think of him as a person, it's more a emotional feeling, empowerment, comforting side […] I don't think of him as a person. I don't accept the Holy Spirit in the way that I feel that I have accepted Jesus or God into my life. I don't know if that's right or wrong but [laughs]. I also felt that the Holy Spirit was always something that comes after that, like a precious things that comes upon me and so I've never really thought of it as a person that you could pray to (Glenda).

> I mean in warfare when I'm praying and sometimes when I'm praying and I want to see something broken in the workplace or at home and I will say, Lord, I just pray by the power of your Holy Spirit let you make this or that or stop this or whatever or give me wisdom. And I do most definitely associate the Holy Spirit as a person and that goes back to once again experiences that I've had where I've felt embraced and it's physical and I've associated that experience with the Holy Spirit, but I still thank the Lord, I thank Jesus and I thank the Holy Spirit (Harry).

I think we would speak to the Holy Spirit a lot. But we don't worship him as such. So, you'll hear 'Holy Spirit do your work'. You hear us pray for people, saying 'Holy Spirit do this' and 'Holy Spirit anoint us', you know 'Holy Spirit bless them'. You know, 'Holy Spirit move on the preacher'. So, we talk a lot to the Holy Spirit. But he's not really an object of worship (Brian).

Discussion

The results of this investigation into the nature of ordinary Pentecostal Trinitarian theology have revealed a number of interesting features and these can be reflected upon in the light of the research questions.

First, the main language of the Trinity, when congregation members are forced to articulate their theology is very much indebted to the unity model of the Trinity. This is the dominant Western theology of the Trinity that emerges from a trajectory that can be traced starting with Tertullian (160-225 CE), through Augustine of Hippo (354-343 CE), and Aquinas (1224-1274) to the Reformed and contemporary Protestant traditions. It puts emphasis upon the unity of essence rather than the three-ness of the persons and is captured in colloquial expression by the phrase 'three in one', that is, three persons 'subsisting' in one divine nature. Article 2 of the 1924 Statement of Fundamental Truths confirms this orientation:

> The unity of the One True and Living God who is Eternally self-existent 'I Am' Who has also revealed Himself as One Being in three Persons, Father, Son, and Holy Spirit. Deut. 6.4; Mark 12.29; Matt 29.19 (*Redemption Tidings*, 1924).

This has been modified 80 years later to read in the 2004 Statement of Faith: 'We believe in the unity of the One True and Living God who is Eternal, Self-Existent "I AM", Who has also revealed Himself as One being co-existing in three Persons – Father, Son and Holy Spirit (Deut 6.4; Mark 12.29; Matt 28.19; 2 Cor. 13.14)'.[2]

It is interesting that there is fundamentally no change in the official statements in that both affirm the Western unity position. However, perhaps with greater awareness of the Oneness Pentecostal

---

[2] See: www.aog.org.uk/church interest.asp.

tradition, 'co-existing' in three persons clarifies the denominational position over and against the Sabellian or modalist posture of the Oneness tradition (Reed, 2008: 256-73). However, in popular language this priority of unity is generally not expressed by the language of official doctrine 'one being [co-existing] in three persons', but in simple shorthand fashion: 'three in one'. This finding suggests that, if anything, there is probably a preference towards the 'Orthodox-exclusivist' model with its emphasis on unity and Christology, rather than the Pneumatic-social model with its emphasis on community and pneumatology.

Second, the preference for a unity over a plurality emphasis in the Trinity suggests that while the Orthodox-exclusivist model might predominate there are other models often aligned to the unity emphasis that are present. The congregation members, when talking about the persons of the Trinity, specified certain tasks as associated with particular members of the Godhead. For example, Jesus is interceding on behalf of Christians to the Father and then he passes on the message to the Holy Spirit who works here on earth. This is underdeveloped but could be seen to resonate with the doctrine of appropriation which states that while the operations of the persons are united *ad extra* (La Due, 2003: 53; Gunton, 2003: 80), there is a sense in which particular tasks can be associated with specific persons, such as creation with the Father and redemption with the Son and sanctification with the Spirit (Cunningham, 1998: 117; Fiddes, 2000: 103). However, it was clear that this sense of appropriation, if not carefully stated, could lead in the direction of a Modalist position. This was explained either in terms of functional language, e.g. offices and operations, or in terms of ontological language, e.g. 'forms'. It would appear that functional Modalism is not that far away from the doctrine of appropriation and perhaps it can be accounted for by means of the imprecision of language, which is what one might expect from ordinary theology. However, the language appears to suggest that Modalism is perhaps more deeply rooted and that functional categories dominate ontological ones. In this regard, the main Western tendency continues to be a conceptual problem for ordinary believers. However, and presuming this is the case, this particular group of Pentecostal Christians simply reflects the dominant popular understanding in the Western Christianity today (Letham, 2004: 5).

Third, the language of prayer and worship suggests that there is a degree of fluidity in how the persons of the Godhead are addressed, with the Father and Jesus being the dominant persons, although the Holy Spirit was addressed by some if not others. There was a view expressed that the role of the Holy Spirit was not to receive prayer as much as to help and empower Christians to pray (Rom 8.26-27). This fits with the view that the Spirit's role is to direct attention away from himself towards the Father and the Son (cf. Gal 4.6; Smail, 1988: 30). As Torrance has stated: 'The Holy Spirit has no "Face", but it is through the Spirit that we see the Face of Christ and in the Face of Christ we see the Face of the Father' (Torrance, 1996:63). The role of Jesus as mediator means that often prayer is regarded as addressed to God or to the Father through Christ, that is, in his name and 'in' the power of the Holy Spirit. The instructions of the Lord's prayer supported this approach (Mt. 6.9-13). This might suggest something of a hierarchy in the Godhead, except that within the context of a unity model all members of the Godhead are equal and can theoretically be addressed, although in practice it will largely be restricted to two: the Father and the Son. This finding resonates with earlier research of New Church members (2004), which discovered that the Father is most preferred in terms of worship, prayer, and thanksgiving, while Jesus Christ is preferred in terms of adoration and fellowship. The Holy Spirit is hardly addressed in these spiritual practices. Therefore, it seems inevitable that when there is a strong unity model in play then two different persons will be approached because of the equality of the persons of the Godhead. The strong Christological centre of Pentecostalism modifies the biblical injunction of Mt. 6.9-13, which advocates that prayer be principally directed to the person of the Father, in favour of a dual direction: Father and Son.

Fourth, participants in the focus groups expressed rather contrasting views regarding the personhood of the Holy Spirit. The emphasis by one member was on the empowering and comforting role of the Spirit subsequent to conversion but conceived in impersonal terms. Another person, also based on his experience, thought of the Holy Spirit in association with spiritual warfare. A third person focused on the work of the Holy Spirit as people invite him to minister to them and others. This was a fascinating conversation revealing different opinions as to whether the Holy Spirit should be conceived in relation to other members of the Godhead. The person and work of the Holy Spirit in the Assemblies of God doctrinal statements (other than the Trinity article) simply speak of 'the baptism in the Holy Spirit' (1924 and 2004) 'and operation of the gifts of the Holy Spirit' in the Church today (2004). However, it must be noted that early Assemblies of God Pentecostal theology unequivocally affirmed both the personhood (although using the older language of 'personality') and divinity of the Holy Spirit (Carter, 1926: 12). It would be unfair to accuse these adherents of the ancient Pneumatomachian heresy outright (Cross and Livingstone, 1997: 1303), especially since the personhood and divinity of the Spirit are clearly established in the other ordinary Trinitarian statements (as above). Perhaps it is the rather impersonal metaphor of baptism into the Holy Spirit conceived in terms of a liquid or substance that has given rise to this understanding by some people, similar to the notion of 'grace as a sort of fluid poured into the person' (Gunton, 2003: 79). It is reinforced more generally when the Holy Spirit is not addressed in personal terms in worship and prayer, as previous studies have discovered (Cartledge, 2004). The lack of an explicit Trinitarian grammar in liturgy (e.g. Basil's second doxology: 'Glory to the Father with the Son together with the Holy Spirit', cited by Gunton, 2003: 83-87) and in hymnody no doubt contribute to this confusion (cf. Parry, 2005: 123-28). Clearly a unity preference within a Western tradition, with a tendency towards Modalism, rather than Subordinationism (*contra* Hollenweger, 1991), also has the effect of eclipsing the Holy Spirit in personal terms. This can be regarded as ironic given the emphasis of Pentecostalism on pneumatology. However, if the emphasis is upon functional Christology (saviour, baptizer, and healer etc.), then it would make sense for the tradition also to support a more functional view of the Holy Spirit as an extension of the one God in the lives of believers, namely: power for witness.

Conclusion

This study has shown that the ordinary theology of Pentecostals in the Assemblies of God tradition in the UK is deeply embedded in the Western (unity) Trinitarian tradition. Given this framework there is a tendency towards functional Modalism and fluidity regarding which persons of the Godhead should be most properly addressed in worship and prayer. Although this fits with the perceptions of some theologians (e.g., Latham, 2004), it stands in contrast to previous empirical-theological research on Pentecostal and Charismatic Christians, which has noted the influence of Orthodox-exclusivist, Social and Subordinationist models (Cartledge, 1999, 2002, 2004, 2006, 2009a). The confusion regarding the personhood of the Holy Spirit is supported to some extent by previous studies and coheres with the Pentecostal emphasis upon empowerment. Therefore, this study suggests that further research is required in order to understand better the nature of Trinitarian theology among ordinary believers. This could be proposed in terms of a study of Pentecostal and Charismatic Christianity but also more generally, as it is likely that the views encountered in this congregation will be replicated in wider British Christianity. Thus, this study can be seen as setting an agenda for research in the field of ordinary theology.

References

AOG 'A Statement of Fundamental Truths Approved by the General Presbytery of the Assemblies of God of Great Britain and Ireland', *Redemption Tidings*, 1.1, p. 19.

Astley, Jeff (2002), *Ordinary Theology: Looking, Listening and Learning in Theology* (Aldershot: Ashgate, 2002).

Astley, Jeff and Christie, Ann (2007), *Taking Ordinary Theology Seriously* (Grove Books, Pastoral Series 110; Cambridge: Grove Books, 2007).

Bevans, Stephen B. (2002), *Models of Contextual Theology* (revised and expanded edn; Maryknoll, NY: Orbis, 2002).

Brown, David (1985), *The Divine Trinity* (London: Duckworth, 1985).

Bryman, Alan (2004), *Social Research Methods* (Oxford: Oxford University Press, 2004).

Cameron, Helen, Philip Richter, Douglas Davies, and Frances Ward, (2005), *Studying Local Churches: A Handbook* (London: SCM, 2005).

Carter, John H. (1926), 'Studies on the Fundamental Truths, No.2', *Redemption Tidings*, 2.2 (1926), pp. 10-13.

Cartledge, Mark J. (1999) 'Tongues of the Spirit: An Empirical-Theological Study of Charismatic Glossolalia' (PhD thesis, University of Wales, 1999).

Cartledge, Mark J. (2002), *Charismatic Glossolalia: An empirical-theological study* (Aldershot: Ashgate, 2002).

Cartledge, Mark J. (2004), 'Trinitarian Theology and Spirituality: An Empirical Study of Charismatic Christians', *Journal of Empirical Theology*, 17.1 (2004), pp. 76-84.

Cartledge, Mark J. (2006), 'Empirical-Theological Models of the Trinity: Exploring the Beliefs of Theology Students in the United Kingdom', *Journal of Empirical Theology*, 19.2 (2006), pp. 137-62.

Cartledge, Mark J. (2009a), 'Socialisation and Empirical-Theological Models of the Trinity: A Study among Theology Students in the United Kingdom', in Leslie J. Francis, Mandy Robbins and Jeff Astley (eds.), *Empirical Theology in Texts and Tables: Qualitative, Quantitative and Comparative Perspectives* (Leiden: Brill, 2009), pp. 269-90.

Cartledge, Mark J. (2009b), 'God, Gender and Social Roles: A Study in Relation to Empirical-Theology Models of the Trinity', *Journal of Empirical Theology*, 22.2 (2009), pp. 117-41.

Christie, Ann and Jeff Astley (2009), 'Ordinary Soteriology: A Qualitative Study', in Leslie J. Francis, Mandy Robbins and Jeff Astley (eds.), *Empirical Theology in Texts and Tables: Qualitative, Quantitative and Comparative Perspectives* (Leiden: Brill, 2009), pp. 177-96.

Creswell, John W. (1998), *Qualitative Inquiry and Research Design: Choosing Among Five Traditions* (London, Sage, 1998).

Cross, F.L. and E.A. Livingstone (1997), *The Oxford Dictionary of the Christian Church* (3rd edn; Oxford: Oxford University Press, 1997).

Cruchley-Jones, Peter (ed.) (2008), *God at Ground Level* (Oxford: Peter Lang, 2008).

Cunningham, David S. (1998), *These Three are One: The Practice of Trinitarian Theology* (Oxford: Blackwell, 1998).

Fiddes, Paul S. (2000), *Participating in God: A Pastoral Doctrine of the Trinity* (London: Darton, Longman and Todd, 2000).

Gunton, Colin E. (2003), *Father, Son and Holy Spirit: Toward a Fully Trinitarian Theology* (London: T & T Clark, 2003).

Hollenweger, Walter J. (1991), 'Priorities in Pentecostal Research: Historiography, Missiology, Hermeneutics and Pneumatology', in J.A.B. Jongeneel (ed.), *Experiences of the Spirit* (Frankfurt-am-Main: Peter Lang, 1991), pp. 7-22.

Krueger, Richard A. (1988), *Focus Groups: A Practical Guide for Applied Research* (London: Sage, 1988).

La Due, William J. (2003), *The Trinity Guide to the Trinity* (Harrisburg, PA: Trinity Press International, 2003).

Letham, Robert (2004), *The Holy Trinity: In Scripture, History, Theology and Worship* (Phillipsburg, NJ: PandR Publishing, 2004).

Macchia, Frank D. (2002), 'Theology, Pentecostal', in S.M Burgess and E.M. Van der Mass (eds.), *The New International Dictionary of Pentecostal and*

Charismatic Movements – Revised and Expanded Edition (Grand Rapids, Zondervan, 2002), pp. 1121-41.

Massey, Richard D. (1987), '"A Sound and Scriptural Union": An Examination of the Origins of the Assemblies of God of Great Britain and Ireland during the Years 1920-1925' (PhD Thesis, University of Birmingham, 1987).

Massey, Richard D. (1992), *Another Springtime: The Life of Donald Gee, Pentecostal Leader and Teacher* (Guildford: Highland Books, 1992).

Parry, Robin (2005), *Worshipping Trinity: Coming back to the heart of worship* (Milton Keynes: Paternoster, 2005).

Reed, David A. (2008), *"In Jesus' Name": The History and Beliefs of Oneness Pentecostals* (JPTSup 31; Blandford Forum: Deo Publishing, 2008).

Schreiter, Robert J. (1985), *Constructing Local Theologies* (London: SCM, 1985).

Smail, Thomas A. (1988), *The Giving Gift: The Holy Spirit in Person* (London: Hodder and Stoughton, 1988).

Stake, Robert E. (1995), *The Art of Case Study Research* (London: Sage, 1995).

Swinton, John and Harriet Mowat (2006), *Practical Theology and Qualitative Research* (London: SCM, 2006).

Torrance, Thomas F. (1996), *The Christian Doctrine of God: One Being Three Persons* (Edinburgh: T & T Clark, 1996).

Woodhead, Linda, Matthew Guest, and Karen Tusting (2004), 'Congregational Studies: Taking Stock', in Matthew Guest, Karin Tusting, and Linda Woodhead (eds.), *Congregational Studies in the UK: Christianity in a Post-Christian Context* (Aldershot: Ashgate, 2004).

Yin, R.K. (1989), *Case Study Research: Design and Method* (London: Sage, 1989).

Yin, R.K. (1993), *Applications of Case Study Research* (London: Sage, 1993).

INDEX OF BIBLICAL (AND OTHER ANCIENT) REFERENCES

Genesis
1.1   94
1.2   70, 88, 92
1.26-28 118
1.26-27 89
1.26   86
1.27   94
1.30   89
2.7   69, 88, 89, 90
3   108
3.1-7   108
6.3   90
6.17   89
10.2   122
26.35   90
40.8   100
41.25   100
41.28   100
41.38   100
41.39   100
45.27   90

Exodus
6.7   91
8.3   101
12.23   107
28.3   97
29.21   98
30.30   98
31.3-4   97, 101
32.28   92
33.24   86
35.31   97, 101

Leviticus
26.12   91

Numbers
3.3   98

11.17   91, 97
11.25-29 98
11.25   91, 97, 102
14.24   90
21.17-19 26
24.2-3   99
27.18-23 100
27.18   91, 100

Deuteronomy
6.4   219
34.9   91, 97, 100

Judges
3.9-10   98
6.34   98
11.29   98
13.25   98
14.6   97, 102
14.19   102
15.14   97, 102

1 Samuel
1.15   90
10.1   98
10.6   98
10.10   98
10.11-12 98
11.6   98
16.13-14 98
16.13   98
16.14   102
18.10-11 99
19.20-21 98
19.23   98
19.24   98

1 Kings
18.29   99

2 Chronicles
15.1-7   99
20.14-17 99
24.20   99

Nehemiah
9.20   91
9.30   99

Esther
1.13   101

Job
27.3   89
32.8   89, 101
33.3   89
33.4   89
34.14-15 89
34.14   89

Psalms
23   25
33.6   88
51.10-12 94
51.10   90, 94
51.11   86, 89, 102
51.12   94
87.2   124
104.29-30 88
104.29   89, 94
132.13   124
139.7   86

Proverbs
9.10   101

Isaiah
1.10-14 154
2.1-5   155

9.7	154	54.1-3	155	36.24-25	91
10.1-2	153	55.1	156	36.26	94
10.13	101	55.3	92	36.29	91
10.24-25	153	55.10-11	152	37.1-14	94
11.1-3	98	57.16	89	37.1-10	90
11.2	100, 155	59.21	98	37.1	99
11.5-9	155	61.1-4	152	37.8-9	90
11.9	155	61.1	93, 98, 99	37.9-10	70
13.11	153	63.7-14	86	37.9	69
14.4-6	153	63.10	87	37.11-14	91
28.11	101	63.11-14	91	37.26	91
29.24	90	63.11	87	38.2	122
30.7	153	63.12	87	38.6	122
30.12	153	63.14	87	38.22	125
32.1	154	66.7-9	155	39.6	125
32.14-15	155			43.5	99
32.15	93	**Jeremiah**			
35.8-10	155	1.2	99	**Daniel**	
36-37	153	1.4	99	4.8	100
40-55	92, 93	7.23	91		
40-47	153	9.17	101	**Hosea**	
40.1-11	153	11.1	99	9.7	99
40.19	153	11.4	91		
41.8	93	11.15	124	**Joel**	
42.1	93, 98	12.7	124	2.1-11	93
42.5	89	18.1	100	2.12-17	93
42.6	93	23.18	100	2.18-32	93
42.19-20	93	23.21-22	100	2.23	93
43.7-8	93	24.7	91	2.28-3.1	96
43.10	93	30.22	91	2.28-32	155
43.16	92	31.31-34	91	2.28-29	93
44.3-4	93	32.38	92	2.28	98, 102
44.8	93				
45.1-2	154	**Ezekiel**		**Micah**	
48.15	7	2.2	99	3.6-7	99
48.20-21	92	3.16	100	3.8	99
49.3	93	3.24	99		
49.5-6	93	6.1	100	**Zeph.**	
49.6	93	7.1	100	1.2-4	92
51.9-11	92	8.1	102		
51.9	92	8.3	99	**Haggai**	
51.10	92	11.1	99	2.4-5	
52.1-2	156	16.60	91, 92	2.5	92
52.13-53.12	156	27.8-9	101		
52.13	67	33.22	102	**Zechariah**	
53.7	156	34.25	91	7.12	99
53.11	156	36	91	14.8	72

Matthew		4.48	83	14.23	72
6.9-13	220	4.50-53	70	14.25-26	68
9.2	73	5.8-9	70	14.26	87, 88
12.39-40	61	5.23	69	14.27	68, 69, 72
16.4	61	5.25	70	14.28	62
28.9	68	5.28-29	119	15.26-27	68
28.18-20	73	5.36-38	69	15.26	70, 87, 88
28.19	87, 219	6.18	70	16.5-15	68
		6.27	111	16.7-8	214
Mark		6.29	60	16.7	66, 68, 70,
2.5	73	6.38-39	69		72, 88
8.31	61	7	156	16.8-10	90
9.31	61	7.12	111	16.12-16	70
12.29	219	7.16	69	16.28	62, 68
		7.28-29	69	16.33	68
Luke		7.37-39	67, 72	17	53
1.67	101	7.39	66, 68, 70,	17.5	62, 68
4	156		79, 80, 102	18.5-6	70
4.16-21	152	7.47	111	19.28	112
5.20	73	8.18	69	19.30	112
9.22	61	8.26	69	19.42	60
10.30	25	8.29	69	20	75, 78, 116
24.15	64	8.42	69	20.1	61
24.31	64	8.44	108	20.2	61
24.36	64, 68	9.7	70	20.3-9	82
24.47-49	78	9.33	111	20.3-8	61
24.49	64	9.39	83, 114	20.6-7	82
24.50-51	64, 65	10.3-4	83	20.8	82
24.50	64	11.12-13	67	20.8b	81
24.51	64	11.43-44	70	20.9	82
		13.1	62, 66, 67	20.11-13	82
John		13.3	62, 66, 67	20.11	61
1-20	78	13.8	120	20.14	61
1.1	81, 95	13.16	69	20.16	62, 83
2.7-9	70	13.27	109	20.17-18	62, 65, 66, 74
2.11	83	13.30	122	20.17	61, 62, 65, 68
2.19-21	61, 67	13.31-32	67	20.17b	63
3.1-10	95	13.33	68	20.17c	63
3.3-7	72	14.6	80	20.18	66, 77
3.8	70, 83	14.12	73, 74	20.19-23	60, 67, 76,
3.9	79, 80	14.15-21	79		77, 83
3.14	67	14.15-18	68	20.19-21	68
3.16	51, 83	14.15-17	72	20.19-20a	80
3.31-32	69	14.16	67, 70, 88	20.20	68
4.10	80	14.17	72	20.21	68
4.13-14	72	14.18	72	20.22	69, 71, 72,
4.21-24	72	14.20	72, 80		74, 75, 77, 78

20.23	72, 74, 77, 78	Romans		3.2	116
20.24-29	79	8.26-27	88	3.7	111
20.24-27	80			3.9	108
20.24-26	78	1 Corinthians			
20.25	82	2.4-5	101	2 John	
20.26	68	2.6	101	7	
20.28-29	81	12, 13, 14	33		
20.29	81, 82, 83	12	32, 36	Revelation	
20.30-31	79, 83	12.8-11	101	1.3	120
20.31	79, 81	12.8	101	1.4	113
21	78, 116	12.10	101	1.6	121
21.15-23	78	12.28	101	1.9	115
21.22-24	82	14.21	101	1.18	116
21.24	78	15.3-7	75	2.8	116
21.25	79	15.4	61	2.9	109
		15.8	63	2.10	108, 109, 110
Acts				2.11	120
1.1-2	64	2 Corinthians		2.13	109
1.2	59	1.22	96	2.20	111
1.3	75	3.17-18	95	2.24	109
1.4-9	65	3.17	149	2.26	116
1.5	59	5.5	96	3.7	111
1.6-11	65	13.13	87	3.9	109
1.8	54, 59, 71, 78, 95	13.14	219	3.12	124
1.9	64, 65, 66, 75	Galatians		3.21	113, 114, 116
2	32, 85	5.16-26	95	4.2	113
2.1-4	74, 75, 78, 83			4.3	113
2.1-2	65	Ephesians		4.4	113
2.4	71, 101, 204	1.13-14	96	4.5	113
2.16	96	4.11	101, 205	4.6	113
2.17-18	93	4.15	38	4.8	126
2.21	96	4.30	87	4.9	113, 117
2.38	83			4.10	113, 117
2.41	92	Colossians		5.1	111, 113
3-7	78	1.9	101	5.2	111
6.3	101	3.16	101	5.5	111
6.10	101			5.6	113
8.1	78	1 Peter		5.7	113
8.4	78	1.2	87, 95	5.9	111
8.25	78			5.10	116, 121
8.26-39	78	2 Peter		5.11	113
8.26-27	220	1.21	101	5.13	113, 126
9.3	25			6.1	111
10.46	101	1 John		6.3	111
11.23-24	101	1.8	111	6.5	111
19.6	101	2.26	111	6.7	111
				6.9	111, 114

6.12	111	11.15	126	17.8	110
6.16	113	11.16	113	17.12	110, 117
7.2	117	12.3	108	17.17	112
7.3	111	12.4	108	18.20	114
7.4	111	12.5	113	18.23	111
7.5	111	12.7-9	108	19	107
7.8	111	12.9	108, 109,	19.3	126
7.9	113		110, 125	19.4	113
7.10	113	12.10	126	19.5	113
7.11-12	126	12.13	108	19.8-9	120
7.11	113	12.14	108	19.9	120
7.15	113, 126	12.18	123	19.10	115
7.17	113	13.2	108, 113	19.11	107, 114
8.1	111	13.4	108	19.15	112
8.3	113	13.5	109, 117	19.17	107
9.1	108, 110	13.14	111	19.19	107
9.2	108, 110	14.3	113	19.20	111, 125
9.4	111	14.4	115	19.21	111, 118
9.11	107, 108, 110	14.11	126	20	107
9.15-22	124	14.13	120	20.1-10	106, 127
10.4	111	15.1	112	20.1	107
10.6	117	15.7	117	20.2	108, 109
10.7	112	15.8	112	20.3	111, 122, 125
11.2	109	16.10	113	20.4	114, 115
11.5	124	16.13	108	20.8	122
11.6	111	16.14	123	20.10	114, 125
11.7	110, 112	16.15	120	20.11-15	106
11.9	110	16.17	113		
11.11-14	118	17.1	114		

INDEX OF AUTHORS AND NAMES

Albright, W.F., 137, 138
Alden, Robert, 99
Allo, E.-B., 122
Anderson, Allan, 11, 13, 14, 16, 17, 23, 44, 156
Anderson, A.A., 94
Anderson, Jamie Capel, 134
Anderson, Robert Mapes, 20
Andrews, J., 45
Aquinas, 214
Archbishop Paul, 30
Archer, Ken, 148, 149, 150
Ash, P.A., 130
Astley, J., 200
Atherton, J. 35
Augustine of Hippo, 214
Aune, D., 118, 119, 123

Balfour, Glenn, 2, 60, 62, 71
Barr, James, 131, 137, 143
Barrett, David B., 12, 14, 15
Barrett, P., 160
Barrett, Thomas Ball, 200
Bartlemann, Frank, 54
Bates, M., 163, 183, 192
Beasley-Murray, George R., 111, 125
Bell, Anthea Ruth, 5
Bergunder, M., 14
Bevans, Stephen B., 200
Beyts, J., 161
Bloom, Anthony, 27
Boddy, Alexander, 29, 45, 52, 200
Bonnke, Reinhard, 52
Brown, R.E., 70, 95
Brown, W.P., 130
Bruce, F.F., 95
Brueggemann, Walter, 9
Bruner, F., 43
Bryman, Alan, 207, 208
Buckley, S.J., 161

Bunyon, John, 27

Caird, G.B., 112, 121, 123
Cameron, Helen, 205
Carson, D.A., 95
Carter, John H., 216
Cartledge, Mark, 2, 200, 202, 203, 204, 217, 218
Casey, P.M., 76
Castelein, J.D., 160
Cho, Jonggi, 55
Christie, Ann, 200
Clines, D.J.A., 132
Coristine, M., 161
Coulson, J.E., 160
Craig, C.L., 165, 171, 180, 185, 187, 193, 196
Creswell, John W., 205, 208
Crookes, T.G., 161
Cross, F.L., 216
Cross, W.P., 161
Crossing Peter F., 12,
Cruchley-Jones, Peter, 200
Culpepper, R.A., 76
Cunningham, David S., 219
Cunningham, Valentine, 4
Cutten, G.B., 160

Darr, Kathryn Pfisterer, 151
Davies, Andrew, 2, 146, 148
Davies, Eryl W., 98, 130, 132
Davies, G. Henton, 85,
Davies, Philip, 139, 140, 141, 142, 143, 144
Dempster, M.W., 43, 44, 48
Dodd, C.H., 72
Droogers, A., 14
Dunn, James, 28, 85, 100
Du Plessis, David, 41, 42, 43, 44, 53
Dyer, Anne E., 39, 45, 56

Eagleton, Terry, 131
Edwards, Joel, 50
Eichrodt, Walther, 89
Eysenck, S.B.G., 160, 161, 162, 163, 171, 173, 180

Father John of Kronsdat, 34
Fiddes, Paul S., 215
Fiorenza, Elisabeth Schüssler, 132, 135
Fleck, J.R., 160
Francis, Leslie, 2, 159, 160, 161, 162, 163, 164, 165, 166, 171, 172, 179, 180, 185, 186, 187, 188, 193, 196
Frcka, G., 161

Gaechter, P., 116
Gause, R. Hollis, 107, 109, 112, 113, 118, 121, 125
Gee, Donald, 42, 51
Gillet, Lev, 31
Goldingay, John, 84, 86, 94, 97, 100, 102, 103
Goodwin, L., 46
Grabbe, Lester, 140
Graham, Billy, 3, 41
Green, Michael, 84, 95, 98
Grudem, Wayne, 87, 95
Gunton, Colin E., 219, 216, 217

Hair, J., 162
Hamilton, Victor, 88, 90
Harper, Michael, 28, 35, 44
Harrell, David Edwin, 52
Henry, Carl, 41
Hickman, Albert W., 1
Hine, V.H., 161
Hinn, Benny, 52
Hollenweger, Walter J., 202, 203, 217
Horton, Stanley, 84, 90, 95, 98
Hoste, D.E., 45
Hunter, H.D., 41
Hylson-Smith, K., 179, 180

Jacobsen, Douglas, 16
James, Lucy, 45
Jameson, Fredrik, 131

Japeth, S., 130
Jobling, D., 130
Johnson, R.W, 160
Johnson, Todd M., 9, 10, 12, 14, 15, 16
Jones, Bryn, 50
Jones, S.H., 162, 164, 165, 171, 174, 186, 187, 193, 196
Jung, Carl, 163, 171
Fowler, R.M., 134

Kärkkäinen, V.-M., 41
Kay, William K., 1, 2, 3, 4, 5, 6, 7, 10, 14, 15, 16, 17, 20, 21, 22, 23, 24, 25, 27, 28, 39, 45, 56, 107, 146, 159, 160, 161, 162, 163, 171, 180, 185, 193
Keirsey, D, 163, 183, 192
Kerr, David A., 42
Kidner, Derek, 94
Kildahl, J.P., 160
Klaus, B.D., 48
Knauf, E.A., 145
Knight, D.A., 136
Koester, C.R., 117, 122
Kroeger, Richard A., 183, 185, 194, 207, 208
Kronenberger, E.J., 160

Ladd, G.E., 112, 116, 118, 124
La Due, William J., 219
Lapsley, 160, 161
Lee, Young Hoon, 55
Lepage, M., 161
Letham, Robert, 215, 218
Levison, John R., 99
Levey, A.B., 161
Lewis, C.S., 27
Lincoln, A.T., 78
Lindblom, Johannes, 98, 99, 100
Lindsay, J. Gordon, 52
Littler, Keith, 159, 166, 172, 174, 180, 186, 193
Livingstone, E.A., 216
Louden, S.H., 162
Luz, Ulrich, 60

Ma, Julie, 51
Ma, Wonsuk, 151

McClung, L. Grant, 43
Macchia, F., 200
Mackie, A., 160
McLeod, Hugh, 11
McQueen, Larry R., 147
Martin, D., 25
Martin, I., 161
Martin, Lee Roy, 147
Martyn, J.L., 69
Massey, A., 161
Massey, Richard D., 205
McCaulley, M.H., 163, 180, 189, 192
Mealy, W., 112, 114, 116, 118, 123
Menzies, R.P., 83
Metzger, B.M., 121
Miller, Donald, 21, 22, 49
Miller, Kathleen, 45
Miller, Patrick, 130, 136
Miscall, Peter, 150, 151
Moore, Rick D., 147
Mooneyham, Stanley, 41
Morris, Leon, 95
Moses, Davis, 37
Mott, John, 40, 41
Mounce, R.H., 112, 122, 125
Mowat, Harriett, 205
Murphy, F.J., 120, 127
Myers, I.B., 163, 180, 192, 195

Neve, Lloyd, 94
Neisz, N.L., 160
Ness, R.C., 160
Nissiotis, Nikos, 36
Nockles, P.B., 180

Oates, W.E., 161
Obolensky, Dimitri, 27
Okoye, James Chukwuma, 97
Osiek, Carolyn, 132, 133
Oswald, R.M., 183, 185, 194

Packer, J.I. 33
Parham, Charles, 44
Parker, Simon B., 99
Parry, Robin, 217
Patte, Daniel, 148
Pattemore, S., 114

Pattison, E.M., 160
Pawson, David, 71, 83
Pearson, P.R., 161
Penhale, F., 179
Petersen, D., 48
Petts, David, 1, 71, 84, 90
Petts, Stanley, 4
Philippon, A.J., 37
Pippin, T., 130
Polhill, Cecil, 45
Popper, Karl, 2
Prigent, P., 111, 119
Provan, Iain, 139, 140, 141, 142, 143, 144

Randall, K., 180
Rea, John, 84, 90, 95, 98, 100, 102
Reed, David A., 215
Rendtorff, Rolf, 91, 99
Rissi, M., 112
Robbins, Mandy, 159, 162, 180, 185, 186, 193, 196
Robeck, Mel, 40, 42, 44
Roberts, Dana, 40
Rose, Hiermonk Seraphim, 31
Robson, 208
Ross, Kenneth, 9, 10, 12, 16, 42
Routledge, Robin, 2, 84, 85, 87, 91, 92, 93, 96, 98, 101, 103

Samarin, W.J., 161
Saward, M., 179
Schreiter, Robert J., 200
Sentamu, John, 56
Seymour, William, 44, 54
Silberman, L.H., 136
Simpson, A.B., 52
Simpson, J.K., 160, 161
Slater, P., 196
Small, H., 45
Smalley, S.S., 114, 120, 126
Smith, D.S., 160
Snaith, Norman H., 86
Spandos, N.P., 161
Stake, Robert E., 209, 212
Staley, Jeffrey L., 134
Stanley, B., 48

Stibbe, Mark, 60
Stoppard, Tom, 139
Stronstad, Roger, 84
Studd, C.D., 45
Sweet, J.P.M., 113, 116, 123, 124
Swinton, John, 205
Symeon the New Theologian, 32
Synan, Vinson, 14

Tappeiner, D., 160
Tate, Marvin, 94
Taylor, David, 55
Taylor, Hudson, 45
Tertullian, 218
Theodore of Mopsuestia, 71
Thomas, John Christopher, 2, 107, 120, 122, 147, 148, 150
Thomas, T.H., 162, 180
Thompson, Thomas, 139, 141, 143, 144, 145
Tilley, D., 199
Torrance, James, 36
Torrance, Thomas, 36, 216

Urquhart, Colin, 35

Village, Andrew, 179, 188
van der Laan, C., 14
Vivien, L.M., 160

Voas, David, 179, 187, 193

Waddell, Robby, 147, 150
Waehrisch-Oblau, Claudia, 54
Wakefield, G., 29
Walker, Andrew, 1, 25, 35
Wall, R.W., 119
Warrington, K., 42
Watt, 187, 193
Weiser, Artur, 94
Wellhausen, Julius, 135, 136, 137
Wenham, Gordon, 88
Wenham, J.W., 76
Westermann, Claus, 90
Whinney, M., 196
Williams, C.G., 160
Wilson, Robert R., 99
Wintrob, R.M., 160
Wood, Leon J., 99
Woodhead, Linda, 209
Wright, Christopher J.H., 84, 89, 90, 98

Yamamori, Tetsunao, 21, 22, 49
Yin, R.K., 205
Yong, Amos, 21, 22, 51

Zegwaart, Huibert, 107
Zurlo, Gina A., 15

www.ingramcontent.com/pod-product-compliance
Lightning Source LLC
Chambersburg PA
CBHW070329090426
42733CB00012B/2409